AF180536

The Financial Markets of the Arab Gulf

Financial markets across the Arabian Peninsula have gone from being small, quasi-medieval structures in the 1960s to large world-class groupings of financial institutions. This evolution has been fueled by vast increases in income from oil and natural gas. *The Financial Markets of the Arab Gulf* presents and analyzes the banks, stock markets, investment companies, money changers and sovereign wealth funds that have grown from this oil wealth and how this income has acted as a buffer between Gulf society at large and the newfound cash reserves of Gulf Cooperation Council states (Saudi Arabia, the United Arab Emirates, Qatar, Kuwait, Oman and Bahrain) over the last fifty years.

By assessing the development of institutions like the Abu Dhabi Investment Authority, the Saudi Arabian Monetary Authority, the Public Investment Fund and the National Bank of Kuwait, *The Financial Markets of the Arab Gulf* evaluates the growth of the markets and provides a detailed, critical snapshot of the current form and function of the Gulf's financial markets. It argues that the markets have been controlled by various state institutions for socio-political reasons. In particular, the Saudi state has used its sophisticated regulatory regime to push for industrialization and diversification, which culminated in the Vision 2030 plan. The UAE, Qatar, Kuwait, Bahrain and Oman have also been strongly involved in establishing modern markets for similar purposes but have done so through different means, with varying results, and each in line with what has been considered their respective comparative advantages.

Along with critically surveying these institutions and their role in global finance, the book also presents case studies depicting transactions typical to the region, including the highly profitable documentary credits undertaken by commercial banks, the financial scandal of certain financiers and the regulatory arbitrage they practiced between Bahrain and Saudi Arabia, a review of the Dubai's trade miracle and an assessment of the value and importance of the privatization of Saudi Aramco.

Jean-François Seznec is Senior Fellow, Center for Global Energy at the Atlantic Council, Adjunct Professor at Johns Hopkins School of Advanced International Studies and Managing Director at The Lafayette Group.

Samer Mosis is Senior Analyst with S&P Global Platts, focusing on commodity markets. He previously was a consultant for The Lafayette Group and holds a Master Degree in International Economics from Johns Hopkins School of Advanced International Studies.

Routledge International Studies in Money and Banking

Finance at Work
Edited by Valérie Boussard

The Development of International Monetary Policy
Christopher Warburton

Pension Fund Economics and Finance
Efficiency, Investments and Risk-Taking
Edited by Jacob A. Bikker

The Rise and Development of FinTech
Accounts of Disruption from Sweden and Beyond
Edited by Robin Teigland, Shahryar Siri, Anthony Larsson, Alejandro Moreno Puertas, and Claire Ingram Bogusz

Money, Markets and Capital
The Case for a Monetary Analysis
Jean Cartelier

Monetary Equilibrium and Nominal Income Targeting
Nicolás Cachanosky

Distance, Rating Systems and Enterprise Finance
Ethnographic Insights from a Comparison of Regional and Large Banks in Germany
Franz Flögel

Financial Markets of the Arab Gulf
Power, Politics and Money
Jean-François Seznec and Samer Mosis

For more information about this series, please visit www.routledge.com/series/SE0403

The Financial Markets of the Arab Gulf

Power, Politics and Money

Jean-François Seznec and
Samer Mosis

Routledge
Taylor & Francis Group
NEW YORK AND LONDON

First published 2019
by Routledge
52 Vanderbilt Avenue, New York, NY 10017

and by Routledge
2 Park Square, Milton Park, Abingdon, Oxon, OX14 4RN

Routledge is an imprint of the Taylor & Francis Group, an informa business

© 2019 Taylor & Francis

The right of Jean-François Seznec and Samer Mosis to be identified as authors of this work has been asserted by them in accordance with sections 77 and 78 of the Copyright, Designs and Patents Act 1988.

All rights reserved. No part of this book may be reprinted or reproduced or utilised in any form or by any electronic, mechanical, or other means, now known or hereafter invented, including photocopying and recording, or in any information storage or retrieval system, without permission in writing from the publishers.

Trademark notice: Product or corporate names may be trademarks or registered trademarks, and are used only for identification and explanation without intent to infringe.

Library of Congress Cataloging-in-Publication Data
A catalog record for this book has been requested

ISBN: 9780815380801 (hbk)
ISBN: 9781351059718 (ebk)

Typeset in Sabon
by Apex CoVantage, LLC

MIX
Paper from responsible sources
FSC www.fsc.org FSC® C013056

Printed and bound in Great Britain by
TJ International Ltd, Padstow, Cornwall

To Thackray Weems Dodds Seznec, with deep appreciation for her unfailing support.

For Joseph, Amany and Monica Mosis; you are my guiding light through the dark and the bright.

Contents

Figures, Maps, Tables

Figures

Map

Tables

Abbreviations

AAOIFI	Accounting and Auditing Organization for Islamic Financial Institutions
ABC	Arab Banking Corporation
ADGM	Abu Dhabi Global Market
ADIA	Abu Dhabi Investment Fund
AFH	Al Futtooh Holding Company
AHAB	Ahmed Hamad Al Gosaibi & Brothers
APG	Advanced Payment Guarantee
ASEAN	Association of Southeast Asian Nations
BAPCO	Bahrain Petroleum Company
BBL	Barrel
BBME	British Bank of the Middle East
BBTC	Branch Banking & Trust Company
BKSE	Boursa Kuwait Securities Company
BMA	Bahrain Monetary Agency
BNY	Bank of New York
BSF	Bank Saudi Fransi
CBB	Central Bank of Bahrain
CBK	Central Bank of Kuwait
CBU	Central Bank of the UAE
CEDA	Council of Economic and Development Affairs
CMA	Capital Markets Authority
DAM	Dar Al Mal Al Islami
DFSA	Dubai Financial Services Authority
DIB	Dubai Islamic Bank
DIFC	Dubai International Financial Center
DME	Dubai Mercantile Exchange
DPW	Dubai Ports World
FAB	First Abu Dhabi National Bank
FTZ	Free Trade Zone
GCC	Gulf Cooperation Council
GDP	Gross National Product
GIB	Gulf International Bank

GOSI	General Organization for Social Insurance
GRF	General Reserve Fund
GTL	Gas to Liquid
HSBC	Hong Kong Shanghai Bank
IFI	Islamic Financial Institution
IGRC	Islamic Revolutionary Guards Corp
IIRA	Islamic International Rating Agency
IOCs	International Oil Companies
IPIC	International Petroleum Investment Company
IPO	Initial Public Offering
IQ	Industries Qatar
ISOP	Investcorp Employee Share Ownership Program
JAFZA	Jebel Ali Free Trade Zone
JASTA	Justice Against Sponsors of Terrorism Act
JCC	Japanese Crude Cocktail
JJC	Joint Judicial Council
JCPOA	Joint Comprehensive Plan for Action
JV	Joint Venture
KCC	Kuwait Clearing Committee
KFH	Kuwait Finance House
KFTCIC	Kuwait Foreign Trading, Contracting and Investment Company
KIA	Kuwait Investment Authority
KIC	Kuwait Investment Company
KIIC	Kuwait International Investment Company
KIO	Kuwait Investment Office
KIPCO	Kuwait Projects Company
KIZAD	Khalifa Industrial Zone Abu Dhabi
KPCT	Khalifa Port Container Terminal
KSE	Kuwait Stock Exchange
KUCLEAR	Kuwait Clearing House Company
L/C	Letter of Credit
LIBOR	London Interbank Offering Rate
LMC	Liquidity Management Center
LNG	Liquid Natural Gas
MbR	Mohammed bin Rashid
MbS	Mohammed bin Salman
MbZ	Mohammed bin Zayed
MK	Markets Committee
MoF	Ministry of Finance
MSM	Muscat Securities Market
NBB	National Bank of Bahrain
NBD	Emirates National Bank
NBK	National Bank of Kuwait
NCB	National Commercial Bank

NGLs	Natural Gas Liquids
NOCs	National Oil Companies
OBU	Off-Shore Banking Unit
P/E	Price to Earnings Ratio
PB	Performance Bond
PDO	Petroleum Development Oman
PIF	Public Investment Fund
PPA	Public Pension Authority
QAFAC	Qatar Fuel Additives Company
QAPCO	Qatar Petrochemical Company
QCB	Qatar Central Bank
QFI	Qualified Foreign Institution
QIA	Qatar Investment Authority
QNB	Qatar National Bank
QP	Qatar Petroleum
QSE	Qatar Stock Exchange
QVC	Qatar Vinyl Company
RBS	Royal Bank of Scotland
RFFG	Reserve for Future Generation
SABIC	Saudi Basic Industries Company
SAMA	Saudi Arabian Monetary Agency (or Authority)
SAMBA	Saudi Financial Group
SAR	Saudi Riyal
SCECO	Saudi Central Electric Company
SFAAI	State Financial Administrative Audit Institution
SIB	Saudi Investment Banking Corporation
SIDF	Saudi Industrial Development Fund
SPC	Supreme Petroleum Council
SPV	Special Purpose Vehicle
SWF	Sovereign Wealth Fund
TASI	Tadawul All Share Index
TIBC	The International Banking Corporation
UAE	United Arab Emirates
WTO	World Trade Organization

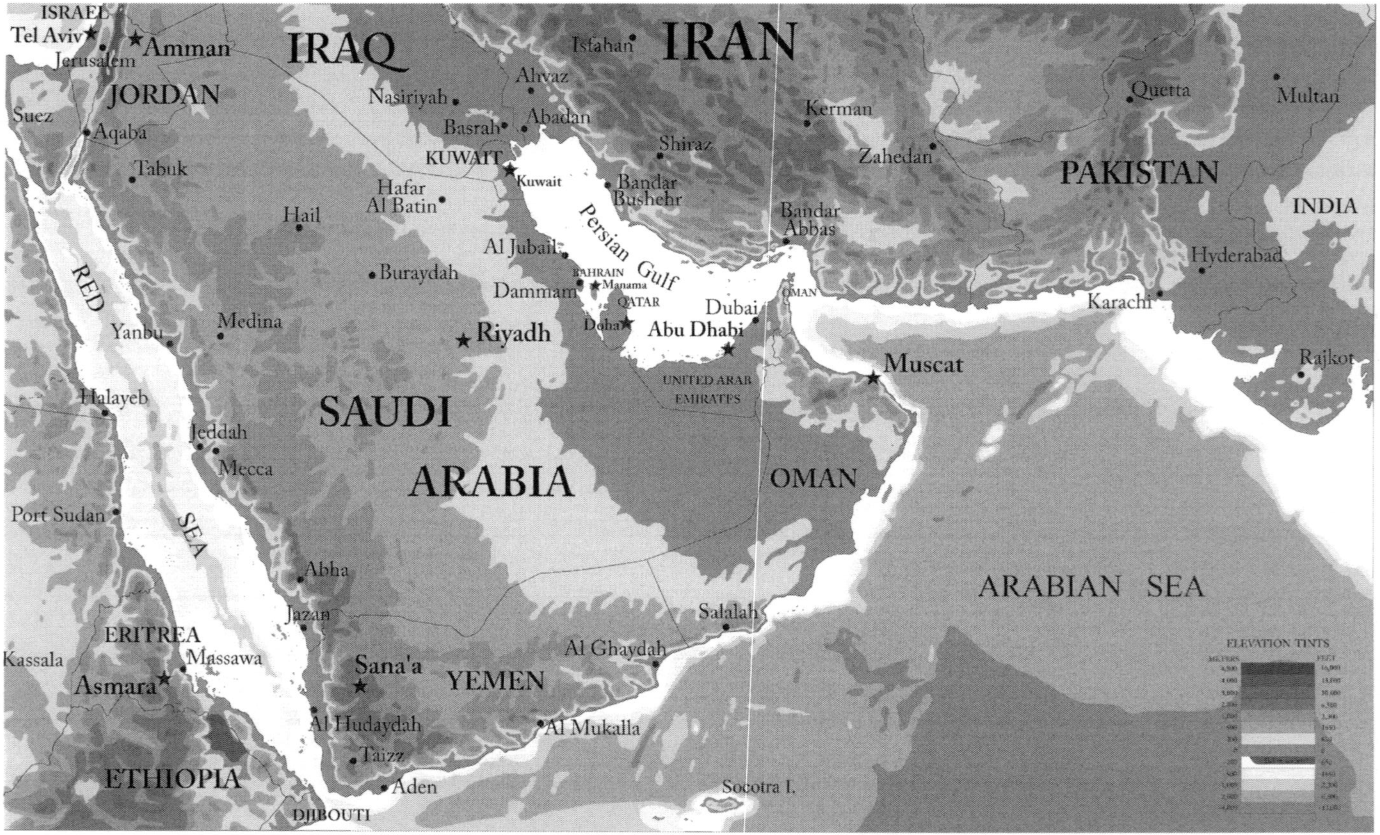

Map 0.1 Map of the Arab Gulf States

Introduction

"Money, money, money makes the world go 'round'" says the song. Definitely this is true in the energy producing countries of the Arab/Persian Gulf.[1] The states of the Gulf Cooperation Council (GCC), Saudi Arabia, the United Arab Emirates (UAE), Qatar, Kuwait, Oman and Bahrain, have been selling oil for almost eighty years, providing them with many tens of billions of dollars. This money has been used for a broad swath of purposes ranging from large military expenses to industrial development and modern state infrastructure such as roads, airports, harbors, schools and hospitals. In some cases, it has been used to pad the Swiss bank accounts of various leading royal or merchant families. In all cases, however, these monies had to pass through financial institutions. This book will describe in some detail the banks, stock markets, investment companies, money changers and sovereign wealth funds (SWF) that grew from this oil and gas wealth and how the Gulf's Arab States funneled the money to people and vice versa.

There are some recurring themes that appear in the various chapters. One is that regional financial markets evolve very rapidly. Countries like Bahrain, which at one time was slated to become a major financial center, has seen its quick growth as an international financial service center stagnate under competition from markets aiming to service growing financial markets in Saudi Arabia and the UAE. As part of its plan to become a global financial platform for investment banks, stock markets and legal services, Dubai created the Dubai International Financial Center (DIFC), which has become an outstanding real estate success, but remains little used as a financial center in the traditional sense. Ultimately, the major financial centers of the region have become a magnet for the big money in the region, i.e. Saudi Arabia and Abu Dhabi. Even in this proviso, one should add that the centers with the most active financial markets are those with truly sizable populations, namely Riyadh. Indeed, Saudi Arabia, with 21 million local citizens, or four times the amount of citizens living in the rest of the GCC, has a natural advantage since, by and large, people are biased toward investing their money close to home.

The Gulf's financial institutions, and the broader regional markets they occupy, are all very closely controlled by the states and their respective leaderships. In Saudi Arabia, the state and its various institutions de facto control all the privately owned banks. The stock markets are highly influenced by the states in the sense that all the companies with shares in the market are dependent on their relationship with the state to get contracts. Also, the markets' legal environments are highly controlled by the state. None of the Gulf judiciaries are independent. For instance, in Bahrain every judge, whether in criminal or civil courts, is appointed by the King. In this sense, the states have complete control over financial disputes.

On the other hand, and perhaps paradoxically, the countries of the Gulf have extremely liberal financial controls. There are no foreign exchange regulations or limits on how funds can be transferred in or out of the region. Individuals, money changers, banks, investment companies can transfer any amount, in any currency, a practice that aided in cross-border investment as well as cross-border fraud, as was seen during the Souk Al Manakh stock market crash. Prior to 2001, it was common to see people opening their briefcases at airport security only to have officers looking through vast sums of cash searching for guns or other suspicious items, totally ignoring the fortune in front of their eyes. Today, cash transfers are less common and under more scrutiny to comply with the anti-money laundering and anti-terror financing regulations, but there are still no regulations on amounts or currencies that can be transferred.

The marketplace in the countries of the Gulf is not as vibrant as that of much older centers like London or New York. The amounts traded are smaller and the relationships between institutions and their employees are relatively unstable, especially in centers where expatriates fill most of the mid- and upper-level management. Top decision makers will mostly be locals, but financial institutions are run day-to-day by their vice presidents and more junior officers. In other words, deals are developed, and in many cases originated, by expatriates who have a short shelf life. Naturally, as the markets mature and the locals become more involved at all levels, this interaction becomes deeper rooted amongst the local population. This is especially true in Saudi Arabia and Bahrain, where locals make up a very large percentage of the employees, thus allowing for more of a true marketplace to develop. The ability of staff to build trust between institutions and the people within them is vital to the strong establishment of syndicated facilities and share issuances.

What has fascinated observers of the region for the past thirty to forty years has been the enormous growth of its markets. Perhaps they are still considered small by New York or London's standards, but, coming from zero, they have now developed sophisticated platforms for real estate, industrial activity and consumer finance, and are home to quickly growing stock markets. It is thus that an underlying theme of this book is to evaluate how these markets have grown over the decades, what factors have influenced the development of societies in the Gulf, and how the societies of the Gulf have, in return, left their mark on the markets' form and function.

The first chapter of the book covers the history of the financial markets in the region. Starting in the 1970s, modern banking technology was badly needed and the states focused heavily on building the adequate infrastructure for longer-term growth, yet these efforts were not always successful. The chapter reviews how Saudi Arabia mobilized funds to rapidly develop the country, how Bahrain took advantage of the opportunity to develop a thriving offshore banking industry, and how large inflows of oil income after 1973 and inadequate regulatory structures caused the Souk Al Manakh scandal in Kuwait. The scandal shook the state to its foundation and stunted the growth of the region's capital markets. The chapter also explores how traditional financial intermediation in the Gulf was undertaken by money changers, which had existed since the start of the pilgrimage to Mecca, long before Islam. These money changers evolved as major financial intermediaries for transfers by the numerous foreign workers and also became quasi-banks. They were eventually brought under the control of the central banks, a trend that would extend further into the financial landscape by the mid-1990s.

The second chapter reviews in detail the markets of the UAE. It focuses mainly on Abu Dhabi and Dubai, as well as the differences between them. Dubai has tried with success to develop its economy without relying directly on oil income. It has built on its trading roots to become a major commercial center with all the services necessary, including financial ones. To maintain its traditional trading business and support its trading families, Dubai most interestingly established more than twenty-five extremely successful free trade zones (FTZ), such as Jebel Ali Free Zone, DIFC and Media City. However, while all the FTZs were runaway real estate successes and JAFZA is one of the most successful ports in the world, the DIFC did not really succeed as a financial center in the sense that London and New York have. For its part, Abu Dhabi has also failed to establish a sizable financial market. On the other hand, Abu Dhabi has become home to some of the largest Sovereign Wealth Funds in the world. The form and function of these SWFs are reviewed in detail, as are questions about what their leadership structures say about power in the UAE, and what their opacity means for the UAE as a whole. The chapter also reviews the evolution of the commercial banks of the UAE, their close connection with royal and merchant elite and the remarkable growth of the UAE's Shari'a-compliant sector.

The third chapter focuses on Saudi Arabia and emphasizes the influence of the state on the financial markets. Banks in the kingdom were never owned by the state, but since the exponential growth of oil income, they have felt the strong hand of the Saudi Arabian Monetary Authority (SAMA), the regulator of the banks, and de facto have come under the control of the state.[2] Ultimately the chapter shows that the state, through SAMA and the Ministry of Finance (MoF) structures the banking sector so that funds in the kingdom would stay in the kingdom and be used to finance either industrial development or the state's budget deficits. It also discusses how the markets are now evolving. The money changers, so successful in the past, have become irrelevant, while the stock market, which was kept small for fear of a new Souk Al Manakh, has now become large and quite sophisticated. Still, the state plays an enormous role in the financial industry in the kingdom. State organizations like SIDF and GOSI still lend money and in fact compete with the non-state institutions. While SAMA and the MoF were the two institutions in charge of finance in the kingdom, the PIF has been separated from the MoF's control and is now independent. It is being groomed to be the SWF of the kingdom and scheduled to receive the proceeds of the Saudi Aramco privatization, as well as surplus oil revenues, a change that would significantly alter the current financial balance of power in the kingdom and potentially undercut the drive to increase transparency in the kingdom.

Chapter 4 reviews the smaller markets of Bahrain, Kuwait, Qatar and Oman. As technological advancements made Bahrain's offshore banking sector redundant, Bahrain focused on establishing itself as the main center for Islamic financial institutions in the Gulf. It has developed a sophisticated regulatory system for Islamic finance, and has had some success establishing new Islamic banks. However, it is under severe competition from the other states in the region, which have now become quite enamored with Islamic banking, a significant change from the past, and have established very large and powerful Shari'a-compliant banking companies. The chapter also discusses cases in which Bahrain has been home to very successful banking companies, including Investcorp. Despite this success, Bahrain's primary asset appears not to be its financial or banking sector, and instead stems from its proximity to, and strong political ties with, the Kingdom of Saudi Arabia.

Compared to its peers, Kuwait's financial markets have remained largely static—a consequence of past failures, namely the Souk Al Manakh crash, as well as the power of Kuwait's National Assembly. This body has distinguished Kuwait amongst its peers politically, but has also placed checks on the monarchical power that has catalyzed development in otherwise lethargic markets elsewhere in the Gulf. Amidst this, Kuwait's markets have become dominated by three major institutions, the Kuwait Investment Authority, which controls the Reserve for Future Generations, the main SWF of the country, the National Bank of Kuwait, and the Shari'a-compliant Kuwait Finance House. The stock market has now recovered from the Souk Al Manakh and is slowly becoming more important, albeit still far from the Tadawul in Saudi Arabia.

Qatar, being a very small, albeit very rich, country is dominated by two institutions, the Qatar Investment Authority, which is reputed to have over US$350 billion in assets under management and the Qatar National Bank, which holds more than 50% of the total banking market of the country. In all cases the financial system of Qatar is dominated by the royal family, who holds the chairmanship of nine out of ten Qatari banks and control the QIA, which is the largest shareholder in the tenth bank. The stock market of Qatar is used by the leadership to spread some of the wealth from natural gas and oil to the people. Some of the country's most important downstream companies have be made into corporations, which have issued shares to the public. Of course all these shares have been bought eagerly by Qataris who now are benefitting from the companies through stock dividends and capital appreciation. The vast majority of Qataris have shares in these firms, thereby creating a sense of community and solidarity with the leadership in spite of their overwhelming control of the economy. While the recent embargo by its neighbors has significant political and financial ramifications, as is shown, Qatar has been able to navigate the financial implications successfully. Moving forward, the ability to continue this successful navigation will be greatly dependent on how Qatar adjusts to fundamental shifts in global natural gas markets.

Oman is a larger country than the three mentioned previously, but is much smaller in terms of wealth and financial sophistication. The banks of Oman are relatively small and so is the stock market, yet the growth the country has experienced as a whole is impressive. That said, the formula which allowed for this development, one based on a bargain struck with leading merchant families during the country's developmental period, may no longer be enough to maintain the political and economic status quo in the country. Oman has sought diversification through trade and finance, but the fruits of these efforts have yet to materialize.

Chapter 5 discusses the role financial markets play in stabilizing the effects of oscillating oil and gas prices. Even though a sudden increase in oil prices creates an enormous effect on GDP figures and vice versa, the people in the street do not immediately feel the fluctuations in GDP. Indeed, as money comes in, it is stored by the central banks or the ministries of finance, who then disburse the money through salaries to the civil service or through contracts to the private sector and through extensive military contracts. The monies not used in the budget are stored in SWFs, or placed overseas by the central banks, or both. Funds received by the public end up in the local banks, which in many cases will lend more money, but who also will place money overseas. The pension funds, which are quite large in the Gulf also invest in local assets but also extensively in foreign government securities. In the reverse, at times of low prices and income, the amounts kept in direct and indirect reserves by the central banks, SWFs, pension funds and banks will be used to finance the same salaries, infrastructure and military needs. In other words, the financial markets of the Gulf act as a buffer between the vagaries of the oil markets and the people.

Whether by intention or not, the portion of this buffer that has been placed overseas has enabled the Gulf states to take on a significant role in global financial markets. This was clearly evident during the 2008 crisis. Yet, the relationship between SWF and central bank assets and global financial crises has a much longer precedent, starting essentially with the oil boom in the 1970s. As global financial flows and trade shift toward developing and formally developing countries, so have the assets of these various states' institutions. With these shifts come implications for broader markets, a dynamic that is unpacked in this chapter.

The Gulf markets have some specificities requiring detailed analysis in order to understand how and why political and financial leadership take the decisions they do. Chapter 6 uses four cases to go into these specificities, and how particular events and financial tools have, or will, influence the evolution of the region's financial markets.

First and foremost, at the time of this writing, there exists the possibility that Saudi Aramco will be privatized. We have provided a short analysis on the valuation of the company based on our observation that Saudi Aramco is managed more like an international oil company, such as ExxonMobil, than a national oil company. The chapter also discusses in detail the motivations behind the privatization and challenges that may stand in its way.

We also review the legal and financial case of a Bahrain offshore banking unit, The International Banking Cooperation (TIBC), which went bankrupt due to fraudulent loans approved by its management. The bank became fairly large and obtained funding from major international banks on the basis of its alleged ownership by the Al Gosaibi family of Al Khobar in Saudi Arabia. This case provides great insight into how unscrupulous investors were able to take advantage of the differences in the regulatory processes between Bahrain and Saudi Arabia and how regulators, foreign banks and service companies failed to prevent the affair.

It is also quite informative to see how Dubai is benefitting from the region's major upheavals. We offer in the third case study a theory on how some in the Iranian leadership have set up companies in Dubai to transfer money from Tehran to the emirate. Undoubtedly, Dubai is staying within the right side of the law, but in the process is receiving large volumes of capital from individuals that are seeking to bypass regulations on foreign exchange and financial transfers, whether it be from Iran, Pakistan or Afghanistan.

Finally, we show in some detail how banks have had great success by working the very traditional banking instruments of documentary credits to facilitate the implementation of hundreds of billions worth of major infrastructure projects since the 1970s. Issuing letters of credits, performance bonds and the like may not appear very exciting but in fact continues to provide steady and substantial returns to the banks.

Ultimately, the states' control of the financial markets has been very strong and decisive in their growth and success in the past forty years. Looking forward, with the swelling of available capital in the region, the tremendous growth of non-petroleum production, and most importantly the increasing sophistication of the youth, it appears that the next forty years in the Gulf's financial markets will see the receding of state control and the rise of characteristics more regularly seen in developed markets across the world.

Notes

1. Persians and Arabs both claim the name Persian Gulf or Arab Gulf for the body of water between Iran and the Gulf Cooperation Council states. This book will refer to it henceforth as "the Gulf."
2. The Saudi Arabian Monetary Authority changed its name from the Saudi Arabian Monetary Agency on December 4, 2016.

1 A Short History of the Financial Markets in the GCC States

The evolution of the Gulf's modern financial markets began in the 1970s in parallel with the exponential growth of hydrocarbon revenues. Prior to this, local financing needs were met through an amalgamation of money changers, some of which had grown substantially in size and sophistication, local branches of foreign banks and directly through the intermediation of bankers from global hubs in New York and London.

In Saudi Arabia in particular, in the 1970s, there was a major effort to diversify the burgeoning economy away from crude oil. Some of the leading civil servants of the time, such as Mr. Aba Al Khail, Khalid al Gosaibi, Ahmed Zaki Yamani, or Hisham Nazer were strongly pushing for modernization of the Kingdom's economy. They felt that the banking system needed to join the 21st century in order for the Kingdom to have a chance at developing beyond crude oil. One of the primary initiatives in this regard was their push for a well-regulated market under the leadership of a strong central bank, the Saudi Arabian Monetary Agency (SAMA). At the time the Saudi financial and capital markets were just beginning to take shape, while Kuwait was already much more sophisticated with both an official stock market and an unregulated stock market called the Souk Al Manakh. Kuwait and the United Arab Emirates (UAE) had an established Islamic Bank, while Saudi Arabia had none. Nearby, Bahrain was becoming a major financial hub for the region, providing services which Beirut-based financial institutions could no longer offer due to civil war. In the UAE, a series of disparate stories were at play across the country's Emirates, with Dubai capitalizing on its position along major trade routes to supplant its waning hydrocarbon revenues, while Abu Dhabi established the framework for what would be one of the world's largest financial institutions, the Abu Dhabi Investment Authority, in an effort to insulate itself from financial volatility.

These institutions established in the mid-1970s have evolved greatly. The volume and type of transactions they host have grown exponentially. Their exposure and openness to foreign markets has been transformed while their role in global markets has grown in prominence and shifted in substance. The Gulf's modern market structure and function, which will be presented in later chapters, has been built upon the foundations that are described in this chapter, which focuses on the developments between the mid-1970s and 1980s in key financial markets in the Gulf.

The Commercial Banks

The first commercial banks of the Gulf were established by the colonial powers to service their local needs or that of their traders on their way to the Far East or India. The Bank of the East, which ultimately became Standard Chartered, was first established in Bahrain in 1920 and primarily served British companies and civil servants in their relations with both London and the Indian Empire, which was managing Britain's affairs in the Gulf. Driven by similar dynamics, the British Bank of the Middle East was established in Jeddah to serve the subcontinent trade from England and the Indian pilgrims to Mecca. The British also established The Imperial Bank, now HSBC, in Kuwait in 1943, to service the substantial British presence in Kuwait at the time. The French established the Banque de l'Indochine in Jeddah very early on to service the trade and ships from France to Indochina. This branch proudly claimed that its address was P.O. Box 1. By the same token, Dutch Algemene Bank established a branch in Jeddah for their trade to Indonesia as well as the numerous pilgrims from Indonesia to Mecca.

The branches of foreign banks were very important to the region's early development. Many merchants used them to trade with Asia, Europe, or the US. They opened cash accounts, which would help them dealing with the bank's worldwide networks. They also provided short-term loans usually linked to trade. However, in the 1950s, some local merchants decided they could go into banking for themselves. They wanted to have the capacity to deposit funds locally, and in general take their business to locally owned institutions rather than be dependent on what they perceived as the whims and decisions of foreign banks in New York, London or Paris. In Saudi Arabia, this gave birth to the National Commercial Bank, established in 1953 by two Hadrami families in Jeddah, the Al Mahfouz and the Kakis.[1] Very rapidly they opened branches in numerous towns in Saudi Arabia, which allowed them to build large local deposits and provide local banking services. The Sharbatly family, also in Jeddah, established the Riyadh Bank in an analogous pattern of events.

Driven by very similar dynamics, leading merchant families in Kuwait and Bahrain started the National Bank of Kuwait in 1952 and the National Bank of Bahrain in 1957, respectively. NBK was established with the full support of then ruling Sheikh Abdullah al Salem al Sabah, who underwrote the bank with an interest-free deposit of 1 million British pounds. In doing so he looked to placate prominent merchant families who felt that British-owned banking interests were unjustly eroding their money-lending and money-changing enterprises.[2] Some of these families were among the founding members of NBK, most notably the Al Kharafi, the Al Sagr, the

Al Hamad and the Al Sayer, all of whom continue to have members represented across NBK's board of directors and executive management.[3] After its founding, NBK quickly took on many of the country's central banking functions, expanded its lending operations and opened new branches throughout the country. By the late 1950s, NBK had surpassed its British counterpart as the dominant bank in Kuwait.

The United Arab Emirates saw the modern history of its banking sector start with UAE Federal Law No. 10 of 1980. Known as The Banking Law, it established the Central Bank of the UAE (CBU) and gave it legal authority to issue and ensure the stability of the official currency (the dirham), organize, promote and supervise the banking sector, oversee credit policy, advise the government on economic matters, maintain foreign reserves and act as the bank for banks in the UAE.[4] As part of these authorities, the Banking Law also provided the CBU with oversight over the registration, licensing and operation of commercial and investment banks, financial institutions and money changers, most of which is carried out by the CBU's Banking Supervision and Examination Department. That stated, as stipulated in the Banking Law's Article 77, a number of important institutions are outside the CBU's jurisdiction including public credit institutions other than commercial banks, governmental development funds, private and pension funds and insurance and reinsurance agencies, effectively placing the country's various sovereign wealth funds outside of its oversight.

Before 1980, there had been no central regulatory actor for the UAE's burgeoning banking and finance sector. The CBU's predecessor, the Currency Board, had been established in 1973 not for regulatory reasons, but with the primary purpose of establishing a new UAE currency. Until then, the prevalent currencies used in the recently formed country were the Qatari Riyal and the Bahraini dinar. The lack of regulatory oversight was not due to lack of foresight, but instead due to the ruling Emirs' reluctance to grant regulatory power over domestic banks, including many which royal family members held financial interest in, to the Currency Board's mainly foreign management.[5] In a time of massive oil-driven financial growth, this lack of regulation led to significant troubles including rampant real estate speculation, bank proliferation and credit expansion, eventually leading to a run on the currency and multiple bank failures in 1977.[6] It is in this sense that the Banking Law fundamentally changed the banking sector, forcing banks to be established as national shareholding companies and binding them to capital and ownership structure limitations.[7] Once in place, the CBU was quick to act, issuing regulations expanding audits and inspections, expanding reporting requirements, establishing a computerized loan risk department, setting minimum capital requirements and limiting loans to bank executives to 5% of the bank's total capital.[8]

In Saudi Arabia, after the first oil boom of 1973, the government, like most other oil-producing countries, started programs to establish physical infrastructure on par with that of Europe or the US. It signed hundreds of billions in contracts for harbors, roads, airports, schools, entire new cities—all at the same time. This level of expenditure brought about a new role for the young domestic banking sector.

To ensure efficiency in the financing of these infrastructure projects, the Ministry of Finance (MoF) supervised the issuance of contracts. It demanded that all contractors involved in this effort provide bid bonds, followed by performance bonds and advance payment guarantees. These performance bonds, which were often written in favor of SAMA, ensured that the Saudi central bank would recoup any losses stemming from incomplete projects, either due to unforeseen circumstances or contract bankruptcy. From 1974 to 1983, the Saudi market required US$1 billion dollars of performance bonds and between US$2 and US$4 billion of advance payment guarantees each year. The bonds and guarantees required were drafted to the same standards of the documentary credits used in the United States. The banks also had to provide letters of credits to contractors for the import of goods related to the contracts, as well as cash advances to tie the contractors over between the time the work was done and the time the government actually paid; all told these financial instruments amounted to roughly US$30 billion per year.[9]

This activity provided an opportunity for the local banks not only to expand their portfolios, but arguably more importantly, to interact with, and learn from, more advanced international banking outfits. This was underpinned by the fact that many of the banking facilities needed for the larger contracts were so large that the local banks had to share their risks with other banks locally and abroad. Since most of the income of the Saudi government was in USD from the sale of oil, the government drafted and paid all contracts over in USD US$100 million and not Saudi Riyals (SAR). Hence, for larger contracts, the banking facilities needed were in the hundreds of millions of USD. On a US$100 million contract, such as road or an airport, which was a substantial amount in the 1980s, contractors needed to provide a 1% bid bond, a 5% performance bond and a 10% advance payment guarantee. The contractors also normally would require about 10% for letters of credit and a similar amount in short-term advances. Thus a contract of the size mentioned would require a total facility of US$46 million, a large sum at the time. Accordingly, banks tried to share the risks with other banks through syndication arrangements, with the largest portion of syndicated risks consisting usually of performance bonds and advanced payment guarantee facilities. A more detailed discussion of this process is discussed in Chapter 6.4.

As such, syndications of large lines of credits for contractors became a major activity between banks in the Middle East, as well as leading international banks, and became a major source of income for many of these banks. This active exchange and spreading of risk was one of the first modern financial activities carried out regularly across the Gulf. In the early 1970s, to ease the strain on local banks, SAMA agreed to accept bonds issued directly by certain well-vetted large foreign banks. These banks consisted of the largest Western banks (Citibank, Chase, Morgan Guarantee, Barclays, Indosuez, Sumitomo, Bank of Tokyo) as well as some of the more established banks from developing countries. All other banks were required to either co-issue with approved banks or local Saudi banks, with which the smaller banks could have a traditional correspondent relationship. The limitation on the number of foreign banks able to issue bonds directly gave SAMA substantial leverage in dealing with the foreign banks.

By the late 1970s, SAMA grew fearful that the still quasi-embryonic local banking sector could lose its dominant role in arranging these various financial facilities to a massive flow of banking services from abroad. It also feared that local banks would grow to seek more lucrative, and less risky, use of their funds by providing facilities to non-Saudi companies active outside Saudi Arabia. To avoid this SAMA took a number of measures. In 1978, SAMA forbade all Saudi banks from participating in foreign led syndications. SAMA also required that Saudi banks request its approval prior to participating in syndications not floated for the Saudi market specifically. In great part, these actions were also driven by SAMA's watchful eye on the problems many banks were having with syndicated loans and facilities in Latin America. It was there that some of the largest banking outfits were facing major defaults, a development which SAMA wanted local banks to avoid.

Until the early 1970s the branches of foreign banks operating in Saudi Arabia were not regulated by SAMA, but instead were technically under the jurisdiction of regulators in their home jurisdiction. SAMA had very little say on what the local branches of these foreign banks could or could not do outside of its ability to limit the amount of local deposits they could take. By and large, the branches of foreign banks were small and unable to cope with a large increasing demand for banking services, some due to lack of infrastructure and some due to lack of capital. Even though the capital of the branches was technically the same as that of the parent bank, facilities to local merchants would have to be approved by remote head offices, which de facto limited the amount of business that was actually done with local merchants. With the inflow of oil income and significant growth in infrastructure expenditures, the potential for business was growing rapidly, especially given the numerous infrastructure projects active during the period, all of which required significant financial facilities.[10] To tap in to the post-1973 booming market, it was important for the foreign banks to obtain more deposits. Getting SAMA's approval to do so proved problematic though, as the Saudi central bank was uncomfortable with them taking the local deposits while practicing outside the Kingdom's direct regulation. It was in light of this environment that SAMA felt it had the leverage to establish a new regulatory environment, one in which these foreign branches would be forced to come under its jurisdiction.

In 1978, SAMA informed the foreign banks that they would be permitted to expand and open more branches, but only if they became locally registered Saudi corporations and increased their capital, but with the proviso that the new capital structure had to give Saudi citizens a 60% majority. Hence, the banks were not nationalized per se, but were "Saudi-ized," which in turn put these foreign entities under the supervision of SAMA rather than under the supervision of their home central banks. The Saudization requirement started lengthy negotiations between the foreign banks and SAMA. The parent banks in Europe and the US feared that Saudization would hinder their ability to manage their overseas branches and control their own banking risks. Moreover, minority ownership positions, even with management control, was against the corporate policy of some banks, such as Citibank, which held out to the longest prior to accepting its new status.

SAMA was able to persuade the banks to go along with the plan because the foreign banks realized that they could increase their deposits, their loans and their fee instruments. More importantly, the banks realized that by moving forward with new regulatory structures they would remain on the good side of SAMA, who at the time had reserves of US$180 billion, which had to be placed somewhere. Thus, in the eyes of these foreign banks, the potential increase for business and profit was strong despite the potential loss of 60% of the new profits to Saudi shareholders. In the end, the foreign banks were still able to maintain a 40% interest, and their fear of being dominated by Saudis shareholders was somewhat assuaged by the fact that no Saudi was allowed to own more than 5% of the outstanding shares, a stipulation that allowed the foreigners to keep effective control of management.

The perception that there was money to be made in Saudi was not wrong. In conjunction with the large increase in oil revenues, the Kingdom's bank deposits increased from US$1.09 billion in 1973 to US$47.49 billion in 1991.[11] However, the larger deposits were not matched by a proportional increase in loan activity. The ratio of bank loans to deposits in the Kingdom went from 61% in 1980 to 46% in 1991.[12] If banks do not lend money to businesses or individuals, they must place their money with other financial institutions or buy corporate or government securities. At the time Saudi banks did not trade in government securities and did not place funds with one another. Hence, the Saudi banks became little more than intermediaries between small Saudi depositors and large Western and Japanese banks.

The declining loans to assets ratio was largely due to the problems banks had collecting bad loans from rich and powerful borrowers. At the time, Shari'a law, which acted as the law of the Kingdom, applied to everyone, including banks and business. The Saudi interpretation of Shari'a, especially the Hanbali interpretation, specifically forbade the giving and receiving of interest.[13] Mortgages that bore interest or that were on movable assets were not acceptable in court and floating liens were specifically forbidden in the Qur'an. The court's conservative interpretation of the Shari'a meant that judgments where usually rendered against banks. Consequently, banks justifiably felt that they could not credibly obtain redress in court, which in turn limited the banks' desire to lend, let alone take risky debt. Further, even in the unlikely event that bank received a favorable judgment, it could not count on obtaining any repayment, as the Saudi legal system has no bailiff or sheriff to enforce core decisions, and police officers asked to enforce judgment would at times even retry the case themselves.[14] For all intents and purposes, banks were lending unsecured.

Even though the absolute amount of loans increased yearly after 1974, the actual ratio of loans to assets declined drastically until 1990. After 1990, the ratio turned around but not because the banks had re-entered the markets as lenders to the private sector, but because government-linked entities, then unable to obtain funds from the state, had been borrowing heavily from the local banks. The Saudi banks formed syndicates to lend to SABIC (the State controlled chemical company), VELA (the shipping company owned by Saudi Aramco), Saudi Aramco or SCECO (the Saudi electric company, also known as SEC). All of these companies were government controlled and therefore seen by the banks as government risk, but with the added benefit of possibly obtaining a higher margin above the interbank cost of funds (LIBOR). For local Saudi bankers it was more profitable to place money with the government by buying the State's treasury bonds or development bonds. Between the limit put by SAMA on local banks participating in foreign syndication and the difficulties encountered by the legal system, the banks were easily coaxed into lending more to the large commercial and industrial names in the Kingdom, thereby promoting large-scale industrialization.

At the same time, SAMA had to fund the very large deficits run by the Saudi government. To fund the government, the MoF had to issue development bonds and treasury bills, which paid proper interest. Of course, the local Saudi banks where eager to buy them, as they offered slightly higher interests than the deposits in foreign banks and were definitely a safer investment than loans to the private sector, legally impaired as seen previously. By the end of 1991, the government had issued US$41.5 billion of Saudi treasury bills. They also issued long-term bonds of US$8.5 billion in 1991, which increased US$14 billion in 1992, mostly bought by the banks. These were primarily issued to local banks, who had extensive liquidity. The state bonds were not tradable. If a bank needed cash, the bonds and bills could only be sold back to SAMA. In other words, no bond market developed in the Kingdom.

An alternative did exist though. The banks could place money into dollar-denominated deposits with their correspondent banks in New York or in Saudi denominated accounts with their branches in Bahrain. It was these branches that, in turn, would lend to the Bahraini Offshore Banking Units (OBUs), which while established in Bahrain, sat outside the country's traditional regulatory structure. In a rather humorous twist, the OBUs would very often borrow from the Saudi banks in Bahrain and lend to Saudi customers in Saudi Arabia who could not get funding from the Saudi banks because of the latter's fear of Saudi courts. Of course, when OBUs found their Saudi merchant debtors unwilling, or unable, to honor their commitments, the OBUs did not fare any better in Saudi courts than their local banking brethren. Indeed, many OBUs spent large amounts on lawyers to no avail.

SAMA made some halfhearted efforts in the 1980s to limit the activities of the Bahrain-based banks in the kingdom. In doing so, SAMA was seeking not so much to limit the Bahraini banks influence in the region as to increase the demand for the products of Saudi banks at home. It was indeed difficult for SAMA to discourage Bahraini offshore business as it would have meant putting limits on Bahraini efforts at creating jobs. It also would have directly or indirectly put restrictions on transfers of money in or out of Saudi Arabia, which was, and still is, absolutely unacceptable to all in the Kingdom. It is central to the structure of financial markets in the Gulf region that there are no foreign exchange controls, a practice still standing unchanged to this day. As a consequence, SAMA could limit the type of foreign lending banks could participate in, but could not stop banks from placing funds in foreign banks directly as regular time or current deposits.

Ultimately, during this period, the commercial banks in Saudi Arabia were left with only four types of profitable business:

1. Documentary credits, like letters of credits, performance bonds and guarantees
2. Short-term facilities to companies and trading firms
3. Medium to long-term facilities to industrial companies with strong links to the government
4. Direct lending to the government through purchases of Saudi bonds and bills.

In Kuwait, the banks and broader financial markets followed a different path, one defined by two major events. First was a 1960 decree by the Emir of Kuwait that required all commercial activity in Kuwait, including banking, to be at least 51% Kuwaiti owned. This gave impetus to the creation of eight 100% Kuwaiti owned banks founded by local interests. This stood in significant juxtaposition to the sector's history, which was dominated by British banking interests. This number of banks is large for a market which, at that time, only consisted of 600,000 local inhabitants and 1.4 million foreign workers. Seven of these eight banks were founded by prominent merchant clans, with the eighth founded by the royal family. Despite threats of overcrowding, the period of rapid growth allowed each to build a sizable portfolio of loans and deposits. Before the Iraqi invasion in 1990, the total assets of the commercial banks reached US$40 billion, including US$17 billion dollars in private deposits.

The main activity of the banks was to finance the trade activities of the merchants. Flush with liquidity, especially after 1980, many banks also became active participants in the investment markets by making loans to merchants to speculate on the stock market. This activity was frowned upon by the central bank. Yet, the largest borrowers often came from prominent merchant or royal families whose power could not be easily checked and who the banks could not easily turn down. Underpinning this dynamic, merchants where often directors on the board of the very same banks they borrowed from, positions that they used to pressure banks into making them large loans. Naturally loans to directors are against banking regulations across modern regulatory environments, including Kuwait. However, the directors argued that the loans were fully secured through their pledging of shares significantly in excess of the borrowed amount. Even so, these loans were a breach of fiduciary responsibility, and, as it would turn out, a grave mistake.

The second defining event for the Kuwaiti banking sector was the Souk al Manakh stock market crash of 1982. In the lead up to the crash, only one bank, the National Bank of Kuwait, chose to abstain from weighing their books down with loans for speculative purposes. After the crash, which wiped out the value of all the shares used to 'secure' the speculative loans, all the banks except National Bank of Kuwait became de facto insolvent and lost considerable credibility. Only NBK remained clean. It was the only bank in the country that managed to maintain real capital and solid assets. By 1995, NBK had managed to gain the trust of many Kuwaitis and held 26% of all the banking deposits and 60% of the loans in Kuwait, twice as much as any other commercial bank. NBK has held onto this dominance ever since.

After the crash of 1982, due to the ensuing systemic insolvency, the government had to intervene in the affairs of the banks. It bought bad loans *en masse* from the banks, paying for them with long-term treasury bonds. The state also provided deposits to the banks so they could maintain their liquidity. Interest on government bonds became the main source of income for Kuwaiti banks, except of course for NBK. Thus, in a small market like Kuwait after 1982, most of the banks had no real business. It was at that point that the governor of the central bank called for the merger of the banks, to no avail. After the liberation of Kuwait in 1991, the governor of the central bank announced again that NBK would remain as is, while all the smaller banks would be merged into one. The potential merger of the banks revealed the rivalry of various merchants amongst themselves and between the clans and the royal family. Certain banks, like Burgan Bank, are very close to the royal family, while others, like the Commercial Bank of Kuwait, are close to the merchant classes. At one point in 1991 it had been rumored that all the smaller banks would be merged into the Burgan Bank. This would have created two large banking institutions in Kuwait. This did not happen, undoubtedly because the boards of directors at banks like CBK or Al Ahli Bank did not want to surrender their institutions to the control of the royal family, which controlled Burgan Bank and wanted to maintain their status as directors on a banking board. Today, discussion of consolidation remains an evergreen topic in the Kuwaiti banking sector.

Starting in the 1960s, in parallel with the growth and decline of domestic banking, Kuwait also saw the rise of large domestic investment companies, many of which were founded with government support. The three largest investment companies became known as the 3-Ks, KIC (Kuwait Investment Company), KIIC (Kuwait International Investment Company) and KFTCIC (Kuwait Foreign Trade and Investment Company). They had some private capital, but ultimately they were controlled by the Kuwait Investment Authority (KIA).

The 3-Ks were seen in the markets in the Gulf and in Europe as very aggressive and imaginative. They took participations in a number of European bond issues. They also started a Kuwaiti Dinar bond market for both locals and foreigners, in turn effectively giving birth to a Euro Dinar. The bonds were issued on behalf of foreign entities based and working outside Kuwait, thus allowing these companies to enjoy the advantage of low interest rate Kuwaiti Dinar borrowings. Of course, they could not use the facilities for paying their suppliers or making Dinar investments, and accordingly, once issued and sold they would exchange the Dinars for USD. Borrowers were taking the risk of any appreciation of the Dinar, but felt safe that the rate, which was based on a dollar-heavy basket of currencies, would change very little. This process of changing Dinars for USD created a Euro-Dinar pool of currency outside Kuwait and outside the Kuwaiti Central Bank's reach.

The 3-Ks even attempted, in vain, to start a Euro-Saudi Riyal market for foreign companies to buy bonds denominated in Saudi Riyals, which was quickly thwarted by the Saudi monetary agency. SAMA rejected the idea because it knew that such bonds would create a pool of Euro-Riyals in the world markets that could not be controlled by the Saudi monetary agency, which was significantly more conservative than the other central banks in the region at the time.

The rapid growth of the 3-Ks was prematurely stunted by the Souk al Manakh' crash, albeit indirectly. In the wake of the meltdown, the 3-Ks were forced by the government to take on a supportive role toward the stock market, regardless of the quality of the assets. They bought or lent against over US$2 billion worth of shares, which were in many cases effectively worthless, forcing them to write off many of the investments as losses in the subsequent years, through to the invasion of Kuwait in 1991. The write downs and liquidity implications severely limited the investment company's activity in other, global, markets. The state tried to merge the three K's in 1987, and again in 1997, but ultimately KFTCIC appears to have been subsumed into the operations of the KIA and is no longer active in the markets. KIIC is still controlled by KIA and does not seem very active but still operates, while KIC is still active in great part on behalf of KIA. It has investment assets of about US$800 million, is profitable and issues audited statements. Financial information on the companies is scant, but Middle East Economic Survey published a small chart of Assets, Equities and Profitability for 1987 and 1988, showing total assets for the three companies of about US$4 billion on a small equity base of about US$490 million.

The Islamic Banks

Shari'a-compliant financial profit making institutions, often referred to as Islamic Banks, are based on the principle that interest (*riba* in Arabic), defined as the making of money on money, is specifically forbidden in the Holy Quran. However, the notion of profit sharing is perfectly acceptable. Hence, over the centuries scholars, business leaders and bankers have often tried to find ways to lubricate the ways of commerce and its needs for financial transactions, without having recourse to interest bearing instruments. By the 1960s and 1970s, Islamic banking managed to become established in some Muslim-majority countries but remained nonexistent in the Gulf.

The fundamental difference between traditional banking and Islamic banking would be that the lenders take on risk with the borrowers, hence the payment for the risk is shared by both the borrower and the lender. Toward the end of the 20th century some merchants and bankers started developing financial structures and instruments that could get the endorsement of Muslim scholars. In principle, the new banks would provide four types of facilities. The International Monetary Fund's Mohamed El Qorchi neatly summarizes three types of Islamic financial instruments as:

- Debt instruments such as the Murabaha, Salam and Istisna which encompasses variations of a purchase and resale contract in which a tangible asset is purchased by a bank at the costumer's request and the resale price or delivery time determined based on cost plus profit markup.[15]
- Quasi-debt instruments like Ijara, which are essentially leasing contracts whereby "a party leases an asset for a specified rent and term . . . and can be structured as a lease-purchase contract."[16]
- Profit-and-loss-sharing instruments, which include "Musharaka, an equity participation contract under which a bank and its client contribute jointly to finance a project," and "Mudaraba, a trustee-type finance contract under which one party provides the capital for a project and the other party provides the labor."[17]

One of the major debt instruments not mentioned earlier is the sukuk, a type of long-term bond that has become a major instrument used by large firms and governments worldwide. The sukuk is a complex instrument that includes the establishment of special purpose vehicles (SPV) owned by the ultimate borrower. Legally, it is the SPV that borrows money long term from banks. The SPV pays rent to its owner and in turn the owner pays this rent to the lenders. This rent is calculated to match LIBOR at any one time plus a profit margin. The legal framework for this type of debt is very complex, but ultimately feels like a regular bond with coupon payments and guaranteed set income to the lenders. Some Shari'a scholars have strongly objected to sukuk saying that they were merely interest bearing instruments clothed in Shari'a-compliant wording. Nevertheless, this instrument is now the paper of choice for large project finance and government debt in many states.

The notion of Shari'a-compliant debt has not had unanimous support, even in deeply Islamic states. One of the main criticisms at the time was provided by Mr. Charles Schotta, who at the time was Deputy Assistant Secretary for Arabian Peninsula Affairs at the US Treasury, at a symposium organized in New York in 1985 by Dar Al Mal Al Islami and Kuwait Finance House. Mr. Schotta explained that commercial banks have a certain amount of regulated capital, which is nothing but a cushion to protect depositors from potential errors by the bank managers. In other words, if a bank has nine parts of deposits for one part of capital on the liability and net worth side, the banks can afford to lose 10%of their assets (their loans), without eating into their depositor's money. The only losers are the owners of the banks, who lose their equity. In Islamic finance theory, the practice of producing profits is fine, but the risk has to be taken by both the depositors and the equity holders. Mr. Schotta affirmed that the line between capital and deposits is sacrosanct and that losses cannot be "shared." The capital of any bank must first be used to cover losses and that until this principle could be guaranteed by the Shari'a-compliant institution, Islamic banks would likely not get licensed in the West.

In reality, the whole issue of capital as safety margin to protect depositors from poor management became moot. Without expressly accepting Mr. Schotta's views, most central banks ensure that Islamic Banks do manage their capital in the manner suggested. The Bank of England has issued banking licenses to a select few Shari'a-compliant commercial banks. In the US, no Islamic banks have been licensed. The main problem in the US has been that potential wealthy shareholders with the means to establish a credible Islamic financial institution would likely be Gulf State citizens who would be unwilling to subject themselves to Federal Reserve disclosure requirements, instead choosing to establish the institution in a regulatory environment more respectful of their privacy, such as the Gulf.

In the Middle East, Islamic banking first appeared in Egypt in 1972 through the Nasser Social Bank, which remained the only Islamic finance institution until 1977, when Prince Mohammed Al Faisal bin Abdel Aziz (a son of King Faisal bin Abdel Aziz of Saudi Arabia) started the Shari'a-compliant banks Faisal Islamic Bank of Egypt and Faisal Islamic Bank of Sudan. The Prince's establishment of these banks is ironic given that Saudi Arabia, home to the holy cities of Mecca and Medina and Islam's founding, strongly discouraged Islamic banking in the latter part of the 20th century. Nearby in Kuwait and the UAE, Islamic banking was more actively supported; this led to the founding of Kuwait Finance House (KFH) in 1977 and Dubai Islamic Bank (DIB) in 1975, both of which quickly became and remain leaders in the industry.

DIB's founding was in large part due to the support of Dubai's Governor Sheikh Rashid bin Saeed Al Maktoum, who granted the bank a license despite an active moratorium on opening new banks.[18] Soon after, Federal Law No. 6 of 1985 was passed, stating that Islamic banks were not exempt from the standard banking regulation and oversight as set out in the 1980 Banking Law. During this period, DIB capitalized on Dubai's position as a regional trade hub to develop a role for itself as a leader in trade financing for Muslim merchants. It did so through the use of *murabaha* contracts, where DIB would buy imports on behalf of a merchant and resell them to the merchant at a predetermined markup, with the markup effectively taking the place of interest. What made the practice distinctly Shari'a-compliant was that the DIB, in buying the imports, would temporarily take ownership and thus legal responsibility and risk for the product, in turn justifying the markup. This practice was advantageous for both Islamic banks and merchants, with the former being able to buy imports in bulk at a discount thus maximizing returns while the latter no longer needed to procure costly letters of credit.[19]

In Saudi Arabia, support for Islamic banking was harder to come by. Puzzling to the outsider was that the two main Arab Islamic banks in the world, Al Baraka and Dar Al Maal Al Islami, were both owned by Saudi nationals but were forced to operate offshore of the standard Saudi regulatory environment. One, Al Baraka, was headquartered in Bahrain, while the other, Dar Al Mal Al Islami (DAM), based itself in Geneva. Both banks had extensive activities worldwide, including in non-Muslim countries, but no operations in the Kingdom.

Al Baraka was founded in 1982 with a paid-in capital of US$500 million by Saleh Abdullah Kamel, a prominent and powerful businessman in Saudi Arabia, and one of the first Saudis to launch an Islamic bank. Al Baraka, which was run directly by Saleh Kamel, was unable to obtain a banking license in Saudi, leading to its establishment in Bahrain, which at the time had a significantly more conducive regulatory environment. One should note that Saleh Kamel was one of the persons detained at the Ritz Carlton in Riyadh in November 2017 in the widely publicized effort to stamp out corruption by the new crown prince of Saudi Arabia. Kamel's association with corruption in the Kingdom is not new. He was known to be very close to Prince Sultan and his family, who many in the Kingdom rumored as highly corrupt—a suspicion that seems to have resurfaced many years later in 2017. Thus, one can speculate that one of the reasons why Al Baraka was not allowed to open in Saudi Arabia was because the civil servants, especially at the fiscally conservative SAMA, were not only unwilling to loosen their tight grip on the domestic banking sector but even more hesitant to do so with businessmen known to be corrupt.

DAM, on the other hand, was founded by a son of the assassinated King Faisal, Mohammed Al Faisal. The Al Faisal clan was highly respected with superb lineage, which made them strong candidates for succession to the

Kingship. Despite this, DAM was still unable to obtain a license to conduct Islamic banking operations in the Kingdom. The inability for someone of his stature and repute to obtain the necessary license sheds further light on why SAMA withheld these licenses for so long. At the time, senior members of the Faisal clan headed the secret service, the governorate that borders Yemen and the Ministry of Foreign Affairs. Thus, to many in the government, the civil service and within the royal family, allowing the Faisal clan to also build substantial power in the Kingdom's financial sector, especially when that financial power would be based on Islamic principles, was too large a risk to the existing distribution of power.

The only Islamic Bank to be licensed in Saudi Arabia during this period was the institution controlled by Suleiman Al Rajhi, the Kingdom's most prominent money changer. Even then, it took Al Rahji Bank four years to obtain the proper banking licenses, completing the task by 1988. Mr. Al Rajhi is from Najd, unlike most other money changers in the kingdom who are from Hadramuth in Yemen. He was known to be the largest landowner in Riyadh and, perhaps because of his tribal affiliation, had very good connections with the royal clans, the religious establishment and the Riyadh business community, thus potentially nullifying some of the concerns DAM and Al Baraka faced.

The fear of Islamic banking in the Kingdom continued until the early part of the 21st century when SAMA saw that the sector's interest free, albeit profit sharing, system was appreciated and desired by the public, carried no political advantage and could be regulated just as other banks in the Kingdom were. SAMA then allowed the creation of four Islamic banks including one, Alinma, which was founded with public funds from the Public Investment Fund and various social security funds, and was even managed by former employees of SAMA.

The Money Changers

The region's money changers make up one of the most fascinating groups in the region's financial architecture. Until the growth of the Gulf's banking sector in the late 1970s, most the region's financial needs were handled by this group of financial intermediaries that had existed from the moment pilgrims began flocking to Mecca to worship, ever since the Ka'aba was built by Abraham. These money changers initially traded in gold and silver but in due course their activity subsumed all currencies, in turn providing pilgrims with the currency required for their stay in Saudi Arabia. As such, a whole industry with long trade routes and networks developed over the centuries as increasing numbers of pilgrims along increasingly diverse routes found their way to the holy site. Money changers in Mecca and Jeddah could take almost any currency used in the world, whether convertible or not. As late as the 1990s, it was a common sight in Jeddah to see money changers walk down the street with wads of currencies, which they had just exchanged for

USD, British pounds or Saudi Riyals. Most of the money changers in Jeddah in the 20th century were from Hadhramaut in Yemen and the larger ones were well known to all. The best known names were Al Amoudi, Bamaoudeh, Kaki and bin Mahfouz. As previously noted, the largest money changer in Riyadh was Saleh Al Rajhi from Saudi Arabia's Najd region. Saleh eventually transformed his establishment into the second largest bank in the Kingdom—Al Rahji Bank.

The money changers main trade was to exchange one currency for another. Ultimately, they had to find various outlets for the odd currencies, which they obtained primarily from pilgrims. This led to the development of interesting connections between the money changers in Saudi Arabia and developed banks in Europe, as well as with other countries across the Middle East. In particular, the money changers have had a historically strong relationship with banks in Basel, Switzerland, many of which specialize in paper currency. The money changers would send a trusted employee to Switzerland with suitcases full of cash in Rubles, Ringits and other uncommon currencies. These trusted employees would return to Jeddah with bags full of dollars. Another iteration of trade links fueled by these money changers took shape during the second half of the 20th century as Egyptians began taking up a larger role in the Kingdom's foreign workforce. The million or so Egyptian workers in Saudi Arabia exchanged their Saudi Riyals for USD, which they would then take home and change on the street in Cairo or Alexandria at the street market rate rather than the very low rate imposed by the Central Bank of Egypt. These transactions made Egypt's exchanges flush with dollar bills, which the Saudi money changers would then buy from local Egyptian money changers and bring back to Jeddah.

The second and perhaps most important and profitable role for money changers was the issuing of bank drafts to foreign workers in the Kingdom. These drafts would then be cashed in their home countries and home currencies. The transactions were simple and quickly became extremely popular with Asian and African workers in the Gulf. In essence, each money changer had accounts in banks in Asian and/or African countries, which could provide the recipient in the local countries with cash against the draft. This system was possible even though the money changers essentially only had one bank account, usually at the then Bank of New York (BNY) in New York. They established relations with banks all over the world who also had accounts at BNY. These accounts would be credited by BNY at the request—usually by standing instruction—of the changers in Jeddah. The changers account in dollars would be debited to replenish their account with the foreign bank's account at BNY. The only responsibility of the money changers was to ensure that their dollar-denominated account held enough currency to cover the transfers from their BNY account to that foreign bank's account. This sale of bank drafts was extremely profitable because the money changers charged a foreign exchange margin (often as low as 1%) and a nominal fee for issuing the draft.

In Jeddah and other towns in Saudi Arabia, the workers would go to the money changer, provide the changer with the amount to transfer plus the fees in Saudi Riyals. The changer would then issue a check in the currency required by the foreign worker, which could be drawn on a bank from the worker's country. The worker could then send the check by mail to his family in India, Pakistan or anywhere else in the world. The family eventually could bring the check to the local bank and cash it or deposit it. At the time, there were no foreign exchange regulations, and the Saudi Riyal's exchange rate to the US$ was basically fixed. Thus, it was easy for the money changers to transfer their SAR to a local bank or even to SAMA, who could credit their US$ account at BNY.

These transactions were very profitable for all concerned. The workers received rapid and decent service at reasonable prices. The large New York bank holding all the accounts of the changers and their correspondent banks built up large balances which provided healthy returns, especially given the high interest rate environment in the 1980s. The money changers received fees from the foreign exchange transaction, fees for the draft, and had use of the float from the moment the money was paid by the worker until the draft was cashed in the foreign bank. This float amounted to many millions of dollars, which the money changers could invest at substantial profit.

The float was used by the changers for a number of transactions. Some would use the float to lend to people and businesses in the Kingdom. Little interest was charged, but profits were shared 50/50. Many of the first factories built in Riyals in the 60s were so financed. Some money changers used the float to provide venture capital to potential entrepreneurs. The changers even provided facilities to their clients to pay others with checks drawn on the money changer, thereby making the changers into de facto banks with checking accounts. One practice most of the money changers partook in was investing in commodities. Even in the early 1980s, the changers had direct purchasing accounts with the Chicago Board of Trade and could buy all manner of commodities in both spot and forward markets. Most seem to have specialized in precious metals and grains, mainly wheat and barley. Until Saudi Arabia enacted large agricultural subsidies in the 1980s, which briefly made it the world's eighth largest exporter of wheat, trade in grains within the Kingdom was dominated by the Jeddah money changers.

Gold was also a favorite of the changers, and most speculated heavily in this metal. In fact, gold trading may have been the downfall of the changers. Indeed, seeing that in most cases large money changers had effectively become commercial and investment banks, the monetary agency, SAMA, was very keen to regulate them as they did banks i.e. obtain audited balance sheets, ask for minimum capital, monitor the quality of their loans and the amount of their foreign liabilities. The money changers were able to actively and successfully fight off these requirements for years because they were popular with everyone, including the ruling families of the Gulf. They provided a necessary economic service, simply and on a large scale, to millions of foreign workers. However, money changers traded on their reputation. Their name was their main asset, a critical factor for workers holding a draft issued by the changer and outstanding for a few weeks until cashed in a remote foreign country.

Starting in the late 1970s, one of Saleh al Rajhi sons, Abdullah al Rajhi, had a well-publicized row with his father and established a competing establishment in Dammam. Abdullah's exchange had around forty branches throughout the Eastern Province, where most of the foreign workers were located, and conducted currency exchanges and issued bank drafts—similar operations to those of his father. There did exist a key difference in the father and son's respective operations though. Where the father dealt with gold and precious metals primarily as a medium of exchange, Abdullah dealt in them primarily for speculative purposes, using the substantial float his operations maintained to do so. He bought gold or gold futures through foreign banks in Bahrain, using the float, his own cash and loans. Some of his largest creditors were located in Bahrain, Belgium, Britain and the United States, including Kredietbank, Belgium's third largest bank at the time, Thomas Cook and Bank of America.[20]

Abdullah's speculative endeavors were very profitable. At the time, the price of gold was on the ascent. Less than a decade earlier, the US had taken the dollar off the gold standard, which had fixed the price of gold at US$35/oz, and by the late 1970s, high inflation due to strong oil prices, Soviet intervention in Afghanistan and the impact of the Iranian revolution all prompted investors to move into the metal. The rally was classic bubble mentality, and as price neared the US$850/oz in early 1980, it popped. The ensuing price swing took the price of gold to around half its peak, where it hovered for a number of years, leading Abdullah's creditors to ask for reimbursement of their loans in 1981. In technical terms, the banks had lent on the margin and issued margin calls. At the time, Abdullah's creditors were reportedly owed as much as US$300 million.[21] Abdullah could not meet the margin calls nor could he maintain the necessary funds in the dollar-denominated accounts in New York. These dollar-denominated accounts were being used to back the bank drafts issued to foreign workers across Saudi Arabia. This meant that Abdullah's correspondent banking relations across the world would no longer honor the drafts Abdullah's exchange had issued. In other words, the foreign workers, most of them very poor laborers, saw their family not receiving the money for which they had worked hard for because Rahji's name was no longer credible.

At the time, Saudi Arabia was eager to maintain a positive externally facing story about its growing domestic financial market, and accordingly, coverage of Al Rahji's hardships was tightly controlled in the press. To its credit, SAMA did take the opportunity to move rapidly on the operation, shutting its doors in July 1982 during Ramadan, when most substantive policy decisions are left for a later date.[22] Saleh al Rajhi, the father and largest money changer in Riyadh, publicly disowned his son and refused to be liable for the son's reckless business. Consequently, the workers asked the government of Saudi Arabia to intervene. SAMA agreed to pay back the workers, but not the banks that had lent to al Rajhi on the margin. More importantly, in the ensuing period, the government gave SAMA the right to control, supervise and regulate the money changers. SAMA then moved to require money changers to obtain a license to operate and forbade them from conducting anything except foreign exchange transactions. If they desired to do any more, they would need to apply to be standard commercial banks, thus opening themselves to the regulation SAMA had so long desired. Most money changers decided to remain solely changers except, ironically enough, the operations of Saleh al Rajhi (the father's company), which chose to become an Islamic bank.

In this sense, speculation in gold brought about the end of an era for the money changers. As will be seen in later chapters, the money changers have in great part become irrelevant. They have de facto been forced out of the market by a vastly increased regulatory environment and technological advances that have made financial transfers instantaneous. Under very strong pressure from the United States after events of September 11, 2011, the Gulf authorities established stringent measures to avoid money laundering, which in turn forced SAMA in particular to establish stringent regulations on who could open accounts, who could transfer money and how they could do so. A major casualty of these newly developed bureaucratic regulations were the easy international wage transfers done through money changer bank drafts. This service is now handled by banks, often faster albeit sometimes at a higher cost. In some increasingly common cases, companies, like Arabtec in Dubai, pay their worker by debit card. The worker can then go to an ATM with the capacity to debit the card and send money electronically to the worker's chosen recipient in his/her home country. This bypasses all needs for the money changers, instead transferring this service to banks, who handle the ATMs, and the correspondent banking relationships needed to process the transfers. The money changers thus lost the fees they earned on bank drafts and foreign exchange transactions and, most importantly, lost the float that had provided them with the financial liquidity and power they previously enjoyed.

The Bahrain Offshore Market

Bahrain is a small country, with very limited natural resources. Its main asset has been its people and their ability to adapt to rapidly changing circumstances in the Gulf. In 1973, at the time of independence from Great Britain, the government established the Bahrain Monetary Agency (BMA), charging it with issuing a local currency and establishing proper financial markets and regulations. At first, the BMA was supervised by seconded employees of the Bank of England, who were tasked with training a cadre of Bahrainis to take over the Agency and to help it establish proper financial procedures in Bahrain. The British advisers, along with their Bahraini colleagues, evaluated the financial needs of the region and quickly saw the dearth of banking services in the Gulf, especially in Saudi Arabia. They also saw that Beirut's foreign and domestic banks, which for some time had functioned as the region's financial center, were no longer in a position to operate because of the Lebanese Civil War that started in early 1975. Hence, they felt that Bahrain could become a major financial center for the Gulf, an opportunity even more attractive given the rapid onset of the oil boom at that time. In this light, offshore markets were seen by Bahraini policy makers as a potential natural resource of their own, on par with the oil resources their neighbors benefited from. Building on this perspective, through attractive regulatory policy in the second half of the 1970s, Bahrain set itself up as an important offshore center for banks servicing the whole region. By the 1980s, Bahrain functioned as a key operating base for as many as 170 banks active in the Gulf, promoted the development of at least two major international institutions and fostered the growth of some of the region's largest insurance companies.[23] In doing so, Bahrain created employment for its people and some wealth for the then-Emirate, now Kingdom. In short order though, a confluence of factors undercut many of the comparative advantages Bahrain enjoyed, unseating it as the region's financial capital.

Bahrain had better international communication linkages than its neighbors. Businesses could get telephone lines easily (not an easy undertaking in Saudi Arabia at the time), could operate telexes and trading terminals and travel to Europe and Asia with direct air links; even the Concorde was flying between Bahrain and London daily. Making these links even more significant, in the 1970s and early 1980s before computer trading became the norm, Bahrain could offer a financial harbor between the time zones of the Far East, Europe and the US; an attribute that appealed to large banks that needed to pass overnight foreign exchange positions between Tokyo and London. This led many of these banks to establish substantial foreign exchange and treasury trading operations in Bahrain as Offshore Banking Units.

One of the main activities these foreign exchange rooms engaged in was the disintermediation of the Saudi Riyals (SAR) versus the US$. At the time, SAMA wanted to keep interest rates low, while interest rates were going through the roof in the dollar markets, with LIBOR topping 14%. Since neither Bahrain nor Saudi Arabia had any foreign exchange restrictions, it was extremely attractive for large banks to borrow Saudi Riyals from their correspondent Saudi banks at 4% or 5% for ninety days, change them in Bahrain for US$ and use the dollars to fund their own portfolios in the US. At the time, the banks' US portfolios were often based on the prime rate, which was at, or over, 15% in 1979 and 1980, while SAR interest rates remained in the 4–8% range. At the end of the ninety days, the banks would reverse the transaction to pay back the Saudi correspondent banks. In effect, these banks were capitalizing on Bahrain and Saudi Arabia's respective financial market attributes to profit from a Carry Trade well before the financial mechanism's popular use in the 1990s.[24] Utilizing these techniques, in 1978 an OBU of a large American bank made more than US$6 million in trading profits, the equivalent of US$23.15 million in 2018-dollars, mostly attributable to the dollar/riyal play.[25]

At the time, SAMA wanted to keep the Saudi Riyal loosely pegged (±7.5%) to the IMF's SDR basket of currencies. Maintaining this peg put tremendous pressure on the Saudi Riyal. The situation became untenable for the Saudi financial authorities who were watching their funds leave the country to the great benefit of the foreign banks. It also put pressure on SAMA's cash reserves, as it had to buy extensive volumes of Saudi Riyals and sell foreign currency to maintain the value of the SAR. Eventually, Saudi Arabia allowed the Saudi banks to open branches in Bahrain and do the transactions for their own benefit. More importantly, by 1981, SAMA allowed the interest rates of the Saudi Riyal to move loosely in tandem with those of the USD, and by 1986 moved to a tight, fixed peg with the USD of US$1 = SAR3.75, where it still is today. This peg effectively eliminated the large and profitable currency arbitrage that these banks had capitalized upon. Through these regulatory moves by SAMA, the advantages that had drawn many international banks to establish operations in Bahrain diminished significantly.

Another interesting development in the OBU business was the establishment of locally registered banking corporations that solely operated as offshore banks. The two main banks that obtained OBU licenses as corporations were the Gulf International Bank (GIB) and Arab Banking Corporation (ABC Bank). GIB, established in 1975, was owned by SAMA, and ABC Bank, established in 1980, was jointly owned by the Libyan Central Bank and the UAE Central Bank. Both rapidly became very active in large international syndication. ABC Bank in particular was known to take extensive positions in the Latin American debt market, which was booming at the time. Later on, GIB became a major provider and syndicator of facilities to the large contractors active in the Kingdom. Both banks are still active today, and GIB has even been able to open a full branch in the Kingdom.

Relatedly, in the 1980s and 1990s Bahrain-based OBUs provided excellent services to companies and contractors in the Kingdom. It was the era of the "suitcase" bankers, who spent the majority of their time in the Kingdom to market their services to Saudi merchants and foreign contractors alike. Business was done by telex, mainly tested telexes guaranteeing the privacy of the communications between the clients and the banks in Bahrain.[26] Bankers could market the taking of deposits, or offer loans, bid bonds, advance payment guarantees, performance bonds and letters of credits, even large syndicated facilities. Bahrain became an important center for syndication of large loans and bonding facilities to contractors and companies across the Gulf, most significantly for those in Saudi Arabia. However, with the tremendous growth in the quality of air transport to the Gulf and the massive improvement in communication technology, the large syndicators no longer needed their expensive staff and offices in Bahrain. Instead, these large banks could market to the clients and syndicate their deals more efficiently directly out of London. By the same token, private banking, which has always been a large share of international banks' business in the Gulf, and foreign exchange operations could be handled out of their respective European, American or Asian headquarters. This dynamic was further exacerbated by local Saudi and Emirati banks that, witnessing and learning from the modern banking services these international banks were offering, began offering a wider variety of services to a larger swath of clients, thus undercutting some of the lucrative business that these OBUs were benefiting from.

Collectively, the modernization of the region's financial markets, coupled with global technological advances, limited the need to maintain large offshore operations in Bahrain, dimming the bright future that Bahrain's offshore market once had. As will be shown later in this work, since the decline of its offshore markets, except for its position as a leading proponent for the standardization of Islamic financial regulation, Bahrain has been unable to develop an equally significant role for itself in the region's financial markets.

The Capital Markets

Until the late 1990s, capital markets across the region were sparse. The only two countries which had active capital markets of note were Kuwait and Saudi Arabia. Whereas their capital markets took on significantly different forms, both Saudi Arabia and Kuwait looked to these financial trading centers as a tool through which to disperse the newfound oil wealth that had begun flooding state coffers.

In the mid-1970s, faced with large inflows and seemingly unlimited energy resources, the government of Saudi Arabia decided to promote the industrialization of the country in order to spread the benefits of oil revenues more evenly across the burgeoning population. To do so, the government first developed a soft planning structure which strived to provide the kingdom with the critical infrastructure it lacked. Despite a tenfold increase in revenues between 1972 and 1975, the country had very limited air and sea access, minimal telecommunication networks, no decent medical facilities and not enough schools. Massive government expenditures were used to fund this infrastructure development, with significant incentives given to local entrepreneurs who created factories that would meet domestic construction and retail needs. In time though, this proved to stymy efforts at expanding the population's personal stake in the Kingdom's industrialization—a challenge that SAMA would turn to capital markets to solve.

Most of the ventures financed by the state were done so through Limited Liability Companies (LLC), a legal structure derived from the French SARL (Société Anonyme à Responsabilité Limitée), via the Egyptian commercial code, which was used as a model for the Saudi legal system. This form of organization is closer to a US partnership than to a corporation, where there are just a few founding members with shares that cannot be sold without approval from other shareholders and only after lengthy negotiations. Due to these dynamics, very few share exchanges took place, which in turn limited ownership to wealthy families and some royals. Moreover, corporations with publicly traded shares were not common mainly because incorporation laws and registration procedures were very onerous. They included showing profits for five years as an LLC and were conditional on approval from the King and SAMA, both requirements that opened the aspiring company to significant political pressure and scrutiny. Consequently, with limited equity trading and ownership, the government was caught in a dilemma. On the one hand, it wished to involve the population in the Kingdom's industrial growth through wider ownership in public stock. On the other hand, it did not wish to allow truly free equity stock exchange where budding entrepreneurs could buy and sell their shares, for fear of losing control of the movement of funds within the country, as well as a fear of experiencing unbridled speculation similar to what was happening at the time in Kuwaiti's Souk Al Manakh. Therefore, the government chose to allow a limited number of corporations to be established in which the State could keep total control of management, but where a minority of the shares would be sold to the public.

The first significant effort came with the Saudization of the foreign banks as discussed previously. By forcing the sale of shares only to small shareholders and demanding to vet all the board members and chairmen of the new joint venture banks, SAMA was able provide the public with a share of the Kingdom's new wealth all while remaining a de facto trustee for the Saudi public and maintaining strong control and regulation of the banks. Further, a number of the bank's new Saudi employees had at one point been trained by SAMA or SIDF and thus had close ties with the Ministry of Finance, ensuring that the government's interests were maintained in daily operations.

The second and most important development was the creation of SABIC in 1979 as a corporation owned by the government. SABIC was founded to start the Kingdom's downstream endeavors and provide sources of income outside of crude oil sales. The State organization that owned SABIC put up 30% of its shares for sale to the Saudi public at large, of which 5% were allocated to GCC citizens more broadly. SABIC rapidly became a major chemical company. By 1984 SABIC had raised US$530 million from Saudi and GCC citizens, thus providing the public with a lucrative stake in the Kingdom's development. In turn, SABIC invested in very large petrochemical projects inside the Kingdom. As a corporation, SABIC has proven very successful, producing significant returns and dividend payments since its initial public offering. Over the years, while SABIC continued to raise large amounts of capital from the public, the government has always maintained 70% of the equity. A number of other state controlled corporations where floated in the same manner in order to provide an opportunity for public participation, including SCECO, the electricity company, SAPTCO, the bus company and Ma'aden, the mining company.

By the late-1980s, the Ministry of Finance began allowing a limited number of private firms to float shares to the public without requiring state control of management. The main beneficiaries of this policy where companies with well-established connections to the Kingdom's financial elite, including Al Rajhi Banking and Investment Company, which floated shares in its fully licensed and registered Islamic bank, and the National Industrialization Company, which was created by Saudi businessmen to market SABIC's downstream products. Despite public ownership, even these newly public companies where dependent on the government either for regulatory controls, for financial subsidies from SIDF, or for access to raw materials from Saudi Aramco. As the market developed, more companies were allowed to register as corporations, yet, the trading in these public companies remained limited.

In 1984, there were only twenty-one companies listed to trade in Saudi Arabia.[27] By 2002, there were still only sixty-eight companies listed on the Tadawul stock exchange.[28] Consequently, with the increasingly large amount of capital looking for investments and very limited options for those investments, the few companies traded on the market were susceptible to rapid overvaluation or, when faced with negative news, to significant market corrections. This was exacerbated by the antiquated structure of markets at the time. In the absence of a proper exchange floor or computerized open trading, shareholders were limited in their knowledge of price changes or of a "market" for any given share. Equity investments were therefore illiquid. It was not until the late 1990s that Kingdom launched an electronic settlement and clearing system. The Saudi stock exchange known formally as Tadawul then handled the clearing and monetary settling operations starting October 2001. At that point, all trading and capital market regulation was controlled by the Ministry of Finance and SAMA, a responsibility that would be taken over by the Capital Markets Authority in 2003. By 2016, there were 67.7 billion shares traded annually, compared to only 154 million in 1994.[29] As this text will show, in the decade and a half that followed, the Tadawul would grow into a key instrument in the growth of the country's financial markets and in the dispersion of oil wealth to the Saudi citizenry.

Kuwait, unlike Saudi Arabia, did not have aspirations of industrialization. Whereas the Saudis have a large diversified population spread over an enormous territory, Kuwait is small and holds more foreigners than local citizens. Despite their differences, both countries found themselves on the receiving end of very large financial inflows starting in the 1970s. While there were few development projects requiring funds in Kuwait relative to Saudi Arabia, there was a need to include the Kuwaiti citizenry in the newfound oil wealth. Like in Saudi Arabia, the government of Kuwait accomplished this goal in a number of ways, including public employment, large land grants to citizens that were repurchased at inflated prices, the issuance of contracts for infrastructure and supplies, and active support of the capital markets.

Kuwait was the first Gulf country to develop real capital markets, with a stock exchange, investment companies and brokers. While free in form, the market was not free in function, with the Kuwaiti government intervening during the country's small stock market crashes in 1963, 1973, 1975 and 1977, supporting stock prices until losses suffered by shareholders were covered. A large portion of Kuwaiti stock market's capitalization at the time was made up of local banks that, because of the high liquidity, were very successful.

Unlike in Saudi Arabia, the central bank's control of the commercial banks and financial institutions with fairly minimal. The banks were all owned by the public at large, and from 1963 on, the shares of banks and investment companies were being traded freely in an informal market and due to the extensive liquidity in the market, prices rose very rapidly. To avoid the sudden decline in values which happened in the years mentioned earlier, the government started a highly regulated and official stock exchange in 1977, the Kuwait Stock Exchange (KSE). With the large amounts of cash available to Kuwaitis, the demand for shares quickly outstripped the supply, and prices again rose very rapidly. Eventually stock prices had little relationship to the economic value of the underlining company, which allowed any fear or rumor to spark significant volatility in share value.

To avoid further crashes, the government started regulating the equity market strictly. It limited the number of shares that could be sold, the number of companies which could issue shares and the number of brokers active in the market. However, the supply of money was huge and thus, with the knowledge that in previous downturns the government had always bailed-out markets, investors started trading outside the official stock exchange. Most of the trading became centered in a shopping mall called the Souk Al Manakh.

The increased supply of money in the region, coupled with the shortage of available investment options, led entrepreneurs and businessmen to feel there was more than sufficient demand to successfully launch new companies through public offerings in Kuwait. Since establishing a new company inside Kuwait was cumbersome, some entrepreneurs started new firms outside of Kuwait with the sole purpose of trading the shares in Kuwait on the Souk Al Manakh. To do so successfully, Kuwaiti merchants had to find companies which were likely to appeal to a broad investor base so that shares could be easily issued and traded. In the booming economic climate of the 1970s and early 80s, most banks in the Gulf were enjoying record profits because strong capital inflows and government expenditures were creating significant demand for their products; indeed, to many, banking seemed like a very attractive proposition. Realizing this, and exploiting the regulatory arbitrage available at the time, the Kuwaiti entrepreneurs found themselves drawn to the idea of establishing offshore banks in Bahrain primarily for the purpose of capitalizing on Kuwait's booming capital markets.

For the Bahraini authorities, the purpose of starting the OBU market was to create employment for Bahrain citizens, not to provide safe harbor to Kuwaiti investors and speculators. Hence, anyone wanting to establish an offshore bank in Manama was required to provide sizable paid in capital and be of good repute. Given most of these entrepreneurs were well-known merchants whose families had been in business for generations with considerable regional presence, including in Bahrain, neither of these requirements were problematic. Not only were the Kuwaiti entrepreneurs easily able to borrow funds in Kuwait to capitalize a new entity in Bahrain, but this capital also acted as a public relations tool, providing a sense of security to potential investors.

Kuwaiti merchants followed a pattern in establishing companies for the sole purpose of floating shares on the Souk Al Manakh. The script appears generally to have followed these steps:

1. A group of well-known merchants would get together and start a venture, most often a bank since banks were considered very profitable.
2. They approached the Bahrain Monetary Agency, who would require at least US$100 million in capital, a very sizable sum at the time. They would also approach the Emir and the Prime Minister of Bahrain for their respective blessings.
3. They would borrow the capital from the banks they controlled in Kuwait as personal loans, thus allowing for the initial capital injection to appear to the Bahraini authorities as cash.
4. As founding members in the new company, the merchants would transfer US$100 million into an existing Bahraini institution to prove that the capital promised was indeed paid, and that this capital would give them an 80% ownership in the new bank under formation.
5. They would sign for and register an offshore banking unit in Bahrain.
6. The would hire a mid-level British, French or US banker, make him President of the bank under formation to add credibility to the newly formed institution.
7. The newly formed company would then float 20% of the shares to investors at par value. This 20% would be traded along with the founders shares on the unregulated Souk Al Manakh in Kuwait.
8. The Kuwaiti merchant would then unload their shares at a huge multiple on the Souk Al Manakh, reducing or exiting their ownership of the new Bahraini offshore bank at a considerable profit.

The floating of shares to the public became the sort of event which people recount to their grandchildren, hardly believing that it actually took place.[30] The merchants were able to develop a public relation campaign, which caused something close to the mass hysteria, a main feature of financial scandals from the price of tulips in Holland in the 16th century, the assignat in France in the 18th century and even the US dot-com bubble. They convinced small investors in the Gulf that if the wealthiest and largest Kuwaiti merchants were placing such large financial sums into a venture, the investors would profit greatly by joining them as early as possible. Further, small investors expected that since the investments were in bank shares, they would be safe and profitable just as other banks in regulated markets appeared to be. Shares were issued at a small par value, in other words as penny stocks, which appeals to small investors since it allowed them to buy multiple shares for relatively small sums, making their personal risk minimal. Further, for those who took on large positions, the sentiment that if things really went bad, the Kuwaiti government would intervene provided a false sense of security. Public announcements were made all over the Gulf press announcing that Mr./Mrs. X, Y or Z, well-known and respected merchants in Kuwait, were starting a venture with a US$100 million in capital and were going to float 20 million shares at US$1 each on a given day. The public rushed to these offerings. The interested investors were told to reserve their shares in Bahrain at the notary public. The notary public would inscribe on people's passports that they wished to acquire X number of shares and had paid a 10% deposit toward the share until final allocation was made.

The requirement that interested investors present their passports to the notary public brought out groups of individuals who went through poorer villages in Bahrain filling large bags with passports from the local denizens, which they rented from any willing participant for up to 100 dinars each. These individuals working for the Kuwaiti merchants also asked the passport holders to sign a power of attorney in favor of the Kuwaiti merchant, making them owners of the shares registered on the passports. This added further hype to the share issues. It triggered a feeding frenzy where everybody wanted to sign-up for the shares, and if not able to do so, to buy the rights to buy shares.

The creation of these offshore banks in Bahrain not only fueled the already booming stock exchange but also gave birth to a vibrant warrant market. In more than one instance the warrants for the shares yet to be issued were trading at fifteen times par value. When the hype and the multiple on the warrants were at their highest, the founding members of these offshore banks where usually able to sell a small portion of their shares while retaining control of the firms and making a substantial profit. As seen previously, these founding members in most cases had borrowed the funds needed to pay for the original US$100 million capital and could repay the loans by selling a small portion of the shares and warrants they controlled. In other words, they could make huge profits with no money down and at no risk to themselves.

By 1980, the attraction of the Souk Al Manakh became irresistible. Profits were enormous and share turnover was accelerating due to the use of post-dated checks in lieu of immediate cash payment. It was this development that would prove to be pivotal in the Souk's future. Within the Souk Al Manakh itself, there were tens of small financial boutiques, all lined up next to each other. Stock brokers would buy shares from any of these boutiques paying with a check postdated for twelve months from the purchase date. The amount of the check was made for the agreed price of the share plus interest for the implied 12-month loan. The seller, having thus obtained a financial instrument (the postdated check), could himself go to another shop on the floor and buy shares, also paying for them with his own postdated checks, which was to mature on the same day as the postdated check he had received earlier but for a much larger amount given that it included expected profits on the second transaction, plus interest for the 12-month implied loan. To a seasoned or even marginally critical investor this practice of postdated checks amounted to nothing more than a check kiting scheme. Yet, to the common Kuwaiti investor at the time, caught up in the hysteria and hype around the Souk Al Manakh and armed with knowledge of historical government market intervention, not investing appeared to put more at stake than investing with a postdated check. Consequently, the practice kept going at a rapid pace for a couple of years, with investors becoming vastly richer on paper, not only because share values were relentlessly appreciating, but also because they were making interest on their investments.

Naturally, with the beginning of the Iran-Iraq War investors became a bit nervous. Many people considered discounting the postdated checks they held to be able to cover their own checks if presented for payment and to realize the paper profits imputed by these checks. Indeed, the law in Kuwait requires that, in theory at least, anyone signing a check must have the funds available in their account, whether or not the check is postdated. In the excesses of the stock market, no one bothered to deposit cash in the accounts to cover postdated checks, since everyone was amply covered by everyone else's checks. Nevertheless, in 1982, with the sound of Iranian or Iraqi guns in the distance, someone tried to actually deposit a few checks ahead of maturity. Of course, the funds were not available. The party whose checks were deposited could not cover them, so they also tried to deposit the postdated checks to cover their debts. Again, the funds were not available. Inevitably, this started a run on all the postdated checks leading to the famous crash of August 1982 when in the space of thirty days shares, which were trading at fifteen times par value found themselves trading as low as 10% of par value.

The crash was traumatic for Kuwaiti society as well as for people in the Gulf, many of whom had been somehow involved in speculation on the Souk Al Manakh. Numerous significant institutions also found themselves harmed by the crash. The Kuwaiti banks, as well as a few banks in Bahrain, suddenly faced the potential for default on loans secured with shares that now had minimal value. Some banks also had used real estate in Kuwait to increase the security on their loans. However, as the crash unfolded, people were unloading property at any price in order to meet financial obligations, leading to a parallel decline in land values. Borrowers were not able to meet their commitments and the banks found themselves holding valueless property and even more valueless shares. By the end of the 1982, the aggregate total capital of banks in Kuwait was US$4.5 billion. However, the estimated value of bad loans was estimated to be between US$6 and US$7.7 billion, thus leaving the aggregate capital base of banks negative.

By September 1982, the government of Kuwait was faced with a major financial crisis. There was a total of US$94 billion worth of postdated checks outstanding, spread out amongst more than 6,000 investors, large and small alike, all of which depended on each other for payment. Certain individuals, including members of the royal family, had billions of dollars in liabilities. As a first response, the government established an organization to net out all postdated checks against one another. The new entity was called KUCLEAR. By 1983 the total amount of debts outstanding had been reduced by KUCLEAR to US$10 billion. In other words, Kuwaitis, who had assumed that their wealth had increased by the amount of checks they held, saw their net worth decline by US$84 billion.

The Souk Al Manakh can be an example of how not to develop the capital markets, a lesson very much learned by the Saudi financial regulatory authorities. However, considering the overall economic situation in Kuwait at the time, the outcome was difficult to avoid. It seems that the fundamental causes of the inflation of the values were:

1. There was enormous liquidity available in the region. People generally prefer to invest their money close to home. Kuwaitis and some Gulf citizens thought that returns on the Souk Al Manakh were ten times larger than if invested in the US or Europe. Thus, with a proper opportunity to invest in Gulf "bank" shares, they did so without hesitation.
2. To protect investors, the government of Kuwait had tightened the controls on the KSE. Again, to protect the smaller investors, the authorities limited the number of share issues, the number of brokers and shares traded daily. However, the restrictions only applied to the KSE, not to any "curb" exchange, like the Souk Al Manakh, upon which the authorities had no leverage. In other words, government interference was impeding the natural flow of trade. Merchants in the Gulf region had managed to adapt to changing conditions for many centuries and always found ways to circumvent government regulations. It appears that, in Kuwait at least, overly tight regulations triggered these same circumventing tendencies, though this time the outcome was to bypass them.

A major consequence of the Souk Al Manakh was the slow development of capital markets in the Gulf as a whole. Certainly the fears of the Saudi Arabian monetary agency with regards to the development of strong equity markets in Saudi Arabia is partly founded on what happened in Kuwait, and their genuine concern that wealthy merchants could take advantage of the unsuspecting public. Since the crash, Kuwait's capital markets have never been able to regain their former prominence.

Conclusion

The remainder of this text picks up where these developments left off. As will be shown, upon its original financial infrastructure, Saudi Arabia has built a system that is increasingly open to foreign investment but also locked into the traditional tight control of government agencies, with the PIF taking on some of SAMA's former duties. In the UAE, both Dubai and Abu Dhabi have found themselves increasingly looking to emulate the successes some of their regional peers have had in regard to foreign investment and capital markets, all while continuing to lean heavily on their own comparative advantages. Kuwait, Qatar, Bahrain and Oman remain integral to larger Gulf sociopolitical balances, but have seen their roles in regional and global financial markets diminish. Many of the markets across the Gulf have made mistakes, as markets do everywhere, but those that that have taken those mistakes and turned them into opportunities to become well-regulated markets, safe for investment by citizens and foreigners alike, have seen the most growth. Collectively, the financial markets of the Gulf have evolved in a manner that has surprised many outsiders, but to those cognizant of the mistakes and successes of the 1970s and 1980s, in many ways the path has been predetermined.

Notes

1. Adam Hanieh, "The Development of Capitalism in the Gulf Cooperation Council," in *Capitalism and Class in the Gulf Arab States*. (New York, NY: Palgrave Macmillan, 2011), pp. 57–84.
2. Mary Ann Tetreault, "Autonomy, Necessity, and the Small State: Ruling Kuwait in the Twentieth Century," *International Organization* 45, no. 4 (1991): 565–591; John R. Presley and Rodney Wilson. *Banking in the Arab Gulf*. (London: Palgrave Macmillan, 1991), p. 50.
3. Pete Moore, *Doing Business in the Middle East: Politics and Economic Crisis in Jordan and Kuwait*. (Cambridge: Cambridge University Press, 2004), p. 45.
4. United Arab Emirates, Union Law No. 10 of 1980 Concerning the Central Bank, the Monetary System and Organization of Banking. Available at: www.centralbank.ae/en/pdf/Law-10-English.pdf.
5. H. C. Metz, *Persian Gulf States: Country Studies*. (Washington, DC: US Government Printing Office, 1993).
6. Ibid.
7. Abdulrahman Al-Shayeb and Abdulnasser Hatemi-J., "The Performance of the Banking Sector in the UAE-La performance del settore bancario negli Emirati Arabi Uniti," *Economia Internazionale/International Economics* 67, no. 4 (2014): 439–448.
8. H. C. Metz, *Persian Gulf States*.
9. For a deeper discussion of these documentary credits see Chapter 6.4—Case Study on Documentary Credits.

10. Underwriting infrastructure-related projects regularly returned 5% on banking assets and 95% on equity during this period due to the size and number of facilities required.
11. Saudi Arabian Monetary Authority, "13th Annual Report of SAMA," p. 33; Saudi Arabian Monetary Authority, "39th Annual Report of SAMA," p. 44.
12. Saudi Arabian Monetary Authority, "30th Annual Report of SAMA," p. 44, table 4.5; Saudi Arabian Monetary Authority, "19th Annual Report of SAMA," p. 43.
13. The Hanbali interpretation is the prevalent but not the only school of jurisprudence in the Kingdom.
14. Personal experience confirmed by interviews with Saudi lawyers.
15. Mohammed El Qorchi, "Islamic Finance Gears Up," *Finance and Development* 42, no. 4 (2005): 46.
16. Ibid.
17. Ibid.
18. H. C. Metz, *Persian Gulf States.*
19. Rodney Wilson, "The Development of Islamic Finance in the Gulf Cooperation Council States," in David Held and Kristian Ulrichsen, eds. *The Transformation of the Gulf: Politics, Economics and the Global Order.* (London: Routledge, 2013).
20. Steven Rattner, "Tale of Saudi Money-Changer," *The New York Times*, August 13, 1982.
21. Ibid.
22. Ibid.
23. Jean-Francois Seznec, *The Financial Markets of the Arabian Gulf.* (London: Routledge, 2017), XII.
24. Jim Rickards, "In 1997, the 'carry trade' Was Born," *Business Insider*, March 19, 2015.
25. Seznec, *The Financial Markets of the Arabian Gulf*, 46.
26. Tested telexes are telexes that carry a code known only to the issuer and the recipient of the telex. The test keys are held securely by each party and guarantees that instructions issued with the right key can be tested immediately.
27. Seznec, *The Financial Markets of the Arabian Gulf*, 53.
28. Listed Domestic Companies, *World Development Indicators.* (Washington, DC: The World Bank, n.d.).
29. Saudi Arabian Monetary Authority, *Annual Statistics 2016.* Stock Markets Indicators Table 1 [2–1].
30. The following events were witnessed in person by the author in Bahrain, Kuwait, and the UAE between 1978 and 1984. Other accounts, mainly second hand can be found in MEED, MEES, the Financial Times and Jill Crystal, *Oil and Politics in the Gulf: Rulers and Merchants in Kuwait and Qatar.* (Cambridge: Cambridge University Press, 1990); Fida Darwiche, *The Gulf Stock Exchange Crash.* (London: Croom Helm, 1986).

2 The Financial Markets of the United Arab Emirates

Introduction

"We came from this hard life, but because of this man—may God rest his soul—we now have a good, beautiful life," said 60-year-old Jumaa Al Shami, who lives in the northern emirate of Umm Al Quwain.[1] Jumaa was speaking of Sheikh Zayed bin Sultan Al Nahyan, better known as Sheikh Zayed, the father of the modern United Arab Emirates (UAE). Now known around the world as a glitzy financial oil-rich playground, it was not long ago that this federation of seven monarchical emirates, dependent on a dying pearling industry and British "benefactors," could barely achieve subsistence.[2]

Over the last four decades, the economic and financial development of the UAE has been nothing short of stunning. The country sits on top of the 8th largest oil reserves in the world (97.8 billion BOE or 6% of global proven reserves) and is the second largest economy in the Gulf, second only to Saudi Arabia.[3] While this oil wealth has been critical for the country's development, like many its oil-rich peers, economic diversification has been a key aspect of national policy for years. Unlike others though, these diversification efforts have been successful, taking the country's non-oil contribution to GDP from 37% in 1972 to 69% in 2015 and laying the foundation upon which the UAE's role as trade and finance hub have flourished.[4] As a testament to this diversification, in 2015, despite uncertainty over the future of oil prices, foreign direct investment inflows were US$10.9 billion, or around 3% of GDP, more than similar metrics for both Turkey and Mexico that year.[5]

As a result of these efforts, the UAE is currently home to some of the world's leading banks and financial institutions, one of the world's largest sovereign wealth funds and has a chance to become the premier financial hub for an expanding region that includes parts of Central Asia, South Asia and Sub-Saharan Africa. Similar achievements can be found in the realm of international trade, a sector in which the UAE has a comparative advantage in both location and deep historical experience. Simple customs procedures, extremely competitive import and export costs and some of the world's most advanced seaport and airport infrastructure have all added to the UAE's global competitiveness in maritime trade, collectively helping the country become one of the world's largest re-export centers which actively trades with over 200 countries.

The UAE's economy does have its share of deficiencies though. Efforts to develop deep capital markets have largely failed. Ruling families, policy makers and business leaders are often one and the same, blurring the lines between private and public sector policy objectives and revenues.[6] Unlike other Gulf countries, most, if not all, of the country's leading banks and financial institutions are closely linked to, or even owned by, ruling family members, raising investor concerns over moral hazard, decision making and transparency. From a broader perspective, growth of the non-oil economy, while acting as a model for diversification, has also intrinsically linked the welfare of the UAE to that of global finance and foreign trade, in turn leading to vulnerabilities that were exposed during the 2008 crisis.

This chapter lays out the various channels through which these financial factors have developed, how they dictate the UAE's role in the global economy and how they have affected the economic standing of those who inhabit the emirates.

Dubai versus Abu Dhabi

The United Arab Emirates' financial markets cannot be assessed as a monolithic commercial environment. In reality, the UAE consists of sets of dissimilar regulatory and financial enclaves contained within larger, relatively independent, emirates, each driven by divergent motivations, but rolled up into a confederation style union. It is a complicated ecosystem that has emerged as one of the region's leading trading and financial hubs.

The main actors in this tale are undoubtedly the emirates of Abu Dhabi and Dubai. Where the former holds the vast bulk of the country's oil wealth, the latter has consistently been the only Middle Eastern city listed among the world's top twenty financial centers. Yet, Dubai and Abu Dhabi's foundations are not exceedingly dissimilar. Both effectively function as tribal monarchies whose ruling families trace their lineage back to the Bani Yas tribe. They share a common defense force, the Armed Forces of the UAE, and a common central bank, the United Arab Emirates Central Bank (CBU). Despite this, since the turn of the 20th century, the two emirates have taken different paths to establishing their roles in the regional and global economic system, with each focusing on their respective comparative advantages.

At the root of this divergence is the disparity in oil wealth. In 1971, the same year the UAE was founded, Abu Dhabi generated oil revenues of roughly US$450 million, more than ten times Dubai's US$40 million.[7] The UAE's confederal structure grants oil ownership rights to the emirate within which it is found, and thus Abu Dhabi's reserves gave it significant financial leverage over other emirates. Without their own significant oil discoveries, resource-poor emirates concluded that their standard of living was now dependent on Abu Dhabi's money, leading many of the northern emirates to ally themselves staunchly with the Al Nahyan, who at the time were the driving force behind the country's fledgling political structure.[8] Dubai took a different route, focusing its relatively limited oil wealth on catalyzing domestic economic activity that would outlast its oil reserves.

To accomplish this goal, Dubai focused on its comparative advantages; its location abreast major global trade routes, its navigable creek and the self-inflicted decline in Persian dominance over the Gulf's mercantile activity.[9] As early as the 1880s, the ruling Al Maktoum of Dubai recognized the key to their emirate's growth would be outward looking. Efforts such as eliminating custom duties and encouraging immigration were exponentially effective given that nearby major Persian ports of Lingah and Bushire were falling out of favor with local merchants due to a series of costly and restrictive regulations imposed by the Shah.[10]

Benefiting from Persia's trade barriers would become a decades long trend that, by the 1920s, cemented Dubai's ports as the preferred regional stop-off point for sea merchants, and by the 1950s, with the assistance of Dubai's Port Rashid and Port Jebel Ali, made the emirate the premier import point for merchants looking to distribute their wares throughout the Arab world. These dynamics led many Iranian businessmen to increasingly view Dubai as the Gulf's trade center, and capitalizing on the emirates laissez faire immigration and business policies, many of these businessmen uprooted their operations and relocated to Dubai to escape the Shah's onerous tariffs, some of which touched 40%.[11] With these merchants came invaluable business acumen, rapidly making this Iranian diaspora the backbone of Dubai's mercantile and professional establishment. Today many of Dubai's most powerful families, including the Gargash and Shirawi, hail from this generation of immigrants.[12]

Since then, an outward looking effort to attract foreign experience and investment has been the core of the Dubai's economic strategy. Collectively, these developments have integrated Dubai into global financial and sociopolitical flows, taking the emirate farther and farther away from its tribal history and drawing it closer to the city's deep rooted cosmopolitan tendencies. Indeed, global integration does not stop at the end of business hours. Dubai has developed a reputation for a having vibrant nightlife, is known the world round for its lavish parties, world class shopping, and eschewing of strict religious practices commonplace in neighboring Gulf states. As Abdulkhaleq Abdulla, famous Professor of Political Science at UAE University, notes, "in terms of identity, Dubai is no longer what it was just a short time ago—Emirati, Gulf, Arab, Islamic or Middle Eastern. It has hurriedly become a global city that is intricately connected to the economic, financial and commercial global network."[13]

Conversely, at the turn of the 20th century, where the al Maktoum had to focus on attracting outsiders and keeping businessmen happy, essentially worrying about an ease of doing business index that had yet to be invented,

Abu Dhabi's al Nahyan relied primarily on the expansion of its oil industry, not domestic infrastructure and development projects, for financial security. Further differentiating the two emirates, Sheikh Shakhbut bin Sultan al Nahyan, who ruled Abu Dhabi from 1928 to 1966 following a period of long family conflict and economic turmoil, was not only a spendthrift, but also feared that spending oil revenues on domestic development or allowing for an influx of foreigners would erode Abu Dhabi's traditional way of life. In fact, in the early 1950s, Shakhbut banned all new construction without his permission which was rarely forthcoming, and actively obstructed the entry of foreign merchants.[14] Shakhbut's tendencies were disastrous for Abu Dhabi's domestic economy, which if it were not for the discovery of vast oil reserves in the 1960s may never have risen to the prominence it holds today.

Shakhbut's successor, Sheikh Zayed, was everything Shakhbut was not; forward thinking, enigmatic and, most importantly, he presided over immeasurable oil wealth; wealth he was willing to use to modernize and unite all the other emirates, from Dubai to Ajman, under one United Arab Emirates flag. Abu Dhabi holds the bulk of the UAE's oil reserves, and unlike Dubai's oil reserves, which began faltering as early as 1991, Abu Dhabi's reserves are expected to maintain production levels for decades to come.[15] This oil wealth has become the foundation for Abu Dhabi's economic strategy. It was not long after the discovery of oil that this strategy became clear. Where Dubai looked to attract foreign capital inward, Sheikh Zayed envisioned Abu Dhabi taking its massive oil-driven financial surpluses and funneling them into assets across the globe, in turn generating revenue streams that would support future generations.

Key to this was and remains the Abu Dhabi Investment Authority (ADIA), the emirate's primary sovereign wealth fund (SWF) and one of the largest SWFs in the world. Since its founding in 1976, numerous other sovereign wealth funds have been formed in Abu Dhabi, most notably Mubadala. While prone to secrecy, these SWFs are now estimated to collectively hold assets worth well over US$1 trillion and generate annualized returns averaging between 7.5% and 10%.[16] This revenue stream feeds the budget of Abu Dhabi, the emirates it supports and acts as a financial safety net for times of oil price volatility.

Alongside vast oil export revenue and overseas investment streams, Abu Dhabi also has invested significantly into capital-intensive, not labor-intensive, export-oriented heavy industries, with a focus on metals, plastics, fertilizers and petrochemicals. Some of the most prominent of these state-owned endeavors are Fertile, Abu Dhabi Polymers Company or Borouge, and Emirates Aluminum.

A deeper discussion of these funds is included further in this text but what is critical to note here is how these institutions have molded Abu Dhabi in comparison to Dubai. Just like many of Dubai's largest companies, many of Abu Dhabi's key financial institutions are staffed with foreign professionals. The same goes for heavy industry, where much of the technical expertise involved is gleaned through foreign input. Yet, unlike Dubai, Abu Dhabi's drive to attract foreigners largely stops where business ends. Dubai on the other hand has historically established its economic prosperity through mercantile trade that is dominated by foreigners. Where in the past this was Iranian merchants, today it is shoppers, businessmen and vacationers from across the globe. Indeed, Dubai was the fourth most visited city in the world in 2017, attracting 16 million international visitors, is home to the world's most visited shopping center, the Dubai Mall, and has seen retail and wholesale activity make up nearly 30% of the Emirate's GDP.[17] Just as in the early years of the emirate's development, this dependency on commercial activity creates a situation where Sheikh Mohammed bin Rashid al Maktoum (MbR), the Emir of Dubai, must ensure that the cultural and economic environment is appeasing to foreign commercial actors, be they Iranian merchants or South Asian shoppers. This dynamic has been a critical factor in Dubai's globally minded, western leaning evolution.

Conversely, while it often tries to, Abu Dhabi does not need to accommodate foreign merchants or modern shoppers. Its SWFs and heavy industries employee just a marginal amount of foreigners when compared to Dubai. Where Dubai's expats outnumbered nationals 10:1 in 2018, the most recent figures released for Abu Dhabi show expats outnumber nationals just 4:1.[18] Due to the sensitive nature of the topic, Abu Dhabi has abstained from conducting a comprehensive census covering the figure since 2010, and while this makes the latter statistic outdated, the outsized nature of Dubai's expat population remains, even if Abu Dhabi's comparable statistic has grown in the last eight years, as it likely has. These population dynamics has prevented many of the cosmopolitan tendencies that now characterize Dubai from ever taking root in Abu Dhabi, allowing the emirate to maintain a tighter grip on its cultural roots.

This economically driven divergence has had many implications. From a positive perspective, the different development paths that Dubai and Abu Dhabi have embarked upon have in large part allowed for a further diversification of the United Arab Emirates collective economy. Whereas Abu Dhabi can draw on massive financial reserves driven by oil wealth, Dubai is able to provide a more diverse range of employment opportunities through its laissez faire development strategy.

From a more troubling perspective, some believe that Dubai's foreigner-focused economy has brought little benefit to nationals, who instead view the modernization as a threat to their culture. As Emirati scholar Abdulla al Suwaidi noted on the fortieth anniversary of the UAE, while globalization has greatly benefited the country, with most nationals embracing or at least accommodating modernization, "no one can know when this accommodation might become a danger to social cohesion."[19] Christopher Davidson has taken it even one step further, warning that

> As foreigners are beginning to make vast profits out of real estate and other activities [in Dubai] that were formerly the preserve of the

> indigenous population, the monarchy and its cronies are beginning to appear as very obvious clients or intermediaries in a metropole-satellite chain of dependent relations.[20]

The divergence also appears to be self-perpetuating. Businessmen and young professionals often express hesitation at working in Abu Dhabi, but are eager to seek out employment opportunities in Dubai.[21] Recently Abu Dhabi has made efforts to counter these perceptions, but the divergent sociocultural realities that have evolved from the policies of the al Nahyan and al Maktoum families will be hard to reverse.

From an agency perspective, Dubai's effort to grow economically independent of Abu Dhabi has had mixed results. While it surely boasts significant financial accomplishments, Dubai still required what was essentially a bailout from Abu Dhabi to survive the 2008 financial crises, in turn leading Dubai to rename the Burj Dubai, the world's tallest building, which was intended to be a sign of Dubai's achievement, to the Burj Khalifa in homage to Abu Dhabi's Emir. To some this puts Dubai in the same category as more northern emirates, like Fujairah and Ras Al Khaimah, who are reliant on Abu Dhabi's funds for major projects. This assessment misses a key factor though. Dubai is not dependent on Abu Dhabi as much as it dependent on global investor perceptions. In fact, the dependency may go the other way. As Karen Young has highlighted, Dubai's bailout was a recognition that the "fate of the two emirates were deeply intertwined and that while they had followed two very different development paths, their financial markets were inextricably linked."[22] This effectively means that Abu Dhabi, who until recently has had the luxury of depending solely on its mineral wealth as sort of perpetual annuity, must also concern itself with how global investors perceive Dubai's financial health. This dynamic has become increasingly important to Abu Dhabi as its efforts to engage with global markets have grown in the wake of the commodity price slump.

As the country approaches its sixtieth anniversary, it faces a series of formidable challenges. Where the lower for longer oil price scenario that took hold in 2014 acts as a threat to Abu Dhabi's fiscal position, protectionist sentiments that began sweeping across the globe in 2015 threaten to slow growth in Dubai given its role as a global trade and finance hub.[23] With this interplay between two distinct financial markets acting as a background, the remainder of this chapter presents a nuanced assessment of the regulatory, banking, sovereign wealth and capital market sectors of the UAE economy, highlighting how, despite notable deficiencies, the nation's two leading emirates have built a diverse arsenal of financial tools to weather both adverse global financial flows and commodity super slumps.

The UAE's Regulatory Environment

Compared to global peers, the United Arab Emirates is perceived to be among the world's most attractive business environments. Regulations are devised explicitly with the aim of attracting foreign investors, expropriations are rare, banking is widely and readily available, taxes are low and corruption is considered to be among the mildest in the region.[24] It has not always been this way though.

The UAE's modern legal structure came to life in the late seventies. It exists in a two-tier system, with the Constitution of the UAE granting each of the seven emirates substantial leeway to conduct legal affairs within their territory, except in matters of defense, foreign affairs, communication, education and health, which are controlled at the federal level. The highest federal authority is the Federal Supreme Council, which is made up of the seven emirates' respective rulers and must ratify all laws. Within the council, Dubai and Abu Dhabi hold the most power and as such all decisions must be approved by their respective rulers and at least three of the other five emirates.

Aside from this, as stipulated in Article 122 of the constitution, individual emirates are constitutionally permitted to independently regulate all local matters not subject to federal legislation. From an economic perspective, this has effectively created a situation where some financial sector regulation, such as bankruptcy proceedings and foreign ownership limitations, are set at federal level, while other more minute details such as incorporation proceedings and trade licenses are devised at the emirate level.

This division of powers was the result of long fought efforts by Sheikh Zayed. Through his personal relationships with other tribal leaders, and the readiness to commit Abu Dhabi's oil wealth to the fledgling union, Sheikh Zayed was able to get all seven emirates to coalesce around a compromise that established a union of equal but sovereign states, each of which retained their own international status and autonomy over economic affairs.

To fund UAE-wide policy spheres, such as defense and health, the federal government was initially intended to collect contributions from all seven emirates as a percent of their annual revenues.[25] Yet, driven by tensions over the unequal dispersion of hydrocarbon revenues and poor financial reporting to the federal government, it was not long before the federal government's fiscal base was funded primarily through the contributions of Abu Dhabi and Dubai.

This dynamic was underlined in 1995, when Sheikh Zayed, in a meeting of the Federation's Supreme Council, declared that "since the income of the UAE's citizens was among the highest in the world, no one in the Emirates should be in need," in turn effectively formalizing the policy that the country's broad resources, and Abu Dhabi's oil wealth specifically, would be shared across all the emirates.[26] While this concentrates the fiscal burden on Abu Dhabi, it also provides the Abu Dhabi's leadership with considerable leverage over the smaller emirates and brings to the fore the question of who owns Abu Dhabi's natural resources—the al Nahyan royal family, who would then have the right to use it for patronage as they see fit, or the citizenry—a topic that will be discussed further in this text.

Until the late seventies, federal-level business regulation was essentially nonexistent or unexercised, with regulation instead conducted primarily at the emirate level in what was largely an informal, discretionary and uncodified manner. Since then though, there has been a stunning turnaround in Federal regulatory oversight, at least on paper. Between 1979 and 1990, federal laws regulating industrial affairs, labor, banking, commercial companies and maritime commerce were enacted. Practically though, most business licensing and oversight is still conducted at the emirate level, although they are increasingly influenced by federal policies.[27]

To ease this process, most emirates within the federation have online portals through which certain services associated with starting a new company, obtaining business licenses and construction permits, as well as registering real estate purchases, among other things, are streamlined. These have allowed for an efficient business environment where opening a business takes as little as eight days, registering real estate just 1.5 days and obtaining permission to construct new infrastructure only forty-nine days, all among the shortest in the region, if not the world.[28] Indeed, UAE is ranked 26th out of 190 in the World Bank's Ease of Doing Business index, the highest ranking of any Middle Eastern nation.[29]

The business environment is not without its deficiencies though. A recent example of this can be found in the country's bankruptcy regulations. Until recently, failing to make a single debt payment was an imprisonable criminal offense. In the wake of the 2008 financial crisis, this drove many small to medium sized business owners in the UAE to pack their bags and flee instead of risking jail time, leaving upwards US$1.4 billion in debt behind.[30] This immediate threat of jail time for debtors underlines how, until late 2016, bankruptcy law in UAE overwhelmingly favored creditors and limited options for debtors looking for restructuring assistance or financial protection. Coupling this with the law's ambiguous text meant that the UAE's 1993 bankruptcy law was time consuming, resulted in low recovery rates and existed as a serious business risk. The inefficiency of the bankruptcy process was actually stunning, with the process taking an average of 3.2 years, costing 20% of the estate and recovering just 30 cents on the dollar, World Bank data shows. This pales in comparison to the United Kingdom, where bankruptcy proceedings take just one year, cost 6% of the estate and recover 88.6 cents on the dollar.[31]

To the UAE's credit, the government has recognized the seriousness of this deficiency, passing a new law in 2016 overhauling the corporate bankruptcy process. The new legislation removes the threat of arrest, applies to all onshore and most free zone companies and was noted as a significant improvement by leading law firms.[32] The UAE's action in this area highlights the country's focus on continuously buffing blemishes off its coat so as to always shine in the eyes of foreign investors.

In this regard, ownership structures in emerging markets often act as another serious concern for foreign investors, and the GCC is no different.

In the UAE, ownership laws are dealt with at the federal level through the Industrial Law of 1979, the Commercial Agency Law of 1981 and the Federal Companies Law of 1984. The laws stipulate that commercial and industrial companies in the UAE must be 51% owned by UAE nationals, branch offices of foreign companies must have a national agent, all general partnerships must be owned by UAE nationals, and foreign shareholders can only hold 49% of most UAE companies.[33] These ownership limitations are more restrictive than in any other GCC country. It remains difficult, if not impossible, to sell anything in the UAE without a local agent.[34] More troublingly, a 2010 amendment made it so that foreign companies cannot end their business engagement with the local agent without first showing "material reason justifying its termination or nonrenewal."[35] Not only is this nearly impossible, but even in the event that the agreement is terminated through court proceedings, the agent is often awarded compensations based on past profits, actual losses incurred and extent of agent's investment.[36] As of 2015, there were over 6,000 registered native agents, with over 90% of those representing foreign companies registered in Abu Dhabi and Dubai, as well as an unknown, but believed to be significant, number of unregistered agents.[37] Most recently, in 2018 the UAE floated potential revisions to these agency and ownership laws, but at the time of this writing, details of the revisions were scant, with those available hinting that the changes would be marginal and applied in a highly selective manner.

While the agency laws are inconvenient for foreign investors, they serve an important purpose for UAE government. During the 1970s, when the country experienced exploding economic activity, largely the result of booming oil wealth, local merchant families quickly found themselves facing unsustainable market competition and petitioned for government protections. It was not long after that emirate-level agency laws were enacted, followed not much later by the Federal Agency Law.[38] According to a US Embassy official at the time, requests for these protections were not simply the result of greed, but "the desire to foster the development of [native] managerial and entrepreneurial class which can control the country's economic future."[39] Since then, the sociopolitical role of the agency law has honed in on this last bit, "control of the country's economic future." For thousands of UAE natives, the Agency Law provides a legal method to tap into the vast wealth streaming into the country. In this sense, while the agency law does effectively act as a non-tariff barrier, it does so at the financial benefit of the native population, in turn establishing one mechanism through which the UAE's ruling families can distribute the country's wealth.

It is important to note that agency laws of this nature are against World Trade Organization (WTO) rules. In fact, to the regret of Saudi merchants, Saudi Arabia had to abandon similar rules when it acceded to the WTO. As one of the WTO's founding members, the UAE did not have to negotiate specific changes to its trading rules, and thereby was able to keep the agency rules in place, in effect protecting the livelihood of many UAE merchants. In repeated Trade Policy Reviews, the WTO has urged the UAE to liberalize these practice, to which the UAE has pointed to its much more liberal Free Trade Zones.[40]

Free Trade Zones

Conceptually, free trade zones are special areas or enclaves that, legally isolated from their surrounding domestic economies, are aimed at driving foreign investment, boosting exports, inducing skills transfer and creating employment for the host country. The UAE's experience with free trade zones is really a discussion about Dubai's experience with free trade zones (FTZs). Since Dubai's 1985 establishment of the Jebel Ali Free Zone Authority (JAFZA), the emirate has seen a proliferation of FTZs with specialties ranging from technology and media to finance and flowers (See Table 2.1).

Table 2.1 Dubai's Free Trade Zones

Free Trade Zone	*Date Established*	*Owner*
Jebel Ali Free Zone Authority	1985	Dubai World
Dubai Airport Free Zone	1996	Emirates Group
Dubai Cars and Automotive Zone	2000	Dubai World
Dubai Internet City	2000	Dubai Holding
Dubai Gold and Diamond Park	2001	EMAAR
Dubai Media City	2001	Dubai Holding
Dubai Healthcare City	2002	Dubai Holding
Dubai Multi Commodities Centre	2002	Dubai World
Jumeirah Lakes Towers Free Zone	2002	Government of Dubai
Dubai Knowledge Park	2003	Dubai Holding
International Media Production Zone	2003	Dubai Holding
Dubai Flower Centre	2004	Dubai Holding
Dubai Industrial City	2004	Dubai Holding
Dubai International Financial Centre	2004	Government of Dubai
Dubai Outsource Zone	2004	Dubai Holding
Dubai Silicon Oasis	2004	Emirates Group
Dubai Science Park	2005	Dubai Holding
Dubai Studio City	2005	Dubai Holding
Energy and Environment Park	2006	Dubai holding
Dubai International Academic City	2007	Dubai Holding
Dubai Logistics City	2007	Emirates Group
Dubai Maritime City Authority	2007	Dubai World
Dubai Textile City	2007	Dubai World
International Humanitarian City	2007	Government of Dubai
Dubai Design District	2015	Dubai Holding

Each of Dubai's twenty-five FTZs is effectively empowered with total control over planning, zoning, regulations, licensing, service provision and facility development within its operational area.

Dubai's FTZs act as an attractive alternative to the complex and restricted investment environment across the general UAE. They are exempt from all licensing, agency, emiratization and national ownership regulations that apply outside of the zones. In most cases this means that businesses located in free trade zones can hold 100% equity ownership in their business regardless of nationality, be fully exempt from import and export taxes, as well as commercial levies, repatriate 100% of their profits and hire employees outside of the heavily critiqued labor sponsorship program. In addition, free zone authorities often provide significant support services, including sponsorship, worker housing, dining facilities, security and labor recruitment. All of this comes with limitations though. FTZ companies are prohibited from commercial activity with the nearby onshore communities without special authorization, foreigners permitted to work for FTZ companies are expected to work only from the company's FTZ offices, and work visas procured through free zone activity, either in the form of capital investment or regular employment, cannot lead to UAE citizenship.

By many metrics these zones have been wildly successful. The emirate's spectrum of quasi-independent enclaves has grown to house more than 20,000 companies and serve as a major re-export center the Gulf region and beyond.[41] A 2016 study of firm level data shows that on average, firms located within free trade zones attract more investment than their comparable onshore peers, are as much as 29% more capital-intensive, purchased an average of 89% of their intermediate inputs from the domestic onshore economy, and were more likely than their onshore peers to seek financing from onshore banks, all factors which add value to Dubai's local economy.[42] Depending on the source, free trade zones generate between a quarter and a third of Dubai's GDP, account for over 40% of the emirates' imports and exports, and have acted as a major source of foreign direct investment and foreign exchange.[43]

The success of these free trade zones is in large part thanks to the continuous support of the Dubai government in the form of land provision, initial infrastructure assistance, financial backing and subsidy accommodation, all of which have provided the projects with an air of credibility from their initial conception. Since the country's first FTZ, JAFZA, the driving force behind this support has been Dubai's Emir Sheikh Mohammed bin Rashid al Maktoum.

MbR's attitude toward outside investors and international commerce was made clear in his 2006 book, *My Vision*, where he stated:

> When a manager of a company that had moved to Dubai asked me if there was anything I wanted from his company. I answered: I want your

> success only. Development is beneficial and so is national participation but what concerns the investor, in the end, is return on investment. If an investor comes to Dubai and starts and enterprise and makes a million, he will invest two million, and if he makes two million he will invest four.[44]

It would be through these FTZ's that MbR would attract global investors to the small Emirate of Dubai.

Dubai's Free Trade Zones

Jebel Ali Free Zone Authority

The 134 square kilometer JAFZA finds its roots in MbR's innovative and entrepreneurial drive to bootstrap Dubai's place in the regional economic order. For Sheikh Mohammed and his closest advisors, including Sultan bin Sulayem, the head of the prominent business family whose son would become CEO of DP World (DPW), one clear solution to this issue was expanding shipping operations at the port of Jebel Ali. At the time, the concept of a FTZ was new to both the UAE and the broader Middle East and initially local businessmen, feeling that Dubai's port infrastructure was sufficient, resisted the idea. Yet, recognizing that the biggest impediment to foreign investment were the emirates onerous ownership laws, in the mid-1980's Maktoum and his advisors decided to transform Jebel Ali into a special economic zone where ownership laws and import fees would not apply.[45] Like many of Dubai's free trade zones, JAFZA would be publicly owned, in this case through Dubai World, whose chairmanship was held by Sulayem and then later his son until 2010, due to fallout from the 2008 Dubai World debt crises. Keeping matters close to the family, Sulayem was replaced by Sheikh Maktoum's uncle Ahmed bin Saeed Al Maktoum.

Today, JAFZA, with its separate areas for commercial, industrial and storage activity, is the largest free zone in the region, is home to the world's largest artificial port and the world's largest dry dock. It generates more than a third of the UAE's total FDI and over 50% of Dubai's total exports.[46] While it has inspired imitators across the region, it still remains the market leader, and as of 2012 was home to more than 7,000 companies, over 120 of which were affiliated with Fortune's "Top 500 Companies."[47]

An important activity of JAFZA is the receiving, repackaging and shipping of goods. For example almost all car companies active in the Gulf have very large warehouses in JAZA. These companies receive parts by container loads through the harbor, store the parts in warehouses, and send specific parts to meet dealer requests throughout the region by using the world's largest cargo airport, which abuts JAFZA. By the same token, some firms bring in parts from all over the world, hire cheap expatriate labor from South Asia and manufacture goods inside JAFZA for export. For example, many Pakistani trading families have set up such shops which allow them to use raw materials and parts brought through the harbor, use Pakistani labor, which they can control, and then export products to Pakistan, allowing them to be paid legally in US$, which they then can park in Dubai.

Trade patterns out of the JAFZA in the decade following its 1985 opening were mostly oriented toward neighboring GCC countries and Iran, a continuation of Dubai's traditional trade flows.[48] Since then though, there has been a distinction diversification in JAFZA's trade patterns. In 2016, the zone's number one trading partner was China with total trade activity valued at US$11.3 billion, largely driven by the numerous Chinese companies capitalizing on JAFZA's logistics infrastructure to establish re-export operations. This dynamic has helped make the Asia-Pacific region JAFZA's number one trading partner (US$32.4 billion) in 2016, followed by the Middle East (US$27.2 billion), Europe (US$9.9 billion), the Americas (US$5.5 billion) and finally Africa (US$5 billion). Nearly half of this trade was made up of machinery and electronic goods, followed by petrochemicals and hydrocarbons at 19%, with the balance equally distributed between food stuffs, textiles and automotive parts.[49]

JAFZA is presently setting its sights on Africa.[50] Through its flagship port operator and developer, DPW, the UAE is offering attractive infrastructure development and port management opportunities to African countries. These projects often come hand in hand with security agreements, training and education for local workers and security forces, and even incentives like visas to the UAE.[51] DPW has infrastructure projects in Djibouti, breakaway Somali states, Rwanda, Mozambique, Algeria and Mali. This web of ports would secure JAFZA as the key logistics and trade hub linking Asia to Africa via DPW infrastructure and management, and act as a defensive move in the face of new ports being built by rivals with similar ambitions, including Iran, China and Pakistan. The development of this activity is not without setbacks. DWP's operations at Djibouti's Dorelah Container Terminal were seized by the host country in early 2018 due to tension between the two states, a conflict that is yet to be resolved. Reflecting the complicated geopolitics and geoeconomics at play, China is also active in Djibouti. It opened its first overseas military base there in 2017 and also recently financed and constructed a 470-mile, US$4 billion electric railroad connecting Djibouti to landlocked Ethiopia, which receives 97% of its imports from Dorelah.[52] There are now rumors that Djibouti will hand over control of the Dorelah Container Terminal to China, which ironically enough, holds a 23.5% stake in Port de Djibouti, DPW's joint venture partner and majority owner of the Dorelah Container Terminal.[53]

The Dubai International Financial Center

In his book *My Vision*, Sheikh Mohammed declared that Dubai should "be on par with the world's most prestigious financial centers, including London and New York." His answer to realizing this vision? The Dubai International Financial Center (DIFC). The financial FTZ was founded in 2004 on prime city-center real estate provided by the ruling family and designed around blueprints set out by the consulting firm McKinsey. By 2008, the DIFC had registered more than 450 firms, including the likes of Goldman Sachs, Merrill Lynch, UBS, Citibank, Credit Suisse and Deutsche Bank, and attracted more than US$18 billion in private sector infrastructure investment.[54] These metrics effectively equate foreign direct investment in the 110-acre DIFC between 2004 and 2008 to all of foreign direct investment in sub-Saharan Africa, excluding South Africa, during the same period of time.[55] Since then, the growth has continued. DIFC is home to more than 21,000 employees and 800 firms as of 2018.[56]

This growth has allowed for the DIFC to become a major real estate success. Every building in its campus is rented out, earning Dubai substantial rent. Most commercial and investment banks active in the region use DIFC as their center from which to operate. Similarly, organizations that service these banks such as accounting firms, consultants, or legal firms have sizable offices there. That said, there have been setbacks in the DIFC's legal environment, which have led many of these companies to resist using the DIFC as a center for arbitration.

Within DIFC, legal and regulatory matters are overseen by the Dubai Financial Services Authority (DFSA). As with most of Dubai's mega projects, the details of DIFC's regulatory environment were put in the hands of Western experts, in this case the hands were of veteran Australian financial regulator Errol Hoopmann, who had been poached from the Australian Securities and Investment Commission to head DFSA.[57] Responsible for licensing and regulating all activity within the DIFC and empowered by an amendment to the UAE constitution, Hoopmann and the DFSA created a legal environment within Dubai that mirrored UK common law. This common law alternative to the complicated and, in the eyes of many, biased onshore civil law legal system has historically been one of the major characteristics drawing foreign firms to DIFC.

Apart from hearing matters specifically related to DIFC companies, the DIFC Courts can also hear civil or commercial actions from outside the DIFC, including outside the UAE. The DIFC Courts have taken even further legal measures to ensure an attractive judicial environment, opening an arbitration center in conjunction with the London Court of International Arbitration, establishing a series of ad hoc agreements with the foreign court systems, including those in Australia, Jordan, Korea, Kenya and Uzbekistan, and initiating legal processes in 2015 that made it the first jurisdiction in the region where a non-Muslim can register a will under an internationally recognized legal structure.[58] Enshrining itself to New York businessmen even further, the DIFC has signed a memorandum with the US District Court for the Southern District of New York that allows mutual enforcement of financial judgments.

In time, these attributes turned the DIFC Courts into what legal professionals called a "conduit jurisdiction," through which foreign firms could enforce foreign-obtained arbitration judgments against local defendants based outside of the financial center, thus bypassing the onshore legal system.[59] As of late, this has drawn the ire of some onshore Emirate-owned companies who felt that the DIFC Courts were acting outside their initial mandate by providing a back door to Dubai's onshore economic environment. Responding to these concerns, the Dubai government established the Joint Judicial Council (JCC) in 2016, which effectively rules on potential conflicts of jurisdiction between the onshore Dubai courts and the offshore DIFC Courts. While it is unclear what the long-term effect of this new legal structure will be, legal professionals have noted that the JCC has been seen as widely favoring the onshore courts and that, if this continues, DIFC risks losing some of its appeal to global businesses.[60]

Dubai Mercantile Exchange

The Dubai Mercantile Exchange (DME), established within the confines of the DIFC in 2007, was founded to provide a platform for traders and buyers to hedge their purchases of oil for shipment East of Suez. Whereas the shipments of crude to the Atlantic basin and to Europe could be hedged through the WTI and Brent markets on the New York Mercantile Exchange and the London International Petroleum Exchange, there were no such platform for shipments East of Suez. Hence, it seemed obvious that a properly designed trading system would appeal to the quickly growing market for crude oil in Asia, and the DME set out to fill this need. Traditionally all the contracts between the major Gulf producers such as Saudi Arabia, Iraq, Kuwait and the UAE have been based on transactions of Oman and Dubai crude oil as aggregated and assessed daily by S&P Global Platts. The price of oil from the Gulf was thus defined based on Platts Oman and Dubai crude benchmark prices with an adjustment for distance and quality. Saudi Aramco, for example, would define its sales of crude to Japan as based on a computed average of Platts benchmarks plus or minus a quality adjustment.

In the Dubai mold, the DME was set up by Tatweer, a Dubai state company, NYMEX and the Oman Investment Fund to trade oil contracts using the Globex electronic trading platform, the same platform which is used in London and New York. DME brought on major investment banks such as Morgan Stanley, Goldman Sachs and JPMorganChase as shareholders to increase the credibility of the exchange with buyers and sellers. The DME offered a platform to auction crude shipments and set contracts for future delivery, primarily through its Oman Crude futures contract. However, the DME did not initially garner much success mainly because buyers were not interested in Oman-Dubai crudes and did not see the need or ability to hedge their purchases of Saudi or Kuwaiti crude using Oman's limited production.

However, on July 4, 2018, Saudi Aramco announced that it was going to change its pricing computation for sales to the Far East by compiling a mix of the Platts prices and the DME Oman crude futures contract. This has the potential to completely transform the DME. Buyers and speculators will now want to hedge at least the DME part of the Aramco's selling prices, which they would now due through the DME's oil futures contracts. Since almost 12 million b/d of crude oil goes to the Far East from all the Gulf's producers, the change will increase the volume of contracts at the DME, especially with hedgers and speculators from Asia.

Abu Dhabi's Free Trade Zones

When it comes to free trade zones, Abu Dhabi undoubtedly takes a back seat to its neighbor. During the 1980s and 1990s when Dubai was worrying about dwindling oil revenues and focusing on catalyzing its international appeal, Abu Dhabi, resting on its oil wealth, remained overwhelmingly inward looking. As of late though, this has changed, with Abu Dhabi looking to develop, if not replicate, some of its own FTZ success. For example, where Dubai has the Media Free Zone, Abu Dhabi has the Two-four54 center, both which focus on attracting foreign press and media. That said, Abu Dhabi's experience with free trade zones is relatively novice compared to its neighbor, with the emirate housing just six free trade zones. Where most of these have been unsuccessful in achieving the same size or grandeur of Dubai's FTZs, Abu Dhabi hopes that its most recent FTZ may buck this trend.

With an eye on Dubai's DIFC, Abu Dhabi's newest free zone, the Abu Dhabi Global Market (ADGM), is an effort to give Abu Dhabi its own finance hub. Just like DIFC, ADGM, which was established in accordance with the same federal laws as DIFC in 2013, has its own regulatory body (the Financial Services Regulations Bureau), has staffed its leadership with foreign experts, applies common, opposed to civil, law, has no corporate or income tax and allows for full repatriation of profits. Those similarities aside, ADGM officials have gone out of their way to point out that they do not intend to compete with DIFC and have instead attempted to complement it by focusing ADGM on wealth management and financial technology, opposed to the DIFC's focus on private equity and international trading.[61] ADGM has launched a number of initiatives centered on these themes, including developing a one-stop shop environment for popular wealth management financing vehicles, as well as funding financial technology incubators.[62] Despite these efforts, ADGM will face an uphill battle, not only due to the well-developed DIFC nearby, but also due to tighter overall liquidity on the back of the lower oil prices and similar efforts to attract FinTech in nearby markets like Bahrain.

ADGM is the not the only arena that Abu Dhabi appears to be emulating Dubai. In the emirates' hinterland, around the Khalifa Port Container Terminal (KPCT), Abu Dhabi is building the Khalifa Industrial Zone Abu Dhabi (KIZAD). The port and industrial zone in many ways mimic JAFZA. KIZAD offers foreign investors the chance to hold 100% ownership in an industrial property, provides land, warehouses, offices and aims to become a major export and re-export hub for metals and petrochemical products. Key to this is Mubadala-controlled Emirates Global Aluminum, one of the largest aluminum companies in the world. EGA has numerous projects set to capitalize on both KPCT and KIDZA. Despite this, while KIDZA and Port Khalifa are part of Abu Dhabi's broader strategy to develop the port as a regional hub, JAFZA's decades of reputation and management experience will make it hard for KIDZA to effectively build a comparative advantage.

FTZ's Unintended Consequences

It is not clear that the FTZs always have their intended effect on the local economy. For example, Dubai's Internet City is in many respects a success. It's initial infrastructure was built in under a year, it went from housing just a handful of companies in a few buildings in 2000 to over 900 companies in more than twenty-five buildings in 2007, and currently is home to some of world's leading technology firms, including Microsoft, Oracle, HP, IBM, Canon and Cisco.[63] Yet, where the initial objective behind the zone's establishment was to draw high tech, high value research and development into Dubai, many of the flagship companies located in the zone do little actual research there. Microsoft, the first major company to open an office in DIC, and doing so only after being given a 50-year rent-free lease, merely uses the DIC to house one of its many service centers that sells and services software developed elsewhere.[64] Conversely, not far away, Microsoft houses an army of coders at multiple locations across Israel as part of its Israel Research and Development Center. The center not only conducts extensive recruitment initiatives with the surrounding technology community but also engages with local institutions through academic partnerships and entrepreneurship training programs; in doing so actively providing the skills transfer that Sheikh Mohammed wished for his own citizens.

These dynamics are even more distinct when looking at DIFC. While the FTZ has undoubtedly become the regional home for global banking, finance and consulting leaders, in many ways it has become little more than that. Companies like CitiBank, Ernst and Young and Goldman Sachs do have offices in DIFC, but the vast majority of these companies' substantive work is done elsewhere. These offices in DIFC act as little more than representative offices. Admittedly, this has allowed the emirate to make vast amounts of money on real estate. Yet, Sheikh Mohammed's goal was to set the DIFC on equal footing with financial centers in New York and London. No metric highlights the failure to achieve this goal better than Nasdaq Dubai, the capital market that sits within the DIFC.

More than a decade after its creation, Nasdaq Dubai is home to only nine equity listings and saw less than 30,000 individual trades in all of 2017.[65] Comparatively, the New York Stock Exchange regularly sees over 4 million individual trades on any given day.[66] While Dubai's other exchange, the Dubai Financial Market, saw around 1 million trades in 2017, it is still ranked 40th globally in terms of total market capitalization, with a total market capitalization of less than 0.5% of the NYSE market cap.[67] In this regard while the DIFC does add a great deal of glitz to Dubai's business appeal, technically speaking it does not do so as a financial center.

Furthermore, many of the freedoms enjoyed in FTZs are also not as free or immutable as initially suspected. For example, Dubai's Media City, a free zone geared toward journalists and television stations that attracted the likes of Reuters, France-Presse, CNN and Dow Jones, was established with promises of press freedom directly from MbR.[68] Yet, in 2007, when Pakistan, a historically close ally of UAE, declared martial law, two Pakistani networks based in Media City, GEO TV and Ary One, refused to comply with request put forth by the Pakistani government and suddenly found the UAE government forcing them to close down. With Dubai Media City's executive director stating that it would "observe the broadcast principles of the country's foreign policy," it was clear that DMC's freedoms had taken a back seat to federal foreign policies.[69]

The Banking Sector

In the early 2000s, the UAE's banking sector regularly found itself receiving high praise for its strong supervision and regulation, yet these accolades only came after the UAE learned from a series of rattling crises.[70] In 1990, in the wake of Iraq's invasion of Kuwait, as much as 40% of total deposits were withdrawn from UAE banks, driving at least two banks to require capital injections from the CBU.[71] Not long after that, in 1991, the Bank of Credit and Commerce International, which Abu Dhabi's ruler Sheikh Zayed was a founding shareholder in, collapsed on a grand scale. Stemming from allegations of money laundering by United States and British authorities, simultaneous action was taken by regulators in seven different countries, eventually leading to the closure of BCCI in sixty nine countries.[72]

The scandals were embarrassing for the UAE and instigated a period of regulatory overhaul that tightened the CBU's supervision and monitoring processes and set strict minimum capital adequacy ratios. Since then, the

CBU and the UAE federal government have incrementally added new layers of regulation through circulars and notices on topics ranging from accounting standards to liquidity requirements. For example, in 2013 the SBU enacted macroprudential measures to temper a resurgent real estate market and in 2015 the CBU began the process of implementing the Basel III capital and liquidity standards, with plans to have them in place by 2019.[73] Amidst all these changes, the 1980 Banking Law still remains unchanged from its original form, with many industry watchers long calling for an overhaul.

From a monetary policy perspective, the UAE dinar is pegged to the US$, thus minimizing the CBU's ability to conduct independent interest rate policy and limiting the tools it has for addressing inflation and painful exchange rate-driven business cycles. For example, between 2015 and 2017, the strength of the US$ contributed to falling investment in UAE's property market and undermined the competitiveness of UAE non-oil exports, a series of events that a central bank overseeing a free, or even managed, floating interest rate would have been able to address through interest rate policy.[74] While the CBU does not have an independent interest rate policy, it does exercise some monetary and credit controls through its sale and purchase of certificates of deposit.

Commercial Banks

As of 2017, the UAE's banking sector was well capitalized and heavily banked, with capital adequacy ratios and Tier 1 capital across the sector both well above the required 12% and 8%, respectively.[75] The sector consists of twenty-three domestic and twenty-six foreign licensed banks, six of which are from elsewhere in the GCC, with numerous other institutions licensed to carry out investment banking and other specialized activities. This saturation has led the CBU to effectively put a moratorium on new banks and limit the number of branches foreign banks can open. Most recent measures show that domestic banks have 846 branches to foreign banks' 85.[76]

Collectively, UAE banks have seen their total deposits grow from around US$222 billion in 2012 to over US$350 billion in 2017, an average annual growth rate of 10%.[77] On the lending side, UAE banks have seen their total loan books grow from US$350 billion in 2012 to over US$460 billion in 2017, of which nearly US$400 billion, over 100% of GDP, was to the private sector.[78]

As far as personal credit goes, as recently as 2004, most UAE banks were reluctant to delve deeply in the personal loan market given the absence of consumer credit reports and a general lack of confidence in the expatriate community, most of which do not have long-term residency status.[79] This dynamic has changed dramatically in the last decade. In one example, personal loans as a portion of all loans in the National Bank of Abu Dhabi's loan book grew from 16% in 2004 to 30% in 2016, well above the average in the US.[80] Much of this personal loan growth occurred during the boom years between 2004 and 2008, eventually causing a spike in non-performing loans, which peaked at over 7% in 2012.[81] Since then though, non-performing loans have stabilized at around 5.2%, the CBU has enacted a number of regulations limiting the size of personal loans, and the private credit-to-non oil GDP ratio has been on a multiyear upward trajectory, surpassing 100% at the end of 2016.[82] Moving forward, credit growth may find new footing given the recent launch of a modern personal credit rating system in the UAE, providing more transparency for banks in the lending process.[83]

Underneath all this, the banking sector has traditionally been, and remains, highly concentrated, with over half of the sector's total assets held by just two banks, First Abu Dhabi National Bank (FAB) and Emirates NBD (ENBD), both of which are the result of mega mergers. ENBD is the result of a merger between Emirates Bank and National Bank of Dubai in 2007 and FAB of First Gulf Bank (FGB) and National Bank of Abu Dhabi (NBAD) in 2017.[84] The latter was the first merger between major banks in Abu Dhabi and Dubai and acted as a milestone in breaking the divide between each respective emirates' banking sector. Market expectations are that the success of the FAB merger is likely to trigger a wave of consolidation across the crowded banking sector, were the multitude of banks cater to a bankable population of roughly 9 million individuals, more than 83% of which already have bank accounts.[85] These dynamics, coupled with the low oil price environment post-2014, have taken a toll on the banks profitability, with asset, return on asset and return on equity growth rates falling considerably between 2014 and 2016.[86]

In a trend that mimics Saudi Arabia, most banks in the UAE are majority government or royal family-owned and managed. ENBD (56% owned by ICD) and FAB (37% owned by ADIC and Mubadala) are no exception, with royal family members dispersed throughout the management structure of both banks. In fact, in a move that mirrored the government-driven merger of Mubadala and the International Petroleum Investment Company (IPIC), the merger of NBAD and FGB, both of which were majority government owned, was spearheaded by the Nahyan family's desire to cut costs in government-owned organizations while simultaneously assisting the emirate become a global financial center.[87] [88] This dynamic is no secret, as FAB's chief executive Abdul Hamid Mohammed Saeed said shortly after the merger, "government-related entities and state entities are one of our main client groups, and in addition to helping them in achieving their goals, they are also our supporter."[89] With operations in nineteen countries and deposits of over US$170 billion at the time of the merger, FAB is in a prime position to do just that.

Contrary to popular perception, direct royal family bank ownership across the GCC is almost nonexistent outside the UAE, whereas in the UAE it has made up as much as 10% of total ownership in the last decade.[90] In light of this complex intermingling of oversight and ownership structures, dominated by royal family members doubling as private sector leaders, there exists the perception that the UAE government would be loath to allow a domestic bank to fail. The belief is not without historical precedent. The UAE government has repeatedly stepped in at times of financial shock to limit systemic fallout and preserve banking sector stability. These interventions have included explicit deposit guarantees, forced consolidations, direct cash injections, and extensions of overdraft facilities.[91] Prime examples of this dynamic can be seen in Abu Dhabi's interventions during the onset of the Great Recession, when between 2008 and 2009 both the CBU and the Abu Dhabi government took extreme measures to limit the effects of the Dubai World debt crises, and separately the CBU issued a temporary 3-year deposit insurance guarantee for all deposits in locally and foreign owned banks.[92]

Islamic Banking

Another critical part of the UAE's banking sector is the country's growing Islamic financial markets. Islamic finance in the UAE has historically been strongly supported by various royals, with Dubai Islamic Bank, one of the region's first modern Islamic banks, founded in 1975 in large part thanks to the support of Sheikh Rashid bin Saeed Al Maktoum.[93] While the UAE's Islamic and conventional banks are established and operate under the same legal mechanisms, it was not until 1998 that the second Islamic bank in the UAE, the Abu Dhabi Islamic Bank, was licensed. By 2015 there were seven Islamic banks across the country, with numerous other conventional banks and financial institutions opening designated 'Islamic banking windows.' In recent years, Islamic banks and conventional banks have been in fierce competition for market share, often competing for the same customers. In fact, Islamic banks in the UAE offer many of the same products that conventional banks do, including credit cards, real estate financing, investment options, car loans and even participating in industrial-scale project financing, usually in a *musharaka* structure, where profits and losses are shared in a predetermined manner.[94] Also similar to their conventional counterparts, many of the UAE's Islamic banks have extended their influence beyond domestic markets, with DIB recently receiving a license to operate in Kenya, supplementing its ongoing foreign operations in Turkey, Jordan and Pakistan.[95]

The key difference between the conventional and Islamic banks though is legal requirement for the latter to have a Shari'a compliance board. This board, which is independently established and run by each bank, must ensure that the bank's actions and products conform with Islamic Shari'a. Despite this added requirement, Islamic banks have shown strikingly strong performance. Islamic banks have grown from holding around 5% (US$2 billion) of the banking sector's total assets in 1996 to holding 20% (US$141 billion) of the sector's total assets as of 2017.[96] A large part of this growth has been due to the UAE's concerted effort to make the country a hub for Islamic finance, a position it is in competition with Bahrain to achieve. The initiative has been wildly successful, with 38% of all global sukuk issued between 2001 and 2015 issued in the UAE.[97] Even relative to its peers, the sector is a success story, boasting asset growth almost twice that of conventional banks between 2015 and 2016.[98] Some of this growth is likely due the generally held public preference for Islamic banks over conventional banks.[99] Arguably more important though has been UAE's accepting regulatory stance toward Islamic banks, opposed to Saudi Arabia, where Al Rahji Bank, now the world's largest Islamic bank, had to wait four years before receiving a banking license.[100]

All this said, Islamic banking in the UAE is not without controversy. Since its rapid growth at the turn of the century, Islamic finance has been on the receiving end of substantial criticism over its Shari'a compliance, with one of the world's most sought after Shari'a scholars and chairman of ADIB's Shari'a Board Sheikh Taqi Usmani stating in 2008 that many, if not most, sukuk currently issued were in fact not Shari'a compliant.[101] Making matters worse for Islamic banking advocates, it was not long after Usmani's statement that a US$500 million embezzlement case involving former senior DIB executives exploded into the public eye.[102]

In hindsight, the sector has weathered these storms healthily, and the true obstacle to growth will likely emerge in the regulatory domain. Similar to challenges facing other countries, for the UAE's Islamic finance sector to grow, expert consensus is that product standardization and regulatory clarification is critical.[103] [104] The UAE Federal Council of Ministers took a critical step to achieving these goals in 2016, establishing a Higher Shari'a Board for Banking and Finance with the stated aim of strengthening the "consistency of the Islamic finance industry across the UAE," by setting rules, standards and general principles for Islamic banking and finance and ensuring that they comply with Islamic laws.[105] Reflecting the UAE's proactive business stance, the Board is a product of recommendations prescribed by a CBU-initiated study that included the Dubai Islamic Economy Development Centre and the UAE Banks Federation.[106] When active, it will standardize and streamline the sukuk approval and issuance process, but will also find itself in direct competition with Bahrain's Accounting and Auditing Organization for Islamic Financial Institutions (AAOIFI), another Islamic finance regulatory institution seeking to standardize practices across the sector.

Sovereign Wealth Funds

Globally, SWFs have been perceived in myriad ways. In the traditional reading, they act as intergenerational savings accounts, investing current revenues in order to create future cash flows, or acting as extended arms of government development policy, investing domestically and regionally to catalyze knowledge transfer and economic growth. In more critical readings, they act as foreign policy tools used to expand economic and political influence globally or domestic policy tools used to build and maintain patronage networks in competitive monarchical political systems. While these differing views are explored in more detail in Chapter 5, in Abu Dhabi, where chronic oil-driven financial surpluses have allowed the emirate to incubate some of the world's largest financial institutions, SWFs have evolved to represent all of these interpretations to some degree.

Abu Dhabi Investment Authority

Considered the largest SWF in the world, ADIA is one of several investment vehicles owned by the government of Abu Dhabi, with other major state SWFs including the Mubadala Development Company and Invest AD. Prone to secrecy, the exact size of ADIA is unknown, with most estimates placing the value roughly between US$700 and US$800 billion, easily ranking it among the world's largest SWFs. Collectively, all of Abu Dhabi's SWFs are estimated to be valued at over US$1 trillion.

Like most of Abu Dhabi's SWFs, underpinning ADIA financially are the emirate's substantial surplus oil revenues. The Abu Dhabi National Oil Company, which has some of the lowest production costs in the world, is believed to have surplus revenues reaching as high as 95% of gross revenues. An undisclosed percentage of these surplus revenues are believed to be paid directly to ADIA with the remainder funneled to the Abu Dhabi government.[107]After meeting its budgetary requirements, Abu Dhabi authorities are believed to divert up to 70% of their surpluses to ADIA as well.[108] In reality this number is likely significantly smaller, considering the plethora of off-budget expenses that must be appropriated for, including tremendous military expenditures and support of smaller emirates. Nonetheless, in times of fiscal surplus, these transfers are likely significant. It is difficult to determine exactly how decisions on the timing and size of these allocations are made, but it is understood that they are made by Abu Dhabi's Supreme Petroleum Council (SPC), making membership in the SPC extremely influential. Moreover, by transferring these surplus revenues to a government held financial institution, opposed to private institutions, this transmission process effectively transforms the royal family's monopoly on oil revenues into a monopoly on capital.

Unlike many of Abu Dhabi's more recent funds, ADIA's primary objective is not to invest in domestic development, but instead to act as traditional intergenerational savings fund with an official mandate of securing and maintaining the future welfare of the emirate. In the decade and a half after its 1976 founding, the fund exclusively invested in sovereign debt instruments of the world's leading currencies.[109] While this seems conservative today, at the time it was considered unconventional for a government to invest in anything other than gold and maybe short-term credit. Since then, ADIA's portfolio has taken on increasingly more risk in a diversified manner, currently holding a global portfolio of private, public and alternative assets, with other SWFs from Norway to Kuwait following suit. In 2012, around 75% of ADIA's holdings were overseen by mostly passive external managers. One of ADIA's defining internal policies since then though has been to transition toward in-house specialization, with the long-term objective of minimizing fees and lowering agency costs but most importantly increasing internal capabilities. As part of this drive, ADIA has brought on managers from some of the world's most reputable institutions including Deutsche Bank, Credit Suisse and BP to lead internal private equity departments.[110] As of 2016, externally managed assets had fallen to about 60% of the fund's total assets.[111]

ADIA is also considered to be one of the most secretive SWFs in the world. The secrecy is ironic given that Abu Dhabi has taken a series of very public steps toward promoting financial transparency at the global level. Most noteworthy among these was the 2008 co-chairing of the World Bank's International Working Group of SWFs. It was as part of this IWG that ADIA played a key role in the development of Generally Accepted Principles and Practices of SWFs, commonly known as the Santiago Principles. Soon after the Santiago Principles were developed, ADIA began publishing annual reports, but even those were scarce on financial details. For example, while the fund's annual reports confirmed that ADIA holds a well-diversified portfolio, the report aggregates the portfolio's returns over 20- and 30-year time horizons, which as of December 2016 ranged between 6% and 7.5%, leaving returns over shorter horizons and for individual asset classes opaque.[112] Considering the large losses that were undoubtedly incurred in the wake of the 2008 crises, the unaudited nature of the reports and the general opacity about ADIA's investments, returns this strong must be taken with considerable skepticism.

Adding to the fund's opacity, aside from select investments, ADIA has a strict policy of holding small equity stakes, allowing it to remain below disclosure requirements. As Jean-Paul Villain, a French banker who has been with ADIA since 1982 and is now their Head of Strategy, has stated, remaining below disclosure requirements maximizes the number investments the fund can make and eliminates the headache that comes with being a public shareholder.[113] Coupling this with ADIA's utilization of external managers makes it hard to map its acquisitions.[114] Moving forward there does not appear to be any near term intention to move toward quarterly reports, disclose more detailed performance indicators or take on larger investment stakes.[115]

While the exact legal and regulatory structure governing ADIA is somewhat opaque, for all intents and purposes, since the 1980s the fund has been independent in terms of its asset allocation decisions. Similarly, there is a dearth of clearly defined regulations governing withdrawals from ADIA, and while ADIA's charter in principle forbids withdrawals from its account, the fund is expected to make its funds available to the government if, and when, they are needed. Practically though, these withdrawals are infrequent and largely only occur during prolonged periods of low oil prices. Yet, even in this case, withdrawals are usually a last resort. For example, to meet its budgetary requirements for 2016 many analysts, including the IMF and Fitch Ratings, projected that Abu Dhabi would dip into ADIA or one of its other SWFs. Instead, Abu Dhabi surprised analysts by tapping global markets in an overwhelmingly successful sovereign debt offering.[116]

Despite statements of independence, a basic glance at ADIA's board of directors shows that the SWF is intrinsically linked with the ruling family and its governmental affairs. Five out of seven of ADIA's royally appointed board members are members of the Al Nahyan family, with the other two, Mohammed Habroush Al Suwaidi and Khalil Mohammed Sharif Foulathi, closely linked to royal affairs. The former has acted as the personal advisor to president of the UAE, and is a board member of the SPC and the Abu Dhabi Investment Council, while the latter is the chairman of the board of the CBU.

With the importance of ADIA's leadership in mind, one could venture that the fund's secrecy acts as a defense mechanism, shielding ADIA and its powerful, royal board members from controversy. This was a lesson Abu Dhabi learned the hard way in the early 1990s when the late Sheikh Zayed found himself embroiled in immensely embarrassing BCCI affair.

There is another, equally likely, rationale underpinning ADIA's secrecy. By keeping the size of its assets secret, ADIA has effectively fueled a rumor mill which has only resulted in increasingly larger estimates of the fund's assets. This in turn has the knock on effect of inflating external managers' interest in ADIA. Indeed, every manager wants to be able to tell their clientele in private that they work with the world's largest and most successful SWF. This would then easily allow ADIA to extract competitive, beneficial terms from external managers who would otherwise charge egregious fees.

Mubadala

Often viewed as the brainchild and policy tool of Crown Prince Mohammed bin Zayed, Mubadala is Abu Dhabi's second largest SWF. It was founded in 2002 and mandated with facilitating Abu Dhabi's diversification through investment in long-term, capital-intensive projects that not only deliver strong financial returns but also have tangible social benefits. In this sense, where ADIA is externally focused, Mubadala is responsible for nourishing growth within the emirate. In line with the English translation of the Arabic word *mubadal*, meaning to exchange, Mubadala's strategy has been to partner with experienced industry leaders, bringing together Mubadala's regional connections and capital with their partners' intellectual capabilities in hopes of creating a mutually beneficial exchange. To date, Mubadala's focused has been technology-centric, with a large amount of its assets held in aerospace, engineering, information technology and clean energy assets.

In this sense, where Dubai looks to initiate knowledge transfer through free zone development, Abu Dhabi looks to Mubadala to initiate knowledge transfer through deliberate investments, which often take the form of joint ventures; one of the fund's distinguishing features. Unlike ADIA, who is prone to secrecy, Mubadala produces audited statements, and often seeks controlling or at least board-level shares in the projects it enters, making its investment strategy relatively public by nature.

Since its founding, the direction and stature of the fund has been closely linked with the rise of Mohammed bin Zayed, commonly known as MbZ. MbZ has increasingly run Abu Dhabi since becoming Deputy Crown Prince in 2003 and then Crown Prince in 2004, when his father and founder of the UAE, the late Sheikh Zayed, died. The fund was established when MbZ was not yet in control of Abu Dhabi's general budget and foreign assets. Since then, the fund has grown immensely in size and prominence. Building on annual government, no-interest transfers that peaked at US$6.8 billion in 2008 and have averaged around US$200 million since, the fund has grown to hold assets valued at US$67 billion in 2016.[117] These assets saw a significant boost in 2017 when Mubadala merged with IPIC, another of Abu Dhabi's SWF, bringing Mubadala's total asset size to US$125 billion, making it the world's 14th largest sovereign fund.[118] As discussed later, IPIC was only the first of two major mergers, which eventually brought Mubadala's total assets under management to US$250 billion in 2018.

Mubadala is managed similarly to a very large hedge fund. Deals are looked at constantly, sometimes almost frenetically and the corporate culture is akin to that of investment companies in New York or London. Further reflecting MbZ's desire to bring Abu Dhabi's financial practices in line with global standards, Mubadala has made it an internal policy to primarily look toward capital markets when in need of additional capital. This dependence on limited leverage is intended to provide self-enforcing financial discipline since lenders would need to check off on the profitability of new deals. In practice though, this initiative may have little real discipline-inducing mechanisms given that Mubadala is viewed with the same credit rating as its powerful sovereign owner. Indeed, Mubadala's credit ratings from the three major ratings companies sit in the highest possible tier, well above other funds its age.

Similar to ADIA, Mubadala's leadership is extremely close to the royal court, with the management of the fund firmly in the hands of MbZ-confidant Khaldoon al Mubarak since its inception. A close friend of MbZ, Mubarak was raised in the ruler's court after the assassination of his father, the UAE Ambassador to France, and holds various other important government roles including membership in the Abu Dhabi Executive Council. In line with this, Mubadala's objectives have often mirrored the emirates broader policy goals. In fact, just five years after its founding, the fund was made the principal agency in actualizing the ambitious diversification agenda put forth in Abu

Dhabi's Vision 2030. The Vision, which calls for sustainable, knowledge-driven economic diversification, has led Mubadala to make major investments in the fields of clean energy and semiconductors, most notably through the Masdar project and the Advanced Technology Investment Company. Yet, even though both these projects aim to create knowledge transfer and domestic job opportunities in the long term, over the first decade of their existence, most of the related investments have gone into foreign companies or wholly owned but foreign located endeavors, with minimal impact seen domestically.[119] Admittedly, this does not negate the forward looking premise of these initiatives, but instead highlights the substantial domestic roadblocks, ranging from vested interest in fossil fuels to a deficit of local expertise, which impede this kind of development and knowledge transfer.

SWFs, Power Patronage and Asset Ownership

From a sociopolitical perspective, Abu Dhabi's sovereign wealth funds play a prominent role in the country's political power structure. As with most monarchies, the al Nahyan depend on the support of the emirate's elite for their political power. Traditionally, key supporters among these elite have been the tribal leaders dominating Abu Dhabi's eastern Al Ayn province, including those heading the Dhawahir, Mazariah and Awamir tribes. Historically, leaders of the al Nahyan who were able to acquire the loyalty of these hinterland tribes were able to establish and maintain power and stability across the broader emirate. Deriving from this, over the last century investment by al Nahyan leaders into al Ayn has been significant, modernizing the city and making it a commercial hub.[120] This patronage continues today. In fact, many of the board positions across Abu Dhabi's smaller SWFs are occupied by members of these powerful tribal allies. For example, Amer Saleh Al Ameri, board member at mid-sized Abu Dhabi SWF Invest AD, is of the Awamir tribe, while Mohamed Ali A. Al Dhaheri, Chairman of Invest AD, hails from Al Ayn's Dhawahir tribe. Similarly, Hareb Al Darmaki, board member of Emirates Investment Authority, another of Abu Dhabi's smaller SWFS, is of the Dhawahir tribe.

This practice of placing members of prominent Al Ayn tribes into influential positions is neither new nor isolated. Members of these powerful families are regularly found throughout other parts of Abu Dhabi's government, with Suhail Faraj al Mazroui, of the Mazariah tribe, currently Minister of Energy and Sultan bin Saeed al Badi, of the Dhawahir tribe, currently Minister of Justice. This practice finds its root in the rule of Sheikh Zayed, who placed competing power groups within the royal family at the heads of different institutions throughout his reign. To ease succession, before his death he put his influential fifth son Sheikh Mansour bin Zayed al Nahyan in charge of the IPIC, gave tribal leaders leadership roles at the Abu Dhabi Investment Company, now known as Invest AD, appointed Sheikh Khalifa to lead the SPC, put a close ally of Khalifa in charge of ADIA, and placed MbZ in charge of the UAE's defense forces, all appointments that in some form remain today.[121]

By continuing to place powerful non-ruling royals and tribal leaders in positions of influence, the al Nahyan effectively extend what has been years of patronage, pacifying the ambitions of potential political rivals by creating common interest among royals in preserving the status quo. This in turn reduced the probability of conflict between the various branches of the royal family. This system of power patronage is especially important given that, prior to its implementation, Abu Dhabi had seen decades of fratricide and conflict all due to issues of succession. In fact, with the death of the late Sheikh Zayed in 2004, Abu Dhabi saw its first uncontested transfer of power in nearly 100 years. This is critical because, at the time, MbZ had amassed substantial power, providing him the opportunity to disrupt Khalifa's succession. In line with these dynamics of power patronage, upon his succession Khalifa not only named MbZ his crown prince but also decreed the establishment of Mubadala, placing it in the hands of MbZ, and gave the IPIC, which was still controlled by Mansour, more autonomy.[122] Without these moves, MbZ and, to a lesser degree, Mansour would have been less likely to rally behind Khalifa's succession.

As Emir, Khalifa has maintained control over ADIA, but recent shakeups have shown that MbZ is preparing the grounds for his own succession ahead of Khalifa's death. For example, the 2010 reshuffle of ADIA's board of directors replaced managing director Sheikh Ahmad Al Nahyan, a close ally of Khalifa who died in a glider accident in Morocco, with his brother Hamed, who is considered an ally of MbZ and is chairman of the Crown Prince's Royal Court. While keeping Khalifa as the chairman, the shakeup moved MbZ and some of his key allies into positions of more influence within ADIA. The merger of IPIC and Mubadala acts as another example, with the merger effectively bringing Mansour's largest source of power and patronage, the IPIC, under the umbrella of MbZ's Mubadala. In another move aimed at consolidating control over the emirate's financial power centers, MbZ took over the chairmanship of the Abu Dhabi Investment Council from Khalifa in 2015.[123] Just a few years later, in 2018, ADIC was merged fully with Mubadala, effectively cementing MbZ's control over two of the UAE's three largest SWFs. With both IPIC and ADIC under its control, Mubadala's total assets under management grew to an estimated US$250 billion in 2018, making it the eleventh largest SWF in the world, just ahead Saudi's Public Investment Fund, data from the Sovereign Wealth Fund Institute indicates.

This amassing of financial and political power has only bolstered what is already considered to be a given case for MbZ's succession to Emir. The succession is also likely to have strategic implications for the ADIA, given that with his rise to Emir, MbZ would also take control over ADIA. This highlights the possibility that MbZ will transmit some of Mubadala's investment and governance tactics to ADIA, who has increasingly been viewed as the outdated older brother of the innovative Mubadala.

Upon this background, it is rational to conclude that the royal family is the ultimate owner of the SWF's assets. Indeed, most outsiders do view it this way. Yet upon closer inspection, ultimate ownership is less clear. Does the government itself own ADIA's assets or does it just manage these assets on behalf of Abu Dhabi's citizens? If the latter is true, are the funds managed by ADIA entrusted to it in the same sense hedge fund managers are entrusted with their investor's assets? If so, why does the royal family have the ability to make major investment decisions without disclosure to the ultimate asset owners, the Abu Dhabi citizens. While it may appear inconsequential, the difference is actually material. If the funds are being managed on behalf of the citizenry, then not only would ADIA's management have a fiduciary responsibility, but also, the people of Abu Dhabi would have a right of regard on the source of the funds, their amount, the risk level, the profits and losses incurred, the type of investments, and ultimately their distribution.

As things stand, it appears that the funds managed by Abu Dhabi's SWFs are state funds which are being managed on behalf of the emirate's citizens. This in turn makes the fund's management, the vast majority of which are royal family members, fiduciaries to the people. While Mubadala's relatively transparent behavior is in line with the traditional understanding of fiduciary responsibility, it is clear that ADIA's board has yet to fully accept its broader fiduciary responsibility. Presumably, if it did, there is a strong argument to be made that the required subsequent transparency would limit the royal family's ability to unilaterally access ADIA's funds, which in turn would fundamentally alter the country's power dynamics.

Conclusion

Sovereign control of national wealth has been the underlying principle behind much the growth across the Gulf. As has been shown, the UAE is no different. This control has given Dubai a chance to become the premier financial center for the Gulf and broad swaths of Central Asia and Africa. Similarly, it has given Abu Dhabi control of one of the world's largest pools of investable assets. These developments have accrued the UAE with global stature well beyond what the 60-year-old Jumaa Al Shami from the northern emirate of Umm Al Quwain would have ever dreamed growing up.

Moving forward, the UAE's ability to rise further will rely on its ability to capitalize on these new assets. The DIFC must find a way to be a true marketplace, one where bankers meet to originate business, not just complete tasks sent in from far off headquarters. Similarly, Mubadala must transform its broad portfolio of investments into measurable domestic employment and consistent streams of knowledge transfer. These metrics differentiate between overly grandiose planning, which many critics level at the Gulf states, from realistic, achievable policy. In the case of Dubai, the ability to apply realistic policy will be seen through the handling of issues like the bankruptcy of Abraaj. Once the world's leading emerging market private equity firm, in 2018, the the Dubai-based company found itself breaching insolvency due to questionable accounting practices and executive decisions made in Dubai. Will Dubai's regulatory authorities seek out, identify and remedy the issues in the emirate's regulatory framework which allowed Abraaj to fail? The rapidity of movement toward reinstalling investor confidence will underline Dubai's commitment to realistically becoming a global marketplace. For Abu Dhabi, consolidation of economic power under MbZ brings with it the potential for efficiency gains and transparency across powerful but opaque investment vehicles. Will the practices Mubadala embraces be spread across ADIA or will the status quo remain at the world's largest SWF? As Al Shami said, "we know have a good, beautiful life." The late Sheikh Zayed set the UAE on a path of development that took the confederation and its citizens to previously unimaginable heights; MbR and MbZ hold the keys to take the United Arab Emirates even further.

Notes

1. "A Lifetime of Perks in UAE Help Cushion Wealth Gap," *Associated Press*, November 4, 2014.
2. Fatma Al Sayegh, "Domestic Politics in the United Arab Emirates: Social and Economic Policies, 1990–2000," in Joseph A. Kechichian, ed. *Iran, Iraq and the Arab Gulf States*. (New York, NY: Palgrave Macmillan, 2001), pp. 161–165.
3. British Petroleum Company, *BP Statistical Review of World Energy*. (London: British Petroleum Company, 2017).
4. Al Sadik and Ali Tawfi, "Evolution and Performance of the UAE Economy 1972–1998," *Ministry of Information and Culture, United Arab Emirates: A New Perspective* (2001): 202–230; United Arab Emirates Ministry of Economy. *Annual Economic Report*, 2015.
5. U.S. Department of State, *Investment Climate Statements: United Arab Emirates*. (Washington, DC: U.S. Department of State, 2017); World Bank, *World Development Indicators*. (Washington, DC: World Bank Group).
6. International Monetary Fund, "United Arab Emirates: Selected Issues and Statistical Appendix," *Country Report* no. 03/67 (2003), p. 27.
7. Karen E. Young, *The Political Economy of Energy, Finance and Security in the United Arab Emirates: Between the Majilis and the Market*. (London: Palgrave Macmillan, 2014), p. 30.
8. Ibid., pp. 29–31.
9. The Creek is a type of natural "fjord" around which Dubai developed. Traditionally the Creek is where merchants operated. Keeping their goods in warehouses on its banks and running the shipping from there.
10. Christopher Davidson, "The Emirates of Abu Dhabi and Dubai: Contrasting Roles in the International System," *Asian Affairs* 38, no. 1 (2007): 34.
11. Ibid.
12. Karim Sadjadpour, "The Battle of Dubai: The United Arab Emirates and the US-Iran Cold War," *Carnegie Endowment for International Peace*, July 2011.
13. Abdulkhaleq Abdulla, "The Arab Gulf Moment," in David Held and Kristian Ulrichsen, eds. *The Transformation of the Gulf: Politics, Economics and the Global Order*. (London: Routledge, 2013), pp. 106–124.
14. Christopher Davidson, *Abu Dhabi: Oil and Beyond*. (New York, NY: Oxford University Press, 2013), pp. 25–43.

15. Christopher Davidson, *Dubai: The Vulnerability of Success.* (New York, NY: Columbia University Press, 2008), p. 101.
16. Christopher Davidson, "Abu Dhabi's New Economy: Oil, Investment and Domestic Development," *Middle East Policy* 16, no. 2 (2009): 59–79; Oxford Business Group, *The Report: Abu Dhabi 2017.* (Oxford Business Group, 2017), p. 34; Abu Dhabi Investment Authority, *2016 Review: A Legacy in Motion.* (Abu Dhabi: ADIA, 2016).
17. Athanasios Tsetsonis, "Dubai's Wholesale and Retail Trade Sector Overview," *Emirates NBD: Sector Economics*, June 30, 2014; Alison Millington, "The 30 Most Visited Cities Around the World in 2017," *Business Insider*, September 26, 2017.
18. Abu Dhabi Statistics Center, *Statistical Yearbook of Abu Dhabi 2017*, 2017; Dubai Statistics Center, *Year Population Estimates*, 2017.
19. Abdulla Al-Suwaidi, "The United Arab Emirates at 40: A Balance Sheet," *Middle East Policy* 18, no. 4 (2011): 50.
20. Davidson, "The Emirates of Abu Dhabi and Dubai," p. 44.
21. Author's interviews.
22. Young, *The Political Economy of Energy*, p. 74.
23. International Monetary Fund, "United Arab Emirates: 2017 Article IV Consultation" *International Monetary Fund IMF Country Report* no. 17/218, July 2017, p. 8.
24. BMI Research, *United Arab Emirates: Country Risk Report. Q4 2017*, p. 32.
25. Young, *The Political Economy of Energy*, p. 30.
26. Ibrahim al Abed, Paula Vine, and Abdullah Al Jabali (eds), *Chronicle of Progress, 25 Years of Development in the United Arab Emirates.* (London: Trident Press for the Ministry of Information, 1996), p. 423.
27. Charles S. Laubach, "United Arab Emirates," in Christian Campbell, ed. *Legal Aspects of Doing Business in the Middle East*, 2nd edition. (Salzburg: Yorkhill Law Pub, 2009).
28. BMI Research, *United Arab Emirates: Country Risk Report. Q4 2017*, p. 34.
29. World Bank Group, *Doing Business 2016.* (Washington, DC: World Bank Group, 2016).
30. Sara Townsend, "Rising from the Ashes: The UAE's Insolvency Dilemma," *Arabian Business*, February 6, 2016.
31. World Bank Group. *Doing Business 2016.*
32. Issac John, "Why UAE's New Bankruptcy Law Is a Boon for Business," *Khaleej Times*, March 1, 2017.
33. Laubach, "United Arab Emirates."
34. U.S. Department of State, *Investment Climate Statements.*
35. Harry Hasting and Donald P. Moore, "Changes in the UAE Commercial Agency Law," *Lexology*, October 14, 2010.
36. James Reagan McLaurin, "Commercial Agency Law in the United Arab Emirates: A Review and Recommendations," *Allied Academies International Conference. Academy for Studies in International Business. Proceedings* 8, no. 2 (2008): 7.
37. United Arab Emirates Ministry of Economy, *Annual Economic Report 2016*, 2016, pp. 16, 52; Howard L. Stovall, "Recent Revisions to Commercial Agency Law in the United Arab Emirates," *Arab Law Quarterly* (2008): 313.
38. Stovall, "Recent Revisions to Commercial Agency Law in the United Arab Emirates," 309.
39. Ibid.
40. Saifur Rahman, "WTO Urges UAE to Liberalize Trade Regime," *Gulf News*, April 2, 2012.
41. U.S. Department of State, *Investment Climate Statements.*

42. Mahmoud Al Iriani, Ibrahim Elbadawi and Dhuha Fadhel, "Economic Linkages between Free Zones and Main Dubai," in Abdulrazak Al Faris and Raimundo Soto, eds. *The Economy of Dubai* * (Oxford: Oxford University Press, 2016), p. 32.
43. Ibid.; Steffen Hertog, *A Quest for Significance: Gulf Oil Monarchies' International Soft Power Strategies and Their Local Urban Dimensions.* (Kuwait: London School of Economics, 2017), p. 12; Dubai Department of Economic Development, *Dubai Economic Profile 2015*, 2016.
44. Mohammed bin Rashid Al Maktoum and A. Bishtawi, *My Vision: Challenges in the Race for Excellence.* (Dubai: Motivate, 2006), p. 145.
45. Jim Krane, *City of Gold: Dubai and the Dream of Capitalism.* (New York: Picador/St. Martin's Press, 2009), p. 126; Larry Nowicki, "Investment and Entrepreneurship in Arab and Muslim-Majority Countries: The Case of Free Zones," in *International Trade and Finance Association Conference Papers.* (California: Bepress, 2007), p. 5.
46. "Our History," *Jebel Ali Free Zone*, 2018.
47. Al Iriani, Ibrahim and Fadhel, "Economic Linkages between Free Zones and Main Dubai."
48. Nowicki, "Investment and Entrepreneurship in Arab and Muslim-Majority Countries."
49. "Dubai's Gem: How Jebel Ali Free Zone Has Turned the Emirate into a Global Trading Powerhouse," *Gulf News*, September 14, 2017.
50. Waheed Abbas, "DP World Eyes Expansion in Africa," *Khaleej Times*, November 2, 2017.
51. Taimur Khan, "UAE and the Horn of Africa: A Tale of Two Ports," *The Arab Gulf States Institute in Washington*, March 8, 2018.
52. Ibid.
53. Josh Rogin, "Can the Trump Administration Stop China from Taking over a Key African Port?" *The Washington Post*, March 7, 2018.
54. "DFSA Licenses 300th Regulated Firm within DIFC," *Al Bawaba*, November 17, 2008; Millstein, I. and J. Kopell, interviewing N. Saidi, W. Foster, I. Odeh and Y. Gamali "What's the View from Dubai?" *Yale School of Management* (Fall 2008); Krane, *City of Gold*, p. 147.
55. Michael Strong and Robert Himber, "The Legal Autonomy of the Dubai International Financial Centre: A Scalable Strategy for Global Free-Market Reforms," *Economic Affairs* 29, no. 2 (2009): 38.
56. Young, *The Political Economy of Energy*, p. 30; Oxford Business Group, "A New Financial Centre in Dubai Will Bridge Western and East Asian Markets," *Oxford Business Group*, 2015.
57. Daniel Brook, *A History of Future Cities.* (New York: WW Norton & Company, 2013), p. 359.
58. Oxford Business Group, "Michael Kerr, Regional Managing Partner, Dentons, on the International Reach of the DIFC Courts: Viewpoint," *Oxford Business Group*, 2016; U.S. Department of State, *Investment Climate Statements.*
59. Reed Smith, "The Dubai Judicial Tribunal—the Beginning of the End for the DIFC as a 'conduit' Jurisdiction?" *Reed Smith Client Alerts*, March 2, 2017.
60. Simeon Kerr, "Legal Wrangles Dent Dubai's Image as Region's Financial Centre," *Financial Times*, October 12, 2017.
61. Economist Intelligence Unit, "Financial Centers Prioritised," *Economist Intelligence Unit*, September 16, 2016.
62. Oxford Business Group, "Abu Dhabi Global Market Becomes Fully Operational," *Oxford Business Group*, 2016.
63. Krane, *City of Gold*, 130.
64. Ibid.

65. Nasdaq Dubai, *Annual Review 2017*, 2017.
66. Daily NYSE Group Volume in NYSE Listed, 2018. Available at www.nyse.com/data/transactions-statistics-data-library.
67. Dubai Financial Market, *Annual Bulletin 2017*, 2017; Daily NYSE Group Volume in NYSE Listed, 2018.
68. Krane, *City of Gold*, p. 131.
69. Lynne Roberts, "Dubai Deals Blow to Pakistan TV," *Arabian Business*, November 18, 2007.
70. International Monetary Fund, "United Arab Emirates: Financial Stability Report," in *International Monetary Fund*. (Washington, DC: World Bank Group, 2001), p. 6.
71. Steven Prokesch, "Huge Withdrawals Hurt Gulf Banks," *New York Times*, August 27, 1990.
72. H. C. Metz, *Persian Gulf States: Country Studies*. (Washington, DC: US Government Printing Office, 1993).
73. International Monetary Fund, "United Arab Emirates: 2017 Article IV Consultation," p. 5; Economist Intelligence Unit, "Industry Report, Financial Services United Arab Emirates," *3rd Quarter 2017*, p. 4.
74. Economist Intelligence Unit, "Industry Report, Financial Services United Arab Emirates," p. 8.
75. UAE Banks Federations, *Annual Report 2016*, 2016, p. 69.
76. Ibid.
77. Economist Intelligence Unit, p. 8.
78. Ibid.
79. M. Anaam Hashmi, "An Analysis of the United Arab Emirates Banking Sector," *International Business & Economics Research Journal* 6, no. 1 (2007): 80.
80. National Bank of Abu Dhabi, "UAE Banking Sector Chart Book: Q3 2016 Review," *NBAD Global Markets*, December 14, 2016; Hashmi, 81.; Federal Deposit Insurance Corporation, "FDIC Community Banking Study," *FDIC 2014*, 5–11 through 5–20.
81. Economist Intelligence Unit, "Industry Report, Financial Services United Arab Emirates," p. 4.
82. International Monetary Fund, "United Arab Emirates: 2017 Article IV Consultation," p. 23; Economist Intelligence Unit, "Industry Report, Financial Services United Arab Emirates," p. 4.
83. Gillian Duncan, "Al Etihad Credit Bureau Launches Credit Scoring System," *The National*, April 17, 2017.
84. S. Khan, "The Changing Dynamics of the UAE Banking Sector," *MEED Business Review* 2, no. 3 (2017): 49–51.
85. Economist Intelligence Unit, "Industry Report, Financial Services United Arab Emirates," p. 3.
86. Alvarez & Marsal Middle East, "UAE Banking Sector Pulse Quarter 2, 2017," Alvarez and Marsal, 2017.
87. Reuters Staff, "UAE Banks NBAD and FGB Confirm Merger Talks, Shares Soar," *Reuters*, June 19, 2016.
88. Jareer Elass, "Merger of Abu Dhabi Funds Streamlines Sovereign Investment Sector," *The Arab Weekly*, August 28, 2016.
89. Laura Noonan, "State Stakes in Gulf Banks Bring Business Advantages—and Risks," *Financial Times*, October 12, 2017.
90. May Y. Khamis, Abdullah Al-Hassan and Nada Oulidi, *The GCC Banking Sector: Topography and Analysis*. (No. 10–87. Washington DC: International Monetary Fund, 2010), p. 8.
91. International Monetary Fund, "United Arab Emirates: Financial Stability Report," p. 26.
92. Khamis, Al-Hassan and Oulidi, *The GCC Banking Sector*, p. 23.

93. Metz, *Persian Gulf States.*
94. Rodney Wilson, "The Development of Islamic Finance in the Gulf Cooperation Council States," in David Held, and Kristian Ulrichsen, eds. *The Transformation of the Gulf: Politics, Economics and the Global Order.* (London: Routledge, 2013).
95. Babu Das Augustine, "Dubai Islamic Bank Confirms License for Kenya Unit," *Gulf News*, May 2, 2017.
96. International Monetary Fund, "United Arab Emirates: Selected Issues," June 21, 2017; UAE Banks Federations, *Annual Report 2016*, 2016.
97. International Monetary Fund, "United Arab Emirates," p. 23.
98. UAE Banks Federations, *Annual Report 2016.*
99. Hassan Al-Tamimi and A. Hussein. "Factors Influencing Performance of the UAE Islamic and Conventional National Banks," *Global Journal of Business Research* 4, no. 2 (2010): 1.
100. Wilson, "The Development of Islamic Finance in the Gulf Cooperation Council States."
101. Reuters Staff, "Most Sukuk 'not Islamic', Body Claims," *Reuters*, November 22, 2007.
102. Colin Simpson, "Dh1.8 Billion Fraud Trial That Rocked Business," *The National*, May 1, 2011.
103. Mohsin S. Khan, "Islamic Interest-Free Banking: A Theoretical Analysis," *International Monetary Fund Staff Papers* 33, no. 1 (1986): 1–27.
104. Parag Deulgaonkar, "How one Dubai Bank, Born in the Eye of the Storm, Made It Work," *Arabian Business*, March 14, 2017.
105. "UAE Cabinet Approves Establishment of Both UAE Council for Fatwa and Sharia Board for Banking and Finance," *Emirates News Agency*, May 30, 2017.
106. Babu Das Augustine, "National Sharia Authority to Strengthen Regulations Islamic Finance Industry to Benefit from a Single Reference on Sharia Rules," *Gulf News*, October 5, 2015.
107. Sara Bazoobandi, *Political Economy of the Gulf Sovereign Wealth Funds: A Case Study of Iran, Kuwait, Saudi Arabia and the United Arab Emirates.* (London: Routledge, 2012), p. 77.
108. Oxford Business Group, *The Report: Abu Dhabi 2017.* (London: Oxford Business Group, 2017), p. 34.
109. Khalid A. Alsweilem, Angela Cummine, Malan Rietveld and Katherine Tweedie, *A Comparative Study of Sovereign Investor Models: Sovereign Fund Profiles.* (Cambridge, MA: Harvard Kennedy School, Belfer Center for Science and International Affairs and Center for International Development at Harvard University, 2015).
110. Ruth V. Aguilera, Javier Capapé and Javier Santiso, "Sovereign Wealth Funds: A Strategic Governance View," *Academy of Management Perspectives* 30, no. 1 (2016): 14.
111. Abu Dhabi Investment Authority, *2016 Review: A Legacy in Motion.* (Abu Dhabi: ADIA, 2016).
112. Oxford Business Group, *The Report: Abu Dhabi 2017.* (Abu Dhabi: Oxford Business Group, 2017), p. 34.
113. Sudip Roy, "Money and Mystery: Adia Unveils Its Secrets," *Euromoney*, Saturday, April 1, 2006.
114. Sara Bazoobandi, *Political Economy of the Gulf Sovereign Wealth Funds: A Case Study of Iran, Kuwait, Saudi Arabia and the United Arab Emirates.* (London: Routledge, 2012), p. 81.
115. Sasha Hodgson, "Abu Dhabi Investment Authority (ADIA)-Documenting the Story of One of the World's Largest Sovereign Wealth Funds," *Middle East Journal of Business* 9, no. 4 (2014): 33–45.

116. "Abu Dhabi to Withdraw Billions from ADIA to Meet Deficit, Fitch Says," *Bloomberg*, February 3, 2016; International Monetary Fund, "United Arab Emirates: 2016 Article IV Consultation," *International Monetary Fund IMF Country Report* no. 16/251, July 2016, pp. 8, 10.
117. Mubadala, *Various Consolidated Financial Statements, Annual Reports 2008–2016*.
118. Stanley Carvalho, "Abu Dhabi Creates $125 Billion Fund by Merging Mubadala, IPIC," *Reuters*, January 21, 2017.
119. For a deeper discussion of Masdar and ATIC please see Sami Mahroum and Yasser Al-Saleh, "The Surrogate Model of Cluster Creation: The Case of Mubadala in Abu Dhabi," *Science and Public Policy* 43, no. 1 (2015): 1–12.
120. Christopher M. Davidson. "After Shaikh Zayed: The Politics of Succession in Abu Dhabi and the UAE," *Middle East Policy* 13, no. 1 (2006): 42–59; Rosemarie Said Zahlan, *The Origins of the United Arab Emirates: A Political and Social History of the Trucial States*. (London: Routledge, 2016).
121. Kyle Hatton and Katharina Pistor, "Maximizing Autonomy in the Shadow of Great Powers: The Political Economy of Sovereign Wealth Funds," *Columbia Journal of Transnational Law* 50 (2011): 17.
122. Ibid.
123. Economist Intelligence Unit, "Crown Prince Takes over Abu Dhabi Sovereign Wealth Fund," *Economist Intelligence Unit*, January 26, 2015.

3 The Financial Markets of Saudi Arabia

Introduction

With the region's largest hydrocarbon revenues, population and cash reserves, coupled with an ultra-wealthy merchant class active in trading, industry and finance, Saudi Arabia is home to the largest financial market in the Gulf Cooperation Council (GCC). Historically, for better or worse, the impetus and direction for the financial markets' development has been top-down, state-driven and government-financed through institutions like the Saudi Arabian Monetary Authority (SAMA), the Public Investment Fund (PIF), the General Organization for Social Insurance (GOSI) and the Saudi Industrial Development Fund (SIDF). Thus, it is not surprising that in the same vein, or perhaps because of it, the largest Saudi industrial companies have mostly been state controlled. Yet, the government has made substantial efforts to increase public participation in domestic financial markets. The main tool for catalyzing this participation has been public share offerings (IPOs) in state controlled companies, of which there have been many. These offerings have fueled the growth of a financially savvy middle class, much of which is active on the kingdom's stock exchange, the Tadawul. Today, IPOs of private sector firms as well as of the state controlled companies alike have become extremely common.

Alongside this, the state controlled financial funds are taking on new roles. The PIF is no longer a mere arm of the Ministry of Finance (MoF) but is instead transforming into a full sovereign wealth fund (SWF). The state managed pension funds, which had taken equity stakes in some of the state-owned companies, now are more lenders than equity holders in an effort to avoid crowding out public sector equity investment. Recent reform efforts have driven further changes to this state-driven dynamic, with key institutions beginning to see their roles evolve. For example, while SAMA remains a strong bank regulator, it has ceded its regulation of the equity markets to the Capital Markets Authority (CMA). Looking forward, SAMA is also likely to start relinquishing some of its role as manager of state cash reserves to the PIF.

Another key group of institutions have been the commercial banks, both traditional and Shari'a compliant, which are playing an important role in providing industrial financing as well as substantial levels of consumer finance. Moreover, there are numerous private equity funds actively financing new and old firms. Collectively, these actors are seeking to provide sustainable financial support to private firms, a significant evolution from the recent past when only state-controlled companies could find this form of support.

Despite all this, the markets are still hampered by a difficult legal environment. For example, there was no bankruptcy law until early in 2018. The new law has finally been approved by the Majlis As-Shura and the Saudi cabinet but as of this writing was not yet implemented. The courts, dominated by Islamic scholars, are not fully proficient in dealing with intricate financial matters and often fail to employ precedent in their rulings, a factor that has notably hindered financial market growth. Looking forward, ongoing reform efforts have the potential to mitigate some of these deficits. Indeed, numerous judges were appointed by the King in 2017 and 2018, but implementation of new financial laws and regulations will take some time.

The government's priority on industrial growth has been a key driving force behind the financial markets since the mid-1970s. The renewed effort on reducing the country's dependency on oil revenues is now epitomized by the new Vision 2030 plan. The effort to continue and emphasize non-oil developments will result in changes to the financial markets of the kingdom. However, prominent in the change and the new vision is that the people of Saudi Arabia must wean themselves away from their dependence on the state, including their reliance of state controlled financial institutions, as the ultimate support and incentive for all investments and financial markets.

This chapter will review in more detail how these aforementioned state institutions interact with the non-state actors. It will also present non-state financial actors including the commercial banks-both Shari'a compliant and traditional, the stock market, and the private equity companies.

SAMA and the Regulatory Environment

The SAMA was established in 1952 to:

- Issue and strengthen the Saudi currency and to stabilize its internal and external value; and
- Deal with the banking affairs of the government of the kingdom and to regulate commercial banks and exchange dealers.

In addition, SAMA's functions in relation to circulation of currency and regulation of commercial banks are as follows:

- To stabilize and strengthen the internal and external value of the currency and take measures capable of strengthening the currency's cover;

- To hold and operate monetary reserve funds as separate funds earmarked for monetary purposes only;
- To mint, print and issue the Saudi currency and handle all matters relating thereto in conformity with Saudi Currency Law No.24, dated 23rd Jumada Awal 1377H (December 14, 1957); and
- To regulate commercial banks and exchange dealers as may be found appropriate.[1]

This mandate is largely in line with central banking regulation and practice across the globe. SAMA has been known to be a strong regulator, with a proven ability to force banks and other financial institution to follow regulations. SAMA's approach toward imposing controls on both banks and money changers, detailed in the first chapter, demonstrate this ability. Similarly, the takeover of banks threatened with failure, like Riyadh Bank, SAMBA, or NCB has shown that SAMA will act swiftly and aggressively to maintain the integrity of the banking system. In this same vein, SAMA can be involved in defining the types of lending that can be done by banks. For example, SAMA has strongly discouraged banks from lending in the Eurodollar market, even though banks have large dollar deposits in foreign banks. SAMA has also intervened in some difficult cases that threatened the financial stability of certain institutions in the kingdom. An example of the less public approach to financial supervision has been the subtle intervention of the agency in the very difficult troubles of two Bahraini banks with strong links to a well-known and reputable Saudi trading family, The International Banking Corporation and Awal Bank, both allegedly owned by a scion of the Saudi merchant class the Al Gosaibi family of Al Khobar. SAMA ensured that the international creditors of the two bankrupted Bahraini offshore banks had no recourse to that family and its accounts in the kingdom.[2] The dynamics behind this case are detailed in Chapter 6.2 of this work.

Saudi banks are all traded on the stock exchange and officially are private, i.e. not owned by the state. However, of the eleven banks registered in the kingdom only two do not have any state stake, the Bank Al Jazira and the Bank Al Bilad, the two smallest in the kingdom. SAMA's efforts to protect the banking sector, and by extension all the bank's depositors, has led to a situation where today the Saudi state is the most important shareholder in the banks. Saudi history has shown that as a bank ran into difficulties, as all do from time to time, state financial authorities always managed to bail them out through a strong influx of management skills from SAMA and capital inflows from the MoF-controlled funds like PIF, GOSI and the Public Pension Authority (PPA).

These inflows have given the state institutions large stakes in key commercial banks. The kingdom's largest bank, National Commercial Bank is de facto controlled by the state, which through three of its investment arms control 64.3% of NCB's shares. Samba, originally called Saudi American Bank, the third largest bank in the Kingdom, was founded as a joint venture between Citibank and Saudi public investors through a public offering. Eventually, Citibank sold its interest, after an epic battle for control, to Al Walid bin Talal, who happened to be the largest shareholder of New York-based Citibank. However, Al Walid bin Talal eventually surrendered his controlling ownership to state funds, which now own 49.7%. The state funds are also the largest shareholders in the second largest bank commonly known as Al Rajhi, also the largest Islamic bank by capital in the world. It is difficult to say whether this de facto control of the Islamic and traditional commercial banking sectors comes from a definite policy by the MoF to actually manage the banking sector, or whether it came about by accident, as some of the banks over the years faced major crisis and had to be rescued by the MoF.

Today, the largest of the state investment funds is the PIF, which has been named the SWF of the kingdom under the chairmanship of HRH Mohammed bin Salman Al Saud (MbS), the Crown Prince. Prior to 2016, when all these banking sector stakes were acquired, the PIF was directly under the control of the MoF. Yet, as of March 2015, the PIF is no longer linked to the MoF or SAMA, and instead sits under the Council of Economic and Development Affairs (CEDA), the new council chaired by MbS.

After de-linking from the MoF's oversight, the PIF held onto key stakes in the banking sector. As of February 2018, financial statements show the PIF owning nearly 45% of NCB, 10% of Alinma Bank, and 22% of Samba and 51.3% of Riyadh Bank. These stakes make PIF the main actor on the commercial banking ownership scene in the kingdom, with the PPA coming in a far second in terms of market share. As PIF is no longer linked to the MoF or SAMA, one could perhaps expect that PIF would relinquish its role as ultimate protector of the banks. If so, it could be expected that the SWF will divest itself from its stake in the banks. On the other hand, considering PIF's objective of developing the domestic economy, one could theorize that the SWF may take advantage of its voting power on the board of the banks to push the banks into lending more aggressively to companies in the kingdom to help create jobs. One fear is that the PIF would use its leverage on the banks to obtain funds for its own acquisitions, especially abroad. However, this would be against the banking regulations where directors (and by extension companies represented by the directors) cannot lend to themselves.

SAMA's International Practice

SAMA has been the sole institution handling the foreign currency reserves of the kingdom. SAMA provides monthly information on the amounts it holds and manages. The actual instruments in which SAMA invests are not disclosed. However, it is known that SAMA keeps a very large percentage of its funds in short-term US Treasury Bills. It also keeps some funds in short-term Euros and Yens. It even had a small portfolio of shares in New York and London managed by Baring Brothers. However, SAMA has always been keen to preserve the liquidity of the funds should the state require cash suddenly, as was the case during the Arab Spring, when SAMA was able to fund almost overnight the US$10 billion decreed by King Abdullah to be distributed to citizens. A broader discussion of these foreign reserve holdings can be found in Chapter 5 of this work.

Besides maintaining a high level of liquidity, SAMA's leadership, especially under HE Hamad Al Sayari, who was SAMA's governor from 1983 to 2009, was very keen to preserve the value of the investments. Indeed, this approach was proven to be extremely prudent and beneficial during the 2008 global crash of bond and stock markets. Most SWFs lost very large amounts of money on their equity-heavy portfolios, even in the best firms worldwide. In juxtaposition, SAMA's portfolio did not decline and preserved the integrity and credit worthiness of the kingdom.

Throughout the history of SAMA it is quite interesting to see that the monetary agency and the MoF were opposed to borrowing money from foreign institutions, whether banks or international bodies like the IMF. Except for a very short period after the Gulf war, Saudi Arabia never borrowed from the international markets, in spite of recurring budget deficits. No doubt SAMA and the MoF wanted to preserve their ability to manage the economy and their financial system in a manner decided in Riyadh and not by international bankers or consultants. Even as the kingdom suffered substantial budget deficits of about US$10 billion per year from 1980 to 1999, the monetary agency and the MoF only funded the deficits by borrowing from local banks. The need for SAMA to ensure that the banks had enough liquidity to actually lend to the state may explain in part why historically SAMA has been so focused on ensuring domestic banks remained healthy, transparent to the regulators and not saddled with extensive Eurodollar loans to questionable creditors such as the Latin American countries. While many of these practices have led large banks in neighboring countries to the brink of bankruptcy, in Saudi Arabia the prevention of these practices has kept domestic banks liquid enough to invest mainly in the kingdom's state companies and bonds.

In the wake of the 2014 oil price crash, SAMA once again turned to domestic banks borrowing US$14 billion through domestic bonds in 2017 alone. In a break from past practice though, the state also began borrowing on foreign bond markets, completing the largest ever bond issue of US$17.5 billion in 2016 and the world's largest ever Shari'a compliant sukuk, valued at US$9 billion, on the Irish Stock Exchange in April 2017.[3] These amounts were not actually necessary to cover any cash shortage. Indeed, the central bank's foreign assets averaged over US$500 billion throughout 2017, when the kingdom was most active in its bond issuance. Since then, SAMA's reserve holdings have begun increasing month to month in tandem with the price of oil. Total reserve assets stood at US$512 billion as of April 2018, compared to an all-time high of US$755 billion in August 2014.[4] Despite these vast sums of money, the leadership of the kingdom felt that the bond issues were necessary. This change in policy could have been decided for a number of reasons unrelated to cash management. Not least of these would be the need for the kingdom to show the world markets it has strong credit at a time of weak oil prices, thereby improving its prestige and image in the eyes of large investors, which the kingdom is seeking to attract to grow its non-oil economy faster.

The Capital Markets

The Tadawul

The stock market of Saudi Arabia, the Tadawul, trades in Riyadh and is regulated by the CMA. The exchange itself is 100% owned by the PIF, and has thirty members, mainly the large investments groups and brokers, both local and international, operating in the kingdom.[5] From a market capitalization perspective, the Tadawul is by far the largest stock exchange in the Middle East, with a market cap of around US$550 billion. From a broader perspective, it is still quite small compared to the US$4.8 trillion Dow Jones, or the US$1.77 trillion DAX in Frankfurt, but close to US$680 billion Singapore Exchange.

By many metrics, the Tadawul is a very modern and successful exchange. The exchange lists, in real time, the trades affected on the exchange in shares of publicly held companies. It computes the Tadawul All Share Index (TASI), the main indicator of the market, similar to that of larger exchanges, such as the Dow, FT index, the DAX in Frankfurt or CAC40 in France. Further, it provides a breakdown of the TASI in twenty different specialized components, such as Banks, Energy, Real Estate, Utilities, Telecoms, etc. It provides details on the volumes traded, as well as information on each of the listed companies, including audited yearly and quarterly statements. It also lists the shareholders holding more than 5% of any company traded on the exchange. From a technology perspective, the Tadawul has used NASDAQ's X-Stream INET platform since 2015. The Tadawul went from trading 5 million shares and an index level of 646 in 1986, to 67 billion shares traded and an index level of 7,250 thirty years later. On February 23, 2018, the index was 7,493 and trading at 154 million shares per day.

The Tadawul has also aided in the growth of Islamic finance by providing a marketplace for sukuk, the Islamic bonds offered mainly in the Gulf. In the past three years, most sukuk listed on the Tadawul have been government bonds (US$2.75 billion in the first two months of 2018 and over US$16 billion in 2017). It also lists sukuk issued by "parastatal" firms like SADARA, the chemical JV between Saudi Aramco and Dow Chemicals. However, these bonds do not appear to be traded often and are instead held by long-term investors. Consequently, traded activity in sukuk has been minimal, with the Tadawul showing no open prices or investors' interest for these bonds, and zero trades in January/February 2018 and only two trades in 2017.

The Tadawul also operates a smaller market called NOMU—Parallel Market. It is only opened to "qualified investors," i.e. not the public at large, and offers shares into companies with lighter reporting requirements. It only lists nine companies, traded mainly by speculators and stock brokers, but provides a less demanding alternative to raising capital.

The Capital Market Authority

In the years directly following the creation of the Tadawul, trading and issuance on the exchange was regulated by SAMA. However, as markets developed it became necessary to establish an independent body somewhat similar to the Security and Exchange Commission in the US. Thus, the Capital Market Authority was established in 2003. The CMA issues rules and regulations for all securities. It seeks to protect investors from unfair practices and fraud, maintain the transparency of transactions and the full disclosure of information by issuers to the public. Similar to international standards elsewhere, corporations issuing shares are required to file an offering memorandum with extensive disclosure and audited statements, which are available to the public in English and Arabic on the CMA website.

The CMA's first president was Jamaz al Suhaimi. Mr. Al Suhaimi was a deputy Minister of Finance and highly respected civil servant both nationally and internationally. He had a long experience in finance at SIDF, SAMA and the MoF before heading the CMA. Under his oversight the CMA was placed on its present solid regulatory base.[6] His daughter, the highly regarded Ms. Sarah Al Suhaimi, is now Chair of the Tadawul stock market as well as Chair of National Commercial Bank Capital.

Potentially the most significant initiative the CMA has led is the Tadawul's slow opening to foreign investors and capital, which began in earnest in 2015. There are now over 120 licensed qualified foreign institutions (QFI) on the exchange.[7] The licenses go from dealing as Principal, Agent or Underwriter, to managing of funds, arranging deals and advisory services. The foreign firms were selected by the CMA, had to come from markets the regulator perceived as having proper supervision and regulation, and be highly experienced with portfolios under management of not less than US$1 billion.[8] As a consequence of the tight requirements, the foreign entities allowed to trade and invest in the kingdom were limited to the likes of Goldman Sachs, Lazard Frères, HSBC, Citigroup, Nomura, Société Générale, Credit Suisse, or Morgan Stanley. Even those QFI's permitted to invest on the Tadawul cannot own more than 10% of the shares of any firms traded on the stock exchange, and all QFIs put together cannot own more than 49% of these shares. Collectively, while this regulatory opening did mark a new era for the Tadawul, the tight restrictions limited the potential upside of foreign capital inflows on the exchange.

In January 2018, the CMA issued somewhat more relaxed regulations to be in line with Vision 2030 and with the purpose of attracting more foreign investors. As of then, the QFIs would have to have "only" US$500 million under management, which may open the door to many other potential investment houses. The maximum amount of shares that can be owned was not changed.[9]

Despite these regulatory changes, foreign ownership still makes up a very small portion of activity on the Tadawul and high-profile investors remain hesitant to enter the market. Notable among these is notorious emerging market investor Mark Mobius who, as of June 2018, was openly tepid on Saudi stocks, "simply because the range of offerings is limited and a number of restrictions are still in place."[10] Sentiment like this has kept foreign participation low, with total foreign ownership as a percent of market capitalization actually lower in the first half of 2018 than in the months following the opening to foreign capital, falling from around 5.13% to 4.6% across the 30-month time span.[11] These levels pale in comparison to other developing country's equities markets, like Brazil, where it hovers around 50% and Turkey where it sits at 65%. On the other hand, should Saudi Aramco get privatized, one could expect more activity from worldwide investors through qualified foreign investors. This dynamic, and their effect on the market and Saudis in general, is discussed in detail in Chapter 6 of this work.

Moving forward, the profile of the Tadawul is expected to get a significant boost from its inclusion in major emerging market indices, a change which would make it the fourth Gulf state to achieve the listing, after the UAE, Kuwait and Qatar. Analysts expect the upgrade to drive as much as US$45 to US$50 billion in capital inflows as investors balance their portfolios to match the new index weightings.[12] This upgrade to emerging market status would not have been possible were it not for the CMA's regulatory overhaul.

The State Controlled Financing Companies

Like many of its regional peers, a key government initiative over the years has been to bring development and economic diversification to the kingdom. In Saudi, this focus first grew in prominence after the increase in oil prices of the mid-1970s, when the bureaucracy believed the kingdom should diversify away from oil as its main source of income. During that period, the main non-royal thought-leaders saw that continuing to rely on oil alone would ensure that the kingdom remained a backward third world country. However, in the 1970s the kingdom's financial and economic infrastructure was almost medieval, with very little emphasis on proper accounting, great reliance on trade and virtually no industry. Thus, with the full support of King Faisal, in the mid-1970s, these financial leaders helped the state establish not only the PIF and SIDF but also the Agricultural Development Fund, and the Real Estate Fund. Initially, emphasis was placed on the PIF and SIDF, with the former focused on financing the equity part of new industry and infrastructure, while SIDF focused on providing loans to small, medium and eventually large industrial firms.

Saudi Industrial Development Fund

SIDF provides loans at no interest for fifteen years to any industrial project deemed credit worthy. SIDF procedures were established alongside commercial banking practices. Applicants both large and small were asked for audited statements of existing operations, detailed descriptions of proposed projects and cash flow projections. The figures were analyzed using credit criteria set up by the Chase Manhattan Bank. Chase had a technical service agreement with SIDF to support the start-up of the fund and establish procedures to assess the credit worthiness of the projects and provide project financing experts to get the fund started on a professional footing. The experts' main job was to train young Saudis to take over the portfolio and run the application process. It was these same Saudi experts who would assist less sophisticated borrowers navigate the stringent application process. This cadre of young Saudis quickly became the backbone of the financial industry in the kingdom, with many of the young project finance officers becoming top managers in the kingdom's banks, the MoF and SAMA. To this day, the SIDF provides advice and consulting services to smaller companies. It also provides loan guarantees to Saudi commercial banks who in turn can lend to smaller companies, otherwise not fully credit reliable for a regular banking practice, somewhat like the Small Business Administration in the US. In 2016, SIDF provided 1,711 such guarantees for a total of US$57 million.

Since its inception SIDF has funded 7,493 projects with a total value of US$36.63 billion. It has 611 employees, mainly Saudis.[13] Its procedures have evolved over time and the amounts lent have become very large. However, the basic tenet of the institutions is still based on lending only to projects with a reasonable chance of success according to standard credit practices. SIDF has focused on lending to the chemical industry (38% of its projects), engineering projects (20.8%), consumer industries (17%) and construction-based projects including cement manufacturing (19%). It has lent to Saudi companies as well as to joint ventures, funding 717 joint venture projects with a total value of US$14.3 billion. This focus on joint ventures is set to grow in the near term. In an effort to attract international companies, and in reaction to plummeting FDI figures in 2017, the Saudi government is setting up a US$13.3 billion fund for developing partnerships with foreign companies, called the International Partnership Fund, which will be run by SIDF.[14]

SIDF has been very successful. However, indirectly it also had a deleterious effect on the long-term financial markets. Indeed, why would a company seek long term lending from banks or insurance companies, or even issue shares on the stock market, at the cost of diluting ownership or paying fairly high interest rates when it could get loans of up to fifteen years at no interest with up to a 5-year grace period. Hence, the very existence of SIDF, which has been very beneficial in helping the state channel some of the oil earnings to productive ends, also limited the development of long-term financial instruments, whether bank loans, bonds or even equity.

Other State Financing Entities

The Real Estate Development Fund was set up in 1975 to provide financing to Saudis wishing to build their own houses, or to small investors to build apartments for rental purposes. Recent information on how many loans have been made is not readily available, but it is known that during the first eighteen years of operations the fund provided almost 412,000 loans, and that total outstanding loans as of 2016 is US$42 billion.[15] The original terms of the real estate loans were very generous by most standards. They consisted of long amortization loans with no interest charged. It also included a cancelation of 30% of the debt if payments were made without default for a period of ten years.[16]

Another of the state financial institutions, The Agricultural Bank, was set up in 1964 to catalyze the development of modern agriculture in the kingdom. The bank became very large when King Fahd decreed that the kingdom should strive to become self-sufficient in food production. Accordingly, loans were provided to Saudi farmers at extremely attractive rates. In short, any agricultural expense, like seeds, could be subsidized by 50%. In some cases, equipment was provided at 100% subsidy. Moreover, the ensuing production of cereals, mainly wheat and barley, were purchased at highly inflated prices.[17]

The major financial incentives provided by the agricultural bank and the Ministry of Agriculture certainly succeeded in developing agriculture in the kingdom. By the late 1980s Saudi Arabia had become the eighth largest exporter of wheat in the world. It also developed a major dairy industry which produced milk products for the Saudi market, some of which are now exported across other Gulf countries.

However, the subsidies created an ecological disaster as most of the agriculture developed was based on irrigation taken from non-renewable water resources. The water table in some of the better agricultural areas of the kingdom went from 100 meters below ground to 1,000 meters, signaling a very rapid decline in water resources. Presently Saudi faces serious clean water supply issues, with this phase of agricultural subsidies likely playing a contributing role. Further, the main beneficiaries of the agricultural benefits ended up being princes and tribal leaders who had obtained title to lands, which in previous generations did not have, nor needed, defined title deeds. The Agricultural Bank still exists and lends but its activities have declined substantially. It now has only US$2.11 billion in outstanding loans, about 30% less than in the late 1980s.

A much smaller, but interesting, state controlled financial institution is the Saudi Social Development Bank. This institution used to be known as the Saudi Credit Bank and was established in 1971 to provide interest free loans to less fortunate Saudis. It focuses on providing loans for marriage dowries, house repairs and personal emergencies. Its total loans outstanding today amount to US$80.64 billion.[18]

The three institutions just mentioned are quite indicative of the support that the Saudi state has provided to the population. They were established in the early part of the oil bonanza, when the state and its leadership felt they could provide the citizens, especially the less fortunate ones, with some of the benefits of the kingdom's newfound oil wealth, a practice that still continues today.

All these institutions are funded by SAMA, which advances loans to them to operate. It is likely that these loans are provided at no interest and are primarily justified as a way for the state to funnel money to the less fortunate.

Perhaps, in the case of the Agricultural Bank and the Real Estate Bank, it could be argued that the funds were competing with the private sector banking institutions and, by crowding them out, actually slowed down the development of a mature financial market. Indeed, why would any borrower go to a bank, when it could borrow interest free for the long term from the government? On the other hand, it seems that the state did not really steal this market away from the private lenders. Instead, it merely responded to a difficult legal environment; especially in the case of real estate lending. Shari'a courts would not look favorably on enforcing the interest portion of debt owed, and in no case would allow foreclosure of a person's home. Thus, not until Saudi Arabia accepted the development of Shari'a-compliant institutions could the interest issue be acceptable in court. Even then, Islamic banking did not solve the issue of foreclosure. These legal risks ostensibly preclude most private sector institutions from entering the mortgage sector in any substantial manner. Hence the actual amount of real estate debt to individuals in all banks in the kingdom is small, and the Real Estate Bank is still needed. On the other hand, large real estate development is easier to finance. More recently, the legal environment was eased substantially with the introduction by the authorities of the Commission for the Resolution of Dispute accepted by the World Trade Organization as a proper venue for legal recourse and which gave the banks a fighting chance against debtors.

GOSI

The General Organization for Social Insurance was established to manage the pension funds of non-government employees. Salaries paid by the private sector to Saudis are debited by 7.5%, matched by the state and then invested by the fund to provide retirement funds to Saudis. The fund's money was by and large managed by SAMA along the line of its own conservative tenets. However, some of the funds were at times used to help in the industrialization of the kingdom, with GOSI becoming a shareholder and lender to some of the kingdom's larger industrial firms. For example GOSI was a major source of equity and subordinated loans to PetroRabigh, the US$10 billion refining and chemical venture between Saudi Aramco and Sumitomo. It also owns 10.25% of Savola a large food processing and distributing company.

GOSI set up an investment fund called Hassana in 2009 to give it more flexibility in investing. At first it was capitalized at US$2.37 billion and tasked with investing abroad. It is clear however, that Hassana has not been very active internationally, but has taken percentages in some of the local Saudi Banks to shore up their capital, usually along-side PIF.

The PPA, which invests and manages public employee's retirement funds, often follows GOSI's lead. Like GOSI, its funds were usually invested by SAMA in conservative foreign, often US sovereign securities, but at times were also used in the industrialization efforts of the kingdom.

Public Investment Fund of Saudi Arabia

PIF was first seen as a provider of equity to newly established state-owned companies. PIF's main investments were in the newly formed Saudi Basic Industries Company (SABIC), established to diversify the country away from mere oil production and into the downstream production of chemicals and fertilizers. PIF also became the main shareholder of SAPTCO, the bus company, Bahri, the shipping company, Ma'aden, the mining and aluminum group, and a number of others. Originally, the bureaucracy wanted to ensure that the public at large would support, and be financially included in, the kingdom's industrial growth. The civil servants in charge of development were therefore eager to ensure that the companies would be successful before involving the public through a broader distribution of shares. Thus, PIF was meant to provide the basic equity, with the SWF planning in due course, after the companies proved successful, to sell its shares to the public in order to spread the benefits of the new economic direction. PIF ended up selling no shares to the public, perhaps for fear of losing control of the main non-oil assets to the private sector or to the royal family or merely to protect the public from potential downturns. However, it did end up running very large companies, which eventually went to external markets to raise capital above and beyond PIF's input. These IPOs were most successful, in great part because the public felt, with PIF as the leading partner, the state was de facto guaranteeing their investments.

From inception to 2016, PIF was very close to the Ministry of Finance, with its managing director sitting right next to the Minister's office. Today, however, the link between the two institutions has been greatly reduced. PIF is now independent from the MoF's direct control and has its own board of directors and staff. The chairmanship has been taken away from the

Ministry and handed over to HRH MbS, who has announced that the institution would from now on be the new Sovereign Wealth Fund of the kingdom. It was even hinted that PIF would become the shareholder of Saudi Aramco, whenever the oil giant is privatized, as well as receive surplus oil revenues, a revenue stream that currently flows to SAMA.[19]

Through its myriad investments, PIF has become involved in almost every aspect of the economy, from mining, agriculture and food processing to banking, technology and chemicals (See Table 3.1). Most of the investments were made not so much to gain control of specific segments of the economy, but merely to support industrial development on orders from the Ministry of Finance. This is to say that, while under the direct oversight of the MoF, the PIF did not seem to have a well-defined industrial strategy, short of helping move the economy away from the mere production of crude oil. It was successful in this endeavor, with many of the kingdom's largest companies having become major players in their respective fields. For example, SABIC and Ma'aden are world scale players in chemicals, fertilizers and metals. Nevertheless, PIF has a very large portfolio of local investments and to some extent has competed with the private sector in backing the country's various industrial companies. In fact, today PIF is the largest investor by far in the kingdom and could be interpreted as basically crowding out the private sector.

Table 3.1 Known Investments of the Public Investment Fund (Saudi Arabia)

Public Equity Investments		
Investment	*Market Value of Investment ($Million)*	*% of Outstanding Shares*
SABIC	$58,800.00	70.00%
Saudi Telecom Co.	$27,300.00	70.00%
Saudi Electricity Company	$16,656.00	74.30%
National Commercial Bank	$13,700.00	44.29%
Saudi Arabian Mining Co.	$7,900.00	49.99%
Samba Financial Group	$3,000.00	22.91%
Riyad Bank	$2,400.00	21.75%
Almarai Co	$2,200.00	16.32%
Alinma Bank	$798.50	10.00%
Southern Province Cement Co.	$698.20	37.43%
National Shipping Company of SA (Bahri)	$696.12	22.55%
Saudi Real Estate Co.	$458.60	64.57%
Tadawul	$320.00	100.00%

(*Continued*)

Table 3.1 (Continued)

Public Equity Investments		
Company	*Market Value of Investment ($Million)*	*% of Outstanding Shares*
Qassim Cement	$251.16	23.35%
Yanbu Cement Co.	$145.90	10.00%
The National Agriculture Development Co.	$136.00	20.00%
Saudi Public Transport Co.	$82.60	15.72%
Dur Hospitality Co.	$79.70	16.62%
National Gas & Industrialization Co.	$66.80	10.91%
Eastern Province Cement Co.	$61.20	10.00%
Saudi Fisheries	$59.30	39.99%
Bidaya	$53.30	22%%
Saudi Ceramic Co.	$19.00	5.40%
Total Known Equity Portfolio	**$135,881.18**	
Investments Abroad		
Company	*Market Value of Investment ($Million)*	*% of Outstanding Shares*
Uber	$3,500.00	5%
Noon (e-Commerce)	$500.00	50%
SoftBank Vision Fund	$45,000.00	45%
Blackstone—PIF Fund	$20,000.00	50%
Posco Engineering & Construction Co. (South Korea)	$1,360.00	38%
Virgin Galactic	$1,000.00	
Clariant AG	$1,980.00	24.99%
Hapag-Lloyd AG	$567.00	10.14%
Adeptio		50.00%
Gulf International Bank (Bahrain)	$2,300.00	97%
Other Known Investments (No Percentage or Value Disclosed)		
Company		
Americana		
Taqa		
AMC Entertainment Holdings		
Ibn Rushd		
Tabadul		

Other Known Investments (No Percentage or Value Disclosed)
Company
Elm Company
Marafiq
Water and Electricity Holding Company
Shuaibah Expansion Holding Company
The Savola Group
SALIC
Grain Silos and Flour Mills Organization
Saudi Global Ports Co.
GDC Middle East
Saudi Railway Company
ArcelorMittal Tubular Products Jubail (AMTPJ)
National Procurement Company (NUPCO)**
PECSA
Taiba Holding Company
Saudi Heritage Hospitality Company
Tatweer Education Holding Company
Tadawul Real Estate Company
GCC Electrical Testing Laboratory

Source: Tadawul as of July 24, 2018 unless otherwise noted

** **Owned 100%;**

While prior to 2016 PIF took direction from the MoF, since it has fallen under the direct oversight of MbS its strategy has somewhat shifted. It is still tasked with investing within Saudi Arabia and outside the kingdom in firms that can bring technological benefits to the kingdom. Yet, where originally, the PIF was merely the silent shareholder of major companies like SABIC, Ma'aden, Marafiq (the water desalination company) and Savola (a leading food producer), today the company has a much more aggressive type of management, in part implemented by foreign consultants. It has begun investing very large amounts in advanced technological firms, mainly overseas. PIF has already invested US$3.5 billion in Uber and US$45 billion a JV with Softbank of China for purchase of technological assets. It has also committed to fund US$1.07 billion to small and medium sized enterprises. The fund's assets totaled between US$220 and 240 billion as of September 2017, with the fund aiming to increase this to US$400 billion by 2020.[20] At this time PIF is still financed by the MoF. However, it is not clear how PIF will fund its highly aggressive US$400 billion target. While this is touched on in more detail in Chapters 5 and 6.1, one key to this may be the Saudi Aramco IPO.

Should PIF be granted the entirety of the shares of Saudi Aramco, somewhat like it's 70% stake of SABIC, it would bring its total assets to over US$2.2 trillion, a staggering amount by any standard. However, it would not necessarily provide the cash to invest the US$400 billion mentioned. PIF would indeed become the main recipient of Saudi Aramco's dividends, which at today's highly speculative guess could mount up to about US$60 to US$70 billion/year, which still would be too low for the amount of investments required to reach PIF's US$400 billion objective. Of course, PIF could very easily borrow substantial sums, but it is unlikely that it could borrow the hundreds of billions required, without endangering the credit worthiness of the kingdom. The sheer size of the amount mentioned would lead one to think that PIF may be aiming to take over the funds presently managed by SAMA, which would imply a total redrawing of the Saudi financial management. In fact, this shift may be what Mohammed Al Tuwaijri, the kingdom's minister of economy and planning, was alluding to when he said, in March 2018, "Whenever oil is above our break-even point, this will all go to the PIF . . . . So in that sense they will have a lot of funding, hopefully."[21]

Much of the plans laid by PIF rely on expected returns on investments of between 8% and 9%, which in today's low interest environment may seem a bit optimistic, and perhaps come from listening to hedge fund analysts, who often forget about major downturns and basic credit risks. Conversely, the money held by SAMA has been invested primarily in very highly liquid, safe, but low performing assets. Many in the MoF and SAMA will argue that it is this conservative investment approach that has saved the kingdom tens of billions of dollars in bearish markets. Furthermore, one cannot foresee how PIF could evolve to manage the size of investments mentioned without surrendering its assets to foreign private managers, somewhat like ADIA has done in the UAE. ADIA is of course famous for its complete opacity, which therefore does not qualify it as a model for PIF, as opacity runs contrary to all the statements made by the present Saudi leadership on having a transparent economy and transparent handling of the country's assets. On the other hand, instead of becoming ADIA, PIF could model itself on the Norwegian SWF, which is fully transparent, with audited statements released to the public regularly, and ultimately answers to the people of Norway through its elected parliament. This switch in foreign asset management from SAMA to PIF in the style of the Norwegian SWF could ensure that funds will be managed by Saudis for Saudis, as long as transparency standards and investment policies are clearly established by the management and not subject of the whims of a few individuals without proper vetting and due diligence. Moreover, seeing as Saudi Aramco is being privatized in great part to make the national oil company transparent to all citizens and investors alike, this shift toward Norway's style of asset management would also assuage concerns that the potential main owner, PIF, is quite opaque, thereby denying the advantage of Saudi Aramco's transparency to the public at large.[22]

Even with the PIF's broad foreign asset portfolio, the Saudi state still depends on oil income to fund itself. Of course, even with the public offering of Saudi Aramco, the state will continue to obtain a 20% royalty on oil leases and a 50% tax on income. However, this would not suffice to fill the state's coffers. At the time of this writing Saudi Aramco has become a corporation registered in the Kingdom of Saudi Arabia, but it is not clear who the main shareholder of Saudi Aramco is. Perhaps the shares will be transferred to PIF at a future date. However, if the shares were passed on to PIF, since the fund is no longer linked to the MoF, it would be unclear how the state would be able to cover the budget deficits, unless it taxed PIF. Nevertheless, it is likely that the state will continue to receive a portion of the oil company's profits, whether as a direct shareholder, or as a shareholder of the shareholder, PIF.

The various state funds of the kingdom have done a yeoman's job in helping develop and diversify the economy. Until 2017, all the funds worked basically in the direction imposed on them by the civil service, whose main goal was rapid industrialization. Hence, in the end, their efforts are not so different than those now expressed in the sleek brochures and plans designed by consultants and presented to the world as Vision 2030. However, their efforts have not been as successful as they could have been; primarily because all the funds, through loan and equity ownership, imposed a bureaucratic, heavily centralized control that stifled the broader economy. By having control of the funds, and almost all of the cash reserves of the state, the Ministry of Finance and SAMA effectively did crowd out the private sector.

On the other hand, the very extensive and strong presence of the state in the largest and most profitable companies of the kingdom reassured investors, especially the smaller ones. Hence, the social change caused by heavy industrialization did get the support of most people. Industry and not oil was seen as the future of the country. The strong presence of the state crowded out the private sector and both commercial and investment banks. They limited entrepreneurship. So, in many ways the bureaucracy prepared the path for the new economic revolution. They created the expectations, which the new blood of young leaders in Riyadh are now driven to fulfill in a decidedly less traditional way.

PIF will play a key role in this process. The fund now has major ownership in almost every aspect of the Saudi economy. It owns controlling interests in the largest companies in manufacturing and mining and even those active in the kingdom's recent push toward domestic military equipment manufacturing. It pretty much controls the financial markets through the banks and has taken over the first SWF of the kingdom, SANABIL, which itself has investments in various funds abroad. It would seem that PIF is becoming the single most important economic actor in the kingdom. Were

PIF to become the equity owner of Saudi Aramco, it would then give it quasi control of the economy. One of the main aspects of Vision 2030 is to promote entrepreneurship and a healthy private sector, yet it seems that PIF and its leadership is in fact taking the counter approach. Certainly, PIF has the great intention to develop high tech investments and obtain technology from abroad to eventually transfer it to the entrepreneurs in Saudi Arabia. Yet having a monopolistic role in the control of the entire economy may in fact work just in reverse. PIF will be able, and already is able, to dictate which sector can develop, who gets financed and what industries get to grow. This indeed is just the opposite of what the leadership is seeking to promote and ultimately not unlike what the older civil servants of the kingdom had established and which is now criticized, with some cause, for stifling the entrepreneurial spirit of the young.

The Money Changers

As seen in the historical review in Chapter 1, the money changers have lost of great deal of their influence. Nevertheless, they still exist. SAMA has provided them with two types of licenses, A & B. While both licenses are allowed to exchange, purchase and sell currency, traveler's checks and bank drafts, only A can make cash remittances inside and outside the kingdom. Their main activities are actually changing money and transferring funds on behalf of the expatriates, many of whom remit a large portion of their income back home.

While still active in the kingdom, the free-wheeling style of the money changers has increasingly been curbed over the years. In the past, money changers could invest on behalf of their clients or invest the large float which they carried between the time the expat workers brought their checks to mail home and when these checks were cashed. Today however, the monetary agency pays very close attention to all transactions, especially those of the money changers. They demand that the money changers abide by the 'know your customer' rules. They make sure that transfers do not end up in the accounts of extreme religious or terrorist organizations. In other words, money changers find that the time of simple, efficient, but easily manipulated transactions are over. Moreover, their ability to earn large fees from foreign exchange transactions is challenged by electronic transfer technologies like Apple Pay and PayPal and the sophistication of the modern electronic banking. Consequently, the float has become much smaller as foreign workers can transfer from their accounts to their home countries using their cell phone. Thus, bereft of fees and a float, money changers are now transforming themselves into old fashioned banks, that or leaving the business altogether to focus on managing their own investments.

Due to this deteriorating business environment, there are currently only four A licenses granted by SAMA. Three of the four, including the largest one, Al Amoudi, had their licenses suspended by SAMA in November 2017 for failure to comply with regulator's anti-money laundering and counter-terrorism measures. B license holders are only entitled to do foreign exchange and are thus extremely limited in their ability to do sizable transactions and de facto have been marginalized, soon to become quasi obsolete. Accordingly, while there were around US$37 billion in remittances leaving Saudi Arabia in 2017, the vast majority of these did not go through money changers.

The Commercial Banks

Competition from state institutions has forced the kingdom's local commercial banks to focus on areas where state institutions are not active, such as short-term facilities, consumer loans, letters of credits and, most significantly, government bonds. As of December 2017, letters of credit (L/Cs) were still a major source of income for banks in the kingdom, a continuation of practices established early on in the sector's history. Since most foreign trade transactions require an L/C with fees of anywhere from a .25 to 1%, one could estimate that the banking sector saw income as high as US$1.4 billion in 2016 from these L/Cs, with confirmation of L/Cs on exports providing a further US$90 million per year.[23] These revenues were further supplemented by income on letters of guarantee and advance payment guarantees on government contracts, figures which are harder to estimate but undoubtedly substantial.

The bank's loan books provide the bulk revenue for the banks, with interest income making up between 60 and 70% of total gross income in the banking sector between 2012 and 2017, compared to an average of 27% from fees.[24] As of December 2017, total loans outstanding to the private sector, which includes most parastatal firms, were US$376 billion, with another US$81 billion in loans to government entities, and US$90 billion in consumer loans. The local banks also kept substantial balances in foreign banks, standing at around US$65 billion at the end of 2017. SAMA's Stability Report estimates banks' profits at US$9.5 billion and that 70% of that came from interest income.[25] Thus, a back of the envelope estimate would tell us that banks manage a very respectable spread of 1.2% on their loan portfolio. Of course, profitability is always impaired by bad loans, which undoubtedly hurt NCB, SAMBA and others, leading to their de facto take over by state institutions. Profitability could easily be improved if the banks could make more loans and provide more letters of credits and guarantees, an opportunity that is presently limited by the size of the domestic market and the limitations SAMA has placed on both outward and inward investment. These limitations are increasingly impactful when considering that, on average, Saudi banks are under-leveraged compared to many banks in the world. Their total, unweighted capital to asset ratio was 13.7% in December 2017. This level is substantially higher than it was only four years prior, when it was 11.93%, and significantly higher than the global average of 10.5%. An even more stringent metric of liquidity, tier 1 capital to risk-weighted assets, was even higher, at 18.3% in December 2017, well above the minimum established by both Basel III and SAMA, and more than 5 percentage points higher than the US banking sector's average at the same time, all which underlines the notion that the Saudi banks have room to grow their loan portfolios.[26]

For Saudi Arabia, these metrics are not abnormal. The Saudi banking sector has been historically characterized by extreme liquidity. For example, despite rapid credit growth and large drawdown in deposits throughout 2016, the Saudi banking sector saw its key liquidity metrics hold at an average of 130% the requirements set forth by Basel III.[27] This liquidity is an intended byproduct of SAMA's regulatory structure. In most other countries where banks have a lot of cash on hand, their extra liquidity could be invested in Eurodollar loans to large triple-A rated borrowing states like the French Republic, or more profitable but vastly riskier loans to various developing countries. However, SAMA had cut this avenue to the Saudi banks in the 1980s. These limitations have the intended effect of funneling the sector's large, liquid depository base toward government development bonds, which de facto cover the state's deficit, and toward loans to government-linked parastatal companies, like SABIC, affiliates of Saudi Aramco and Ma'aden.

Of course, loans to the state, either as loans to 'parastatal' entities or directly, could make the banks overly reliant on one customer, threatening to breach limits applied across the global banking environment. All the banks within the kingdom are required to have extensive relations with other banks, especially the large international ones, like JPMorganChase, Citibank and Deutsche Bank. However, due to internal regulation, these international banks have exposure limits with respect to their correspondent banks as well as the clients of those correspondent banks. Therefore, each bank, each year, goes through an analysis of the credit worthiness of their correspondent banks, with an extensive review of how much exposure these banks have to their respective clients, organized in various tiers of risk as defined by the Basel agreements. This review includes how much each potential correspondent bank is liable to any one customer, including sovereign states. In the case of the kingdom, this brings a dual struggle to the fore. Most foreign banks want to maintain correspondent relations with Saudi banks in order to benefit from their large deposits and fees from letters of credits or guarantees. However, if these Saudi banks are too exposed to Saudi state risks, then the correspondent banks in New York or London would have to limit their relations with the Saudi banks. It is in this regard that lending to parastatal firms can be beneficial for the Saudi banks given they can do so without the parastatals providing guarantees from the MoF. This set up could allow foreign correspondent banks to argue the Saudi banks were in fact quasi state quality credits, because of Saudi state ownership, while also maintaining that they did not breach costumer exposure rules. This latter would be due to the fact that technically each of the parastatals was independent from the government and their loan guarantees did not come from the MoF.

The state's role in the banking sector goes beyond lending regulation and government bonds and is better seen through a discussion of the National Commercial Bank. Some of the problems which the bank ran into and how they were dealt with were discussed in Chapter 1. During the travails of NCB in the 1990s, SAMA and the MoF saved the bank though capital intervention, but in doing so ensured that the Bin Mahfouz and Kaki families were excluded from the bank ownership and no longer had any say in the future of the bank, which they had gravely jeopardized. In a practice established by the MoF and SAMA with many other banks in the kingdom, NCB was changed into a publicly held firm with part of the bank's recapitalization accomplished by issuing shares to the public. SAMA and the MoF maintained their controlling stake through their role in the recapitalization that had taken place prior to the flotation on the Tadawul. MoF, which at the time controlled operations at the PIF, dictated to PIF to take a strong stake in the bank, which the PIF has maintained to this day. When the stake by PIF appeared too large, the MoF arranged for GOSI and its investment fund Hassana to take significant financial stakes in the bank, which they have also maintained to this day. Long before NCB ran into major troubles. Riyadh Bank had been taken over by the MoF through PIF, Hassana and the PPA and staffed at key levels by persons close to the MoF. The same is applicable for SIB and SAMBA. Thus, it is quite telltale to see that four of the five largest banks in the kingdom are de facto controlled by the state (See Table 3.2).

The exception to the five is Al Rajhi Bank—now the second largest bank in the kingdom. The bank's founder, Saleh Al Rajhi, was a very pious man and was likely to seek to establish a more Shari'a-compliant financial institution, more like money changers than traditional interest-taking commercial banks. Also, Al Rajhi had a difficult relationship with SAMA from the days when Saleh Al Rajhi was the largest money changer in the kingdom. The bank may have tried to maintain its independence from SAMA by applying to become the kingdom's first Islamic, Shari'a-compliant institution, which SAMA was not able to regulate as thoroughly as the traditional banks. To this day Al Rajhi bank has managed to maintain its independence from the state. Although PPA is a stakeholder in the bank, the Al Rajhi family is likely to be the largest stakeholder in the bank. Al Rajhi is no longer the only Islamic bank in the country, with most commercial banks in the kingdom now offering their clients Shari'a-compliant deposit facilities as well as loans based on the main products of Islamic banking. Even foreign banking joint ventures have adopted the Shari'a-compliant products to appeal to their own Saudi clients, who seem to favor them.

The local Saudi banks operate a number of branches, which serve their customers. Naturally the large banks have more branches. NCB has 352 branches, closely followed by Riyadh bank with 334. On the other hand, Al Rajhi bank, which serves large numbers of smaller customers and heavily focuses on consumer lending, has 525 branches established across in the country. The banks with some foreign ownership like Saudi French (Credit Agricole), Arab National Bank (Arab Bank of Jordan), Saudi Hollandi

Table 3.2 Bank Ownership and Asset Size in Saudi Arabia

Commercial Banks	Total Assets (Q3 2017, US$ Bil.)	Main Shareholder 1	Main Shareholder 2	Main Shareholder 3	% Listed
National Commercial Bank (Al Ahli)	$120	PIF 44.3%	GOSI 10%	PPA 10%	25%
SAMBA Financial Group	$62	PIF 22.9%	PPA 15.0%	Hassana Investment Co. 11.8%	73%
Riyadh Bank	$59	PIF 21.8%	Hassana Investment Co. 16.7%	PPA 9.18%	58%
Saudi French Bank	$54	Kingdom Holding 16.2%	Credit Agricole 14.9%	Hassana Investment Co. 13.3%	45%
Saudi British Bank	$48	HSBC 40.0%	Olayan Financing Co. 17.0%	Hassana Investment Co. 9.74%	28%
Arab National Bank	$44	Arab Bank Plc 40.0%	Hassana Investment Co. 11.3%	Rashed Abdul Rahman Al Rashed & Sons Group 9.97%	33%
Saudi Investment Bank	$27	PPA 17.3%	Hassana Investment Co. 17.3%	JPMorgan Chase 7.49%	52%
Bank Aljazira	$18	Ibrahim Al Sultan Family 6.59%	National Bank of Pakistan 5.83%	Saleh Kamel 5.0%	83%
Islamic Banks	**Total Assets (Q3 2017, US$ Bil.)**	**Main Shareholder 1**	**Main Shareholder 2**	**Main Shareholder 3**	**% Listed**
Al Rajhi Bank	$91	Hassana Investment Co. 10.2%	Suleiman Bin Abdulaziz Al Rajhi Endowments Co. 6.61%	Abdullah Sulaiman Abdulaziz Al Rajhi 2.17%	83%
Alinma Bank	$30	PPA 10.7%	PIF 10.0%	Hassana Investment Co. 5.10%	84%
Alawwal Bank	$27	Royal Bank of Scotland 40.0%	Olayan Financing Co. 21.7%	Hassana Investment Co. 10.5%	28%
Bank Albilad	$17	Subaie Mohammad Ibrahim Mohammad Al 19.1%	Abdullah Ibrahim Mohammad Al Subaie 11.1%	Khalid Abdul Rahman Saleh Al Rajhi 10.5%	48%

Source: Tadawul

(formerly ABN/AMRO, now RBS), Al Jazira (National Bank of Pakistan) or Saudi British Bank (HSBC) have significantly less branches, which are largely clustered in population centers. These banks offer much more specialized services, working often with their foreign counterparts to assist in the advanced needs of their clients within the kingdom. They do handle some retail banking but by and large focus predominantly on wholesale strategies.

Currently regulation also allows some foreign banks to open 100% owned branches in the kingdom. Some banks from across the GCC have capitalized on this. Gulf International Bank (actually based in Bahrain but owned by the PIF) has three branches, while Emirates National Bank NBD of the UAE, National Bank of Kuwait, Bank Muscat and National Bank of Bahrain each have one branch within the kingdom. Other foreign banks with one branch each include JPMorgan Chase, National Bank of Pakistan, TC Ziraat Bankasi of Turkey and the State Bank of India. It is interesting to note that in the 1980s many foreign banks had branches within the kingdom, mainly to serve their home country's pilgrims out of Jeddah or serve their colonial routes. However, in the 1980s, SAMA and the MoF forced them to Saudi-ize as part of government efforts to steer domestic banks toward servicing the Saudi market and catalyzing domestic industrialization. Today, with the growth in the economy and the need to attract more foreign capital, this policy has been reversed and high quality foreign banks are now welcomed back, especially if they have a natural market such as the State Bank of India or the National Bank of Pakistan, who can and do service the millions of foreign workers in the kingdom.

Conclusion

With the sudden growth in the wealth of the region, it became important for the Gulf States' authorities to regulate the flows of money and protect the middle class and less sophisticated investors. In many cases, the local banking establishments and the money changers and banking sector leaders were not pleased with these efforts at regulating areas they had, until then, controlled. They were afraid that their independence would be gravely impeded by bureaucrats. In Saudi Arabia, they lobbied heavily with the King to stop SAMA and the MoF from regulating them. Their view of a central bank and MoF was that these institutions should stick to issuing currency, managing the clearing of instruments and the country's foreign exchange reserves and the disbursement of public funds.

In the struggle between the banks and SAMA about regulation, the banks and the money changers were often their own worst enemies. When the banks put themselves in difficult straits by making risky loans, they had to come to SAMA for help, which SAMA was pleased to do, provided they could then establish strong regulation of the banks, and in some cases even take over their management.

Riyadh Bank founded in 1957 is one of the first purely Saudi banks. It was also the first one to get into trouble by making risky loans. SAMA had to intervene to protect the depositors. In the process, SAMA took over the management and brought in state-owned shareholders to shore up the capital and arranged for PIF to take 51.3% stake in the bank. Later on, in the 1980s, NCB, which has become a very large bank, ran into problems. The bank suffered greatly from the association of its Chairman Mr. Khalid bin Mafouz with BCCI. The BCCI scandal rapidly led to the downfall of Mr. Al Mahfouz followed by the writing off of the banks total equity. The bank was then recapitalized by the Monetary Agency, through PIF, and shares floated to the public, leading to the eventual takeover and control of the bank by the monetary agency. Today, Riyadh Bank and NCB are two of the largest, and most powerful, banks in Saudi Arabia. This is to say, state control has usually led to stronger, not weaker, institutions in the Kingdom of Saudi Arabia, and often does so to the benefit of the broader population.

These steps to regulate, if not control, banks and money changers is symbiotic with the kingdom's broader economic and political strategy. Over the years since the oil boom of 1973, SAMA and the MoF, and through them the King, have pursued a systematic takeover of all the levers of the economy through the control of the financial markets. No firm could truly get established and be successful without the full support from all three institutions (SAMA, MoF, King). The massive industrialization of the kingdom, such as the enormous development of the petrochemical industry and the creation of industries servicing households, was not only encouraged but also shepherded by SAMA and the MoF either through PIF, SIDF or the pension funds of the kingdom.

By manipulating the markets to foster industrialization, the King was able to obtain support of various coalitions of citizens. The princes of the royal family were kept satisfied by having control and commissions on the extensive military expenses. Merchants were assured commissions on all sales and exchange of goods by having the assurance that all imports had to go through one of them. Young people had assurances that they could always count on employment from the public sector or from the growing industrial concerns, such as SABIC or Ma'aden. The development of industry was able to help unite a rather diverse population. The new industries were institutions which all tribal and religious groups in the kingdom had in common. To a certain extent, the effort to industrialize has cut into the historical weight of tribal and religious influence on Saudi society, creating a unifying factor across the breadth of diversified socioeconomic groups. Industrialization brought about by the financial markets seems to provide the state with socioeconomic control, which the regime will likely not risk losing through political liberalization.

Notes

1. Charter of The Saudi Arabian Monetary Agency, Royal Decree August 19, 1957.; The Saudi Arabian Monetary Authority changed its name from the Saudi Arabian Monetary Agency on December 4, 2016.
2. Interview with a high official of Saudi Arabia on the bankruptcy of Awal Bank and TIBC in Bahrain 2012.

3. Davide Barbuscia, "Saudi Arabia Hires Banks for Third International Bond," *Reuters*, September 25, 2017; Peter Hamilton, "Saudi Arabia Lists Largest Ever Sukuk on Irish Stock Exchange," *The Irish Times*, April 26, 2017.
4. "Saudi Arabian Monetary Authority," *Monthly Statistical Bulletin*, April 2018.
5. The Tadawul Members Directory. Available at www.tadawul.com.sa/wps/portal/tadawul/market-participants/members/members-directory.
6. Mr. Al-Suhaimi eventually became chairman of Gulf Investment Bank in Bahrain. Mr. Al-Suhaimi was highly respected in international circles. He died in late 2017. Euromoney published a highly complementary but, as the writer can vouch, accurate obituary. For more see: "Obituary: H.E. Jammaz bin Abdullah Al-Suhaimi," *Euromoney*, November 29, 2017.
7. Capital Markets Authority, "Saudi Stock Exchange Joins FTSE Global Equity Index Series," *Press Release*, March 28, 2018.
8. See Rules and Regulations. Available at https://cma.org.sa/en/Market/QFI/Documents/QFI-EN-amended.pdf.
9. Capital Markets Authority, "Saudi Stock Exchange Joins FTSE Global Equity Index Series," *Press Release*, March 28, 2018.
10. Filipe Pacheco, "Mobius Not Convinced by Saudi Stocks Set for Status Upgrade," *Bloomberg*, June 13, 2018.
11. Tadawul, "The Saudi Stock Exchange Announces the Publication of the Monthly Stock Market Ownership and Trading Activity Report (by Nationality and Investor Type)," *Multiple Press Releases*, Various Dates.
12. David French, "Saudi Bourse Will Be Ready for Capital Inflows after MSCI EM Inclusion," *Reuters*, June 20, 2018.
13. Saudi Industrial Development Fund, "SIDF Lending Activity." Available at www.sidf.gov.sa/en/Achievements/Pages/AccumulatedLendingActivities.aspx; Saudi Industrial Development Fund, "Historical Review," Available at www.sidf.gov.sa/en/AboutSIDF/Pages/HistoricalReview.aspx.
14. Rory Jones, Margherita Stancati and Summer Said, "Saudi Arabia to Spend Billions to Revive Foreign Investment," *Wall Street Journal*, July 22, 2018.
15. Saudi Arabian Monetary Authority, *Annual Statistics 2016*, 2016: table 4–2.
16. Saudi Arabia Ministry of Planning, *Achievements of the Development Plans, Facts and Figure 1970–2002*. (ISSN 1658–0729), p. 74.
17. Barley is used extensively in the Gulf to feed animals, somewhat like corn in the US or Europe.
18. Saudi Arabian Monetary Authority, *Annual Statistics 2016*, 2016: table 4–2.
19. Anjli Raval and Simeon Kerr, "Oil Cash Set to Boost Saudi Arabia's Sovereign Wealth Fund," *Financial Times*, March 9, 2018.
20. Public Investment Fund, *The Public Investment Fund Program (2018–2020)*, 2017, p. 12.
21. Raval and Kerr, "Oil Cash Set to Boost Saudi Arabia's Sovereign Wealth Fund."
22. A larger discussion on the purpose and impact of the proposed Saudi Aramco public offering is included in Chapter 6.1 of this work.
23. These estimates are computed using the amount of imports and exports in 2016 and multiplying by 1% for the imports and 1/20th % for confirmation of foreign L/Cs to the exporters [mainly Saudi Aramco and SABIC].
24. Saudi Arabian Monetary Authority, *Financial Stability Report 2017*, 2017, p. 28.
25. Ibid., p. 30.
26. The figures on loans, exposure to the private and public sectors as well as the leverage come from Saudi Arabian Monetary Authority, *Monthly Statistical Bulletin*. (Saudi Arabia: December 2017): tables 11a, 15a and18; The World Bank, *World Development Indicators*. (Washington, DC, n.d.)
27. Saudi Arabian Monetary Authority, *Financial Stability Report 2017*, p. 31.

4 The Financial Markets of Bahrain, Qatar, Kuwait and Oman

4.1 The Financial Markets of Bahrain

Introduction

As seen in Chapter 1, Bahrain played in important role in the early stages of the region's financial development, primarily through its offshore banking units (OBUs), which acted as a hub for negotiating and syndicating large financial facilities for industrial projects across the region. However, the nature of the region's financial markets changed dramatically between the mid-1970s, when OBUs were first established, and the early part of the 21st century. Toward the middle and late 1990s, with improved communication and more efficient air links between regional hubs in the UAE, Kuwait, Saudi Arabia and the rest of the world, London, which was already the global leader in large-scale syndication, took on the role Bahrain's OBUs had held; doing so more efficiently and at a lower cost. Similarly, the Kingdom of Bahrain's role as a hub for foreign exchange trading dissipated as technology reduced the need for physical trading across time zones. Bahrain's 'suitcase bankers,' who had serviced the commercial needs of Saudi Arabian businesses, were also no longer necessary as local Saudi Arabian banks increasingly offered first-rate, sophisticated instruments. This evolution rendered the notion of OBUs effectively obsolete, undercutting the role Bahrain had thought it would fill in the region's financial evolution. Since then, Bahrain has found limited success in establishing a new niche for itself, and its dwarfed role in regional finance has become a testament to this. Further dimming Bahrain's prospects, the small island nation, barely the size of New York City, has limited hydrocarbon wealth and has failed to realize the financial sector growth that it once foresaw. Consequently, Bahrain's most valuable asset is not economic in nature. Instead, underpinning the survival of the Bahraini economy in many ways is its geographic proximity and strong political ties to Saudi Arabia.

The Banking Sector

Bahrain's banking and finance sector has remained relatively active despite the growth and sophistication of regional banks, especially in areas that

OBUs historically served heavily, like Saudi Arabia. In 2006 the Bahrain Monetary Authority, which had been at the forefront of making Bahrain an important financial center in the 1980s and 90s, was renamed the Central Bank of Bahrain (CBB). The change in name better reflected the duties of the country's financial authorities, which had grown to include the regulation of the hundreds of insurance companies, traditional and Shari'a-compliant banks, brokers, actuaries and adjusters present in Bahrain. The CBB also took on the critical responsibility of issuing the Kingdom of Bahrain's short-term and long-term debt, which came in both traditional and Islamic instruments. Given Bahrain's limited natural resources and chronic budget deficits, these borrowings are increasingly critical. As of early 2018, Bahrain's debt to GDP ratio was nearing 90%.[1] Due the country's prolonged deficit, the island Kingdom has repeatedly turned to its larger, more liquid neighbors, namely Saudi, Kuwait and the UAE, for un-written but implied financial assistance guarantees. Without these potential assurances, Bahrain would be unable to attract enough international investors to the sovereign debt it must issue to remain solvent. This dynamic was clearly at play in the summer of 2018 when Bahrain's dinar recovered from 17-year lows and its bonds rebounded just hours after the three Gulf peers pledged aid to Bahrain.[2] This dynamic is also not new, in fact, in 2011, during reported capital flight amidst popular protests, Gulf peers stepped in with a US$10 billion aid package to shore up Bahrain's domestic economy.[3] The highly regarded technocrat Mr. Rasheed Mohammed Al Maraj, who has been the CBB Governor since its founding, will likely have to continue dealing with these debt issues considering the difficulty Bahrain has had passing tax and spending reform.

Al Maraj has overseen some considerable regulatory changes though. In the evolution of the BMA into the CBB, the system of OBUs was replaced by the new category of 'wholesale banks.' The new name represented much more than a mere change in etiquette. The new 'wholesale banks' included investment banks and investment companies. They were now allowed to work with Bahraini residents and were regulated using the same criteria as the local banks. The only restrictions were that, in their dealing with Bahrainis, they had a minimum transaction amount of US$250,000. In other words, wholesale banks in Bahrain are exactly what they are labeled as, financial institutions offering services ranging from real estate to international trade finance to large account holders across the entire Gulf region, all while remaining under the relative purview of the CBB and not crowding out local retail banks.

All of this said, the Bahraini banking sector is still relatively small. In 2018, total banking assets held in the retail and wholesale space averaged around US$190 billion held across 102 institutions, of which twenty-nine were retail banks and seventy-three were wholesale banks. This sum does not include the seventeen foreign banks which keep representative offices in Bahrain. Of the twenty-nine retail banks, thirteen are locally incorporated banks and sixteen are branches of foreign banks, including Standard Chartered and HSBC. The wholesale banks held the bulk of these assets, with about US$104 billion in total assets in early 2018, while retail banks held roughly US$84 billion. The number of institutions also includes twenty-three Islamic banks with total assets of US$27 billion.[4] To put Bahraini banking sector's size into perspective, Kuwait's NBK, with total assets of around US$80 billion, is as large as all of Bahrain's local retail banks combined, Saudi's National Commercial Bank, with total assets of around US$120 billion, is larger than all of Bahrain's wholesale banks combined, and North Carolina-based Branch Banking and Trust Company (BBTC), with total consolidated assets of just under US$215 billion is larger than Bahrain's entire banking sector, including Islamic banks.[5] In other words, the entire Bahrain market is smaller than the twelfth largest US bank by assets. Further underlining the diminished size and role of the Bahraini banking sector, at US$104 billion, total assets of wholesale banks are barely higher in absolute terms than they were in the mid-1980s, when they hovered around US$100 billion, or the early 1990s, when they had fallen to US$85 billion, and are dwarfed when making the comparison in inflation-adjusted terms, which takes assets in the 1980s and 1990s to around US$195 billion and US$150 billion in 2018 dollars, respectively.

One area in which the Bahraini financial industry has excelled is in hiring and training of local talent, regardless of origin or religion. The sector's employment is predominantly made up of Bahraini nationals, who account for 65% of its total workforce, vastly above levels in other sectors.[6] This heavy role of Bahraini locals can largely be credited to the Bahrain Institute of Banking and Finance, which, established in 1981 by the Bahraini government and affiliated with the BMA and now CBB, has worked with the banking community to establish effective education for Bahraini natives seeking employment in the financial sector.

While the wholesale banks have recently seen their mandate expanded, in practice they are not new. In fact, Bahrain's wholesale banking community is home to one of the region's most successful financial institutions, Investcorp Bank BSC. Investcorp was founded in 1982 under the leadership of Mr. Namir Kirdar. At the time, Mr. Kirdar worked in Bahrain as the Vice President of Chase Manhattan Bank in charge of marketing and general management across the Gulf. Based out of Dubai, Kirdar saw that there was large demand amongst wealthy merchants for investment opportunities akin to what is today considered private equity, a practice that traditional commercial banks operating in the region were unable to satisfy at the time. Capitalizing on this, he brought together a small group of investors that read like a who's who of the Gulf's investment community, obtained an offshore banking license in Bahrain, and hired the brightest minds from Chase, Citibank and other large Western institutions. The group of initial investors provided US$100 million in initial capital in two US$50 million tranches, one in 1982 and the other in 1986. Investcorp would use this capital to make itself a self-described "bridge between surplus funds in the Gulf region and alternative investment opportunities on both sides of the Atlantic."[7] It only took a few years for Kirdar to become the most reliable investment banker in the region.

Investcorp understood immediately that to attract capital from the region, one had to offer investments in well-known companies with brand names respected across the Gulf. With this in mind, among Mr. Kirdar's first investments was the 1984 purchase of Tiffany & Co., the famous American jewelry company. Investcorp invested directly in the company, raising the money through a separate fund managed by Investcorp which then took controlling interest in the jeweler. Investcorp made very substantial fees from the fund as well as from its investment in the company. It was able to hire the right management, reorganize the company and resell a few years later at a substantial profit for itself and its investors. The purchase of this famous brand put Investcorp on the map. It was quickly followed by the purchase of Gucci, perhaps the most famous brand in Italy at that time. Later on, Investcorp arranged for the takeover of Saks Fifth Avenue. Once on the radar of Gulf investors, Investcorp could capitalize on its international linkages to package funds for investment into industrial and technical companies in the US and Western Europe. It also established real estate portfolios, which it could also sell to investors in the Gulf. During the first decade of operations, the bank completed over forty deals in the United States and Europe with a total value of nearly US$5 billion.[8] Investcorp immediately generated money on the loans it made in the acquisition process but made the bulk of its profits through the fees on the sale and management of the funds.

Just as Investcorp recognized that brand recognition was a key factor in attracting Gulf investments, it also understood the need to cultivate its own brand, one of subtle but solid wealth. For instance, all its offices in the world were designed by the same firm, using similar colors and wood paneling and all the board members were chosen on the basis of their reputation and included scions of the Gulf's most prominent trading families. Mr. Kirdar had an excellent knowledge of the US investment markets and with the help of some of the best tax lawyers structured the bank's deals in the US so that foreign investors, such as those in the Gulf, could benefit from the investments without tax liabilities. For example, the major US investments were marketed from New York by Investcorp's large operations on Park Avenue, but no investment decisions were made there. Instead, they went to Bahrain for full analysis and investment decision. Once finalized, the deal was financed through bonds on which no US tax on interest would be levied.

The bank's financing structures were complex, but were all above board and publicly disclosed. The same went for Investcorp's ownership structure. Mr. Kirdar established the bank in Bahrain and floated part of the bank's shares on the Bahrain Bourse, but ensured the bank's employees, especially the senior officers, would be able to control and benefit from the company's operations. To this day, voting at Investcorp is controlled by the Investcorp Employee Share Ownership Program (ISOP), through a structure of holding companies in fiscal paradises, which, while complex, is fully disclosed in its publicly available annual report. The ISOP guarantees that no less than 144 key employees past and present work and remain faithful to the company.

After thirty-five years at the helm of the company, Mr. Kirdar stepped down from his post as Chairman in 2017, handing the chairmanship to his long-time partner H.E Mohammed Bin Mahfoodh Al Ardhi of Omani descent. Investcorp continues to grow and invest in increasingly sophisticated products, including a hedge fund. Having started with US$100 million in 1982, it has assets under management of nearly US$22 billion as of 2017.[9] In sum, Investcorp has been, and still is, the most successful investment bank in the region, and certainly the one closest in form and function to heavy hitting Western institutions. It is the only Gulf financial institution to successfully operate at the crossroads of private equity, fund management and traditional investment banking, an accomplishment that has been aided by Bahrain's regulatory environment. In fact, Investcorp has domiciled some of its investment funds in Bahrain purposefully so as to benefit from a regulatory regime that allows it to "structure, more easily and rapidly, joint ventures in the Gulf region," not to mention the aforementioned tax incentives.[10] That said, its home country may also be a prime factor in Investcorp's low ratings by Moody's and Fitch, both of which remain below investment grade despite the institution proving consistently profitable and holding relatively low leverage compared to its regional peers. Unfortunately, it is probably being impacted by the fact that its home country, Bahrain, is itself rated below investment grade in light of its unsustainable debt levels, unresolved sociopolitical tensions and relative lack of natural resources.

The Capital Markets

Like the banking sector, the Bahrain capital market is quite small. The official exchange, the Bahrain Bourse, hosts only forty-three firms, down from just over fifty in 2008. As of 2017 the total market capitalization of these forty-three firms stood at roughly US$21 billion, up slightly from US$20 billion in 2008, but still paltry compared to Saudi Tadawul's US$500 billion-plus capitalization or even the US$90 billion Kuwait Bourse.[11] While some say that the country's small capital market derives from Bahrain's small size, this relationship has not always been foretold. In the last part of the 20th century, when the region's financial services were very poor, Bahrain had, and eventually lost, the opportunity to become a regional financial hub. At the time, it focused on developing an offshore regulatory haven that would attract commercial banks who could provide for the immediate needs of companies, contractors and investors seeking financial intermediation during the regional oil boom. As discussed in Chapter 1, during this period, it was very difficult to establish share-issuing corporations in any of the GCC states. Most share-issuing corporations at the time were closely government-related and hence not encouraged to obtain capital from non-local investors, and certainly not from non-GCC members. It was in this void that Bahrain had the opportunity to develop a truly free regional capital market, one that capitalized on the country's relatively simple incorporation process. Yet, Bahrain took very limited action in building on these advantages, waiting until the late 1980s to even establish an official exchange, and even then, doing so without the technological sophistication necessary to attract foreign capital.

For its part, Dubai tried to capitalize on this opportunity by establishing a regional market through the DIFC. Yet, despite its sophisticated trading platforms and extensive legal structure, it did not succeed. Had Bahrain been able to establish a trading platform similar to that of Dubai, which was modeled on NASDAQ, it may have been able to succeed where Dubai failed. This is bolstered by the fact that Bahrain's economy has historically had the general support of Saudi Arabia, or at the very least, has not been impeded by authorities in Riyadh as markets in Dubai have. Perhaps what muted Bahrain's efforts at developing a regional capital market was the major failure of the Souk Al Manakh in Kuwait. It does appear that the US$100 billion scandal that shook Kuwait to its foundation also shocked Bahraini authorities. Many of the firms traded on the Souk Al Manakh were technically Bahraini corporations, mostly banks. The local Bahraini authorities were somewhat hoodwinked by fast playing, heavy hitters from Kuwait. When some of the banks created specifically for the Souk Al Manakh went bankrupt, like Kuwait Asia Bank, Bahrain's name as a capital market was sullied. Even though some of the managers of these banks paid for their errors with lengthy jail sentences, Bahrain's financial reputation did not recover for many years. Of course, time erases wounds, but unfortunately, time also erased the opportunity. In the 1990s and the early part of the 21st century, the industrialization of Saudi Arabia in particular required large amounts of capital which could have been raised on a Bahraini capital market. But, by then, the Saudi Tadawul was established and properly regulated, thus eliminating the need for an external exchange. Today, whatever surplus capital is available in Bahrain for regional investments would most likely be invested in Saudi Arabia. This goes for the Gulf more broadly, not only Bahrain. Certainly, Saudis will invest on the Saudi Tadawul first, before they invest in Bahrain. The same can be said for the UAE investors. Ultimately, there is no room for a capital market platform in each of the GCC countries. Had the markets in Bahrain or Dubai been successfully established in the 1990s, they may have prevented the Tadawul from holding the mantel as the region's primary exchange.

Islamic Financial Regulation: A New Niche?

To fill the space left by the decline in offshore banking, over the last two decades Bahrain's financial markets have increasingly focused on developing a space for offshore Shari'a-compliant institutions. Like Bahrain's identification of the need for OBUs in the 1970s, toward the end of the 20th century, there existed a need for a unified Islamic banking regulatory structure across the region in order to catalyze the sector's development and credibility. In the early days of Islamic banking in the Gulf, banks found it difficult to establish religious credibility because their policies and controls were defined and approved internally, opposed to sector-wide. The actual definition for what could be construed as profit sharing, and therefore Shari'a compliant, versus interest-taking, which is not Shari'a compliant, was hotly debated; a dynamic that in the eyes of many made the very of notion of Islamic banking unreliable. Furthermore, each bank's respective Shari'a boards included Sunni legal scholars that often did not have substantive background in finance and business, which chipped at the practice's credibility in the eyes of financial professionals. In fact, there were so few of credible scholars that some ended up being part of numerous boards. The lack of established practice led many of these boards to cast aside any notion of establishing a unified jurisprudence, instead favoring opinions of their own boards, regardless of what other scholars and boards had accepted.

Recognizing this gap in credibility and jurisprudence, Bahrain looked to establish credible structures to advise and regulate Islamic financial institutions (IFIs). The first significant milestone in this effort was the founding of the Auditing and Accounting Organization for Islamic Financial Institutions (AAIOFI). The organization was established in 1991 by The Islamic Development Bank of Jeddah—an international Islamic institution modeled around the World Bank—Dallah Al Baraka, Faisal Group (Dar Al Maal Al Islami), Al Rajhi Banking & Investment Corporation and Kuwait Finance House. The AAOIFI was registered as not-for-profit in Bahrain and provided a space for Islamic banks to develop a standardized set of credible and consistent regulations, which Islamic banks could follow and which other institutions, including the Central Bank of Bahrain (CBB) could use to evaluate and regulate Islamic financial institutions. Most scholars argue that these standards were, and continue to be, critical to the development of IFIs. Equally important, AAIOFI also took on a proactive educational role, providing research and education certificates on the intricacies of Islamic banking and Shari'a-compliant financial instruments. In its efforts to establish universal standards for the foundational aspects of Shari'a-compliant finance, AAOIFI has integrated the opinions from scholars and Islamic finance experts from across the Islamic world. It has its own Shari'a board consisting of twenty scholars from Malaysia, Saudi Arabia, Turkey, Pakistan and the UAE, amongst others, and has numerous committees that review the statutes, regulations and opinions on financial activities ranging from debit cards to various Shari'a-compliant loans.[12] By encouraging the development of the AAOIFI, Bahraini financial authorities were able to bring common ground to all the banks. Of course, the AAIOFI's rules and suggested practices are not necessarily followed everywhere. For example, only a small set of countries other than Bahrain have made AAOIFI standards compulsory. As of 2018, these countries were Jordan, Qatar, Syria, Sudan and Oman.[13] While research shows that there has been industry interest in applying AAOIFI standards in Saudi Arabia for as long as a decade, the standard are not actively used by most Saudi IFIs.[14] In fact, it was not until 2017 that the Saudi Arabian Monetary Authority officially joined the Islamic banking standards institution. SAMA has not expanded on whether it planned to make AAOIFI standards enforceable or if it would adopt all or some of them.[15] Nevertheless, the AAOIFI has provided a welcomed set of standards to a growing financial industry and is most likely a factor in why Bahrain has had success in welcoming numerous large IFIs.

One area of Islamic finance that Bahrain hoped to capitalize on was the growth of the sukuk market, sometimes referred to as Islamic bonds. These instruments effectively acted as fixed income, Shari'a-compliant investment certificates. In Western markets, bonds are predominantly used by sovereigns and corporations to borrow for lengthy tenors. In order to remain Shari'a compliant, sukuk often become quite legally cumbersome. Once accomplished, a large company or sovereign would be able to issue sukuk that pays a coupon comparable to LIBOR plus margin, just as a traditional bond would. However, this coupon is deemed to be profit sharing rather than interest bearing.

The beauty of the sukuk was that banks, states or large corporations could for the first time issue Shari'a-compliant long-term paper, which was not normally available to them in regional markets. So not only did the sukuk offer convenient durations to match the cash flow of long-term projects, but it was also religiously acceptable. Sukuk rapidly became a favorite of borrowers and today most large facilities for industrial projects in the region include a portion of Shari'a-compliant sukuk. The sukuk were structured in such a way that they could be used by borrowers in the same facilities with traditional financial instruments. Most of the syndicated borrowing facilities in the Gulf nowadays include a Shari'a-compliant portion of debt, which is shared by Islamic banks as well traditional foreign lenders and is reflected in the facilities' prospectuses written by the various accounting firms and consultants and subject to inter-creditor agreements signed by all parties, regardless of whether they are Shari'a compliant or not.

Throughout the late 1990s and especially by the turn of the century, Shari'a-compliant instruments, especially sukuk, became increasingly important to regional economic growth. The people of the region, through the assurance of institutions like the AAOIFI and the CBB, had grown comfortable with the tenets of Islamic banking. During this period, Saudi Arabia was still reluctant to embrace IFIs. This gave Bahrain an opportunity to provide this service to the biggest financial market in the region. A number of banks were developed in Bahrain solely to provide Shari'a-compliant services to the Kingdom next door. However, Saudi Arabia, like the rest of the region, came to accept and embrace Islamic finance, in turn making Bahrain-based offshore IFIs less attractive to Gulf clients, who could find similar services directly in the Kingdom.

While Bahrain saw itself as playing a key role in the region's embrace of Islamic banking, and thus a natural home for IFIs and a leader for sukuk offerings, it has been eclipsed in sheer volume of sukuk issuance by the UAE, which is the regional base for the world's leading financial advisors, consultants and lawyers. This financial ecosystem has allowed the UAE, more specifically Dubai, to host over a third of all global sukuk issuance in the last decade. That said, Bahrain still punches above its weight, hosting over 5% of global sukuk issuance between 2001 and 2016, more than Turkey's share, and on par with Indonesia and Qatar.[16]

While Bahrain may not lead in volume of issuance, it has remained a leader in innovation. In 2001, Bahrain became the first Gulf country to offer a sovereign sukuk, a practice that has become widespread in the Gulf, and in 2005 became home to the only IFI rating agency, the Islamic International Rating Agency (IIRA). The first secondary market for short-term sukuk, the Liquidity Management Center (LMC), also calls Bahrain home. Established in 2002, the LMC provides a market for short-term Shari'a-compliant treasury instruments for Islamic banks, helping to boost the liquidity and creating additional investment opportunities for IFIs and conventional banks alike. This innovative and inclusive approach to finance has paid off. Bahrain has the largest concentration of IFIs in the GCC region, including Islamic banks, Takaful and Re-Takaful firms. These IFIs have played a large role in maintaining the strength of Bahrain's financial sector as other avenues for profit were closed either by technological advancement or liberalization in nearby markets. As a testament to this, in 2016, the financial services sector was the single largest non-oil contributor to the Bahraini economy, accounting for 16.5% of real GDP.[17]

During the 1990s, Bahrain was seen as a regional leader in offshore Islamic finance, and many believed that its role in the space would only grow with time.[18] In some ways it has. From a regulatory and innovation perspective, Bahrain has often led the pack. Its numerous IFI-based regulatory and financial services firms are a testament to this. Yet, this role continues to be constrained by size of the island's financial markets. Moving forward, growth in stature, if not size, will be dependent on Bahrain's ability to provide innovative solutions to the sector's challenges, and not necessarily on hosting the financial activity itself.

Bahrain's Unique Natural Resource

Before the oil era, Bahrain was best known for being the center of the region's blossoming pearling trade, with numerous boats plying the coastal oyster beds and frequenting the island nation's vibrant trading post. In a foreshadowing of Bahrain's luck, the pearl market crashed in the 1920s due to unsustainable supply growth fueled by Japanese Mikimoto cultured pearls, significantly depreciating the value of Bahrain's main source of income. Fortunately, oil was discovered in 1932, providing a new source of wealth for the country. Nevertheless, Bahrain was never a large oil producer, with

Bahrain's main onshore field, the Awali field, producing a peak of 79,000 b/d in 1971. Production steadily declined through the turn of the century, falling as low as 35,000 b/d in 2011, but has risen to an average of 45,000 b/d through the use of enhanced oil recovery techniques.[19] Due to these small volumes, Bahrain has never been a member of OPEC. OPEC's smallest producers, Equatorial Guinea and Gabon, produced 135,000 and 200,000 b/d, respectively, in 2017, while Saudi Arabia produced well over 9 million b/d.[20] Oman is the only other GCC state not a member of OPEC. Luckily for the then Emirate, now Kingdom, of Bahrain, in 1972 Saudi Arabia began sharing production from a large offshore Abu Sa'fah field located in Saudi waters a few miles north of Bahrain. This field currently produces around 320,000 b/d and is operated by Saudi Aramco, although the sale of Bahrain's share of production, roughly 160,000 b/d, is handled by the Bahrain Petroleum Company (Bapco). Bahrain also receives from Saudi Arabia 230,000 b/d of crude which comes by pipeline from Abqaiq in Saudi Arabia. This imported oil, plus production from Awali, is sent to Bapco's Sitra refinery, which sells petroleum products locally and abroad. The refinery's largest client is the US Navy's 5th fleet, which is based in Bahrain.[21]

The Awali field also provides about 2.1 bcf/d of dry and associated natural gas production, which Bahrain uses for water desalination, power generation and industrial feedstock. The island Kingdom's primary industrial assets are state owned and, outside of the aforementioned refinery, include the 850,000 t/y aluminum plant, ALBA. It is the fourth largest aluminum plant in the world, and its size and technology were market-leading when it was founded in 1968. This size does come with costs though. ALBA consumes nearly 20% of locally produced natural gas in order to generate the electricity needed for smelting imported alumina. This level of consumption is not opportune as Bahrain's gas reserves are declining very rapidly, with a risk of complete depletion within a few years. This is a major problem for Bahrain, which is entirely dependent on natural gas for desalination and electricity generation. In attempts to remedy the matter, Bahrain is building an 800 mmcf/d floating LNG import terminal although it is only a few miles from Qatar's North Dome gas field, the largest in the world. The terminal is expected to be operational before the end of 2018, with Bahrain taking out a US$740 million loan to finance the project. The LNG import terminal may not be necessary for long with Bahrain announcing in 2018 the discovery of some 80 billion barrels of oil and 13.7tcf of gas in place.[22] However, these reserves are in tight unconventional formations offshore between Bahrain and the Saudi coast. Since offshore tight gas production would be an industry first, commercial production viability, total recoverable reserves and production timeline remain a guessing game at best. In fact, serious doubts remain on whether these assets will ever actually prove economically transformative as Bahrain hopes.

Until more significant developments arise from the Bahrain's new find, its economic outlook will continue to be tied to the aforementioned resources.

Whereas the Bapco refinery's output does provide significant income, Bahrain's largest source of energy revenue comes from the oil it receives from the Abu Sa'fah field. Over the last decade, oil and gas earnings have made up between 70% and 90% of government revenue, and of this, as much as 70% derives from Abu Sa'fah's production. The arrangement stems from a 1958 maritime border agreement that gave oil rights to Saudi Arabia in exchange for Bahrain receiving half the net revenues from production. Repeatedly since the agreement, Saudi Arabia has provided Bahrain with more than its 50% share, giving the island country 100% of the revenues between 1996 and 2004 and continuing to give it payments in 1986 despite Abu Sa'fah being mothballed due to low oil prices. While the benefit to Saudi Arabia is not immediately clear, Saudi's largesse does have strategic purpose. Bahrain sits within throwing distance of critical Saudi oil infrastructure, including the Ras Tanura export terminal and the Abqaiq processing facility. If any foreign or hostile entity were to control Bahrain, it would create an intolerable threat to Saudi's crown jewels. In the eyes of Saudi Arabia, this risk is not unfounded. Iran has historically made claims on Bahrain, maintaining that the island was unfairly removed from Iranian sovereignty by Britain in the 19th century.[23] For its part, Bahrain has also voiced concern to US officials about Iranian intentions.[24] These dynamics are further aggravated by domestic sociopolitical tensions between the Sunni monarchy and the majority-Shi'a local population.

Collectively, these factors have led Saudi Arabia, and increasingly the UAE, to prioritize the economic and political stability of the Bahraini Monarchy. In the extensive 2011 popular protests in Bahrain, Saudi Arabia played an important supporting role in putting down widespread popular protests in Bahrain. Economically, Saudi Arabia and its peers positively counter negative credit ratings and support the broader economy by the sharing the Abu Sa'fah field, selling 250,000 b/d of crude oil to the Sitra refinery, extending verbal assurances to creditors, and, from a broader perspective, through the large number of Saudi tourists that frequent the island, many of whom buy real estate.[25] With these factors a seeming constant, it is hard not to conclude that Bahrain's primary natural resource today is its proximity and strong political ties to Saudi Arabia.

Conclusion

In Bahrain, in the 1970s, as seen in the first chapter, employment of locals was a priority and the growth of the banking industry was seen as a good way to service the region's poor financial infrastructure. The growth of the offshore banks was stunning and banking became the major employer in the island. However, with the development of very sophisticated banks in the region and the growth of Dubai as a major service center, the need for an expanded banking industry declined in Bahrain. Today, the country must rely on other sources of employment and income. In many ways, the failure of IFIs to create a more significant source of revenue and employment has left Saudi Arabia and the UAE as the primary sources of support for the Kingdom of Bahrain. This patronage is unlikely to change given the importance of Bahrain's stability to its Arab neighbors. In this sense, even though Saudi Arabia's financial sector is growing by leaps and bounds, Bahrain will always be allowed to offer cross-border services to Saudi's financial sector, thus keeping one avenue of financial intermediation open in perpetuity albeit one of diminishing importance. A byproduct of this relationship, especially in light of Saudi Arabia's critical impact on Bahrain's perceived credit worthiness, is that the island nation has abdicated its foreign policy to its more powerful Arab brothers. This has been apparent in the blockading of Qatar, of which Bahrain is the only GCC state to participate besides Saudi Arabia and the UAE. In the case that Bahrain's recent oil and gas discoveries do materialize, the relationship may change substantially. Saudi Arabia's own gas supply issues are not insignificant and a more equitable two-way relationship may develop. Yet, this scenario is beyond reputable forecast, and the more likely scenario is that Bahrain, effectively missing its chance at developing into the region's primary financial hub, will remain in the shadow of its regional peers, hindered by the mistakes of financial crises from decades past.

Notes

1. International Monetary Fund, "IMF Staff Completes 2018 Article IV Mission to Bahrain," *Press Release* no. 18/201, May 30, 2018.
2. Reuters Staff, "Bahrain Dinar, Bonds Rebound after GCC Allies Promise to Avert Debt Crisis," *Reuters*, June 27, 2018.
3. Reuters Staff, "Bahrain Central Bank Governor Rasheed Mohammed al-Maraj," *Reuters*, May 24, 2011.
4. Central Bank of Bahrain, *CBB Statistical Bulletin*, April 2018.
5. Federal Reserve, "Insured U.S.-Chartered Commercial Banks That Have Consolidated Assets of $300 Million or More, Ranked by Consolidated Assets," March 31, 2018. Available at www.federalreserve.gov/releases/lbr/current/.
6. Bahrain Banks Association, "Banking in Bahrain," Avaiable at www.banksbahrain.org/banking-in-bahrain/.
7. Investcorp, *Investcorp 2014 Annual Report*, 2014.
8. Kenneth N. Gilpin, "Profile, from Political Prisoner to a Banker for Billionaires," *The New York Times*, May 9, 1993.
9. Moody's Investors Service, "Credit Opinion: Investcorp Bank B.S.C. Annual Update," April 24, 2018.
10. Investcorp, "Investcorp Bahrain Boost," *Press Release*, December 1, 2007. Available at www.tradearabia.com/news/CM_134961.html.
11. Central Bank of Bahrain, *Statistical Bulletin*, February 2018, pp. 41–43.
12. Readers interested in Shari'ah compliant issues should refer to the AAOIFI website (www.aaoifi.org), its publications, conference reports and its handbook of standards.
13. Yosra Mnif Sellami and Marwa Tahari, "Factors Influencing Compliance Level with AAOIFI Financial Accounting Standards by Islamic Banks," *Journal of Applied Accounting Research* 18, no. 1 (2017): 137–159; Accounting and Auditing

Organization for Islamic Finance Institutions, "Adoption of AAOIFI Standards." Available at http://aaoifi.com/adoption-of-aaoifi-standards/?lang=en.

14. Sultan Abdullah Al-Abdullatif, "The Application of the AAOIFI Accounting Standards by the Islamic Banking Sector in Saudi Arabia," (Durham thesis, Durham University, 2007). Available at http://etheses.dur.ac.uk/2594/.
15. Reuters Staff, "Saudi Arabia Joins Islamic Finance Body, Could Boost Cross-Border Deals," *Reuters*, October 22, 2017.
16. Yasuharu Ogino, "Developments of Sukuk (Islamic Bond) Market and Challenges of Japanese Market," *Institute for International Monetary Affairs Newsletter*, January 16. Available at www.iima.or.jp/Docs/newsletter/2018/NL2018No_2_e.pdf.
17. Eckart Woertz, "Bahrain's Economy: Oil Prices, Economic Diversification, Saudi Support, and Political Uncertainties," *Barcelona Center for International Affairs Notes Internacionals* 189 (February 2018).
18. John R. Presley and Rodney Wilson, *Banking in the Arab Gulf*. (London: Macmillan Academic and Professional Ltd, 1991), p. 86.
19. Tatweer Petroleum, "Bahrain Oil Field." Available at http://tatweerpetroleum.com/bahrain-oil-field/.
20. The Organization of Petroleum Exporting Countries, *Annual Report 2017*, 2017, p. 27.
21. "Bahrain Takes $300mn Oil Revenue Hit from Abu Sa'fahh Outage," *Middle East Economic Survey* 61, no. 22 (June 1, 2018).
22. "Bahrain Eyes Unconventional Oil for Economic Reboot," *Middle East Economic Survey* 61, no. 14 (April 6, 2018).
23. Mitchell A. Belfer, "Iranian Claims to Bahrain: From Rhetoric to Interference," *RIPS: Revista de Investigaciones Políticas y Sociológicas* 13, no. 2 (2015).
24. "US Embassy Cables: The Documents. Bahrain," *The Guardian*. Available at www.theguardian.com/world/us-embassy-cables-documents/164906.
25. Saudi Arabia is connected to Bahrain via the 16-mile King Fahd Causeway, which many Saudi citizens use Bahrain in order to escape the moral and cultural strictures of Saudi Arabia. In 2016, 12.2 million visitors crossed the causeway to enter Bahrain, making the tourism sector another major area of Bahrain's economy.

4.2 The Financial Markets of Qatar

Introduction

Five decades ago, there was little in Qatar that financiers and world leaders in New York or London would find of importance. Today, the picture is much different. It owns expansive swaths of prime real estate and corporate equity in the most developed markets the world, is home to the Arab world's largest news network, and will host the World Cup in 2022. This change has overwhelmingly come on the back of one development. As of 2016, Qatar provides the world with a third of its total liquefied natural gas supply (LNG). Indeed, LNG and the related production of Natural Gas Liquids (NGLs) has made the state of Qatar is a very rich country. In an oft repeated metric, the country has the world's largest GDP per capita based on purchasing-power-parity, one well over US$125,000.[1] This largely derives from the fact that it is also a very small country. It has 2.6 million inhabitants, of which only 300,000 are citizens, on a territory smaller than Connecticut.

With these factors in mind, Qatar's current footprint in global dialogue is significantly outsized. This, though, comes primarily from its space in the energy markets, with the country largely unable to diversify significantly away from its lifeblood—LNG. Away from this, Qatar's financial markets are not as large as those in Saudi Arabia or even Dubai. As global natural gas markets evolve, the large role of LNG puts Qatar in a precarious position, especially given the growing animosity between Qatar and its Arab neighbors.

Qatar's Energy Markets

The wealth of the country is fundamentally rooted in Qatar's natural gas reserves. The third largest in the world, Qatar has used these natural gas reserves to become the largest producer of LNG in the world, producing a third of global LNG supply in 2016. Historically, more than 80% of Qatar's export volumes have been sold to just eight countries, Japan, South Korea, Taiwan, India, China, Spain, the UK and Italy.[2] Qatar also produces around 600,000 b/d of crude oil, which makes it the second smallest oil producer in the GCC, only larger than Bahrain. The production of natural gas and LNG also brings with it an associated 750,000 b/d of natural gas liquids (NGL), like propane and butane, which helps lower the break-even cost of Qatar's LNG production and, combined with the sale of crude, pads the country's financial position. Qatar is the largest producer of NGLs in OPEC and exports about 500,000 b/d of its NGLs, with the rest being used locally in a splitter refinery for use in domestic chemicals production.[3]

Some of the natural gas produced by Qatar is used locally. This domestic use is primarily to produce electricity. However, it is also using the gas to run a steel plant. The plant receives iron ore from places like Australia and reduces the ore into steel by using natural gas. Qatar also has a large ammonia plant, which sees its feedstock transformed into urea, a major fertilizer, for export. Qatar also boasts the largest Gas to Liquid (GTL) plant in the world. GTL takes methane and transforms it into diesel fuel or other basic liquids using the Fisher-Tropp formula. Natural gas is also used domestically to power the Qatalum aluminum plant, a joint venture with Norway's Norsk Hydro, which produces 600,000 t/y.

While these industrial and downstream activities are significant, it is Qatar's LNG industry that is the heart of the Qatari economy. Qatar has eleven LNG plants (called 'trains') which produce 77 million tons of LNG annually. As of 2018, the country is actively pushing forward with significant expansions that would take its total capacity to 100 million t/y, potentially requiring two or three additional trains. The expansion is widely seen as Qatar's effort to show global markets that it intends to continue building its energy industry despite the ongoing embargo by its Gulf neighbors. It is also undoubtedly an effort to defend the country's position in global LNG markets in the face of growing Australian and US LNG exports, the former of which is expected to eclipse Qatar as the largest producer of LNG by the early 2020s. Qatar's expansion is expected to be completed by 2025–2026. Any additional capacity will be aided by Qatar's strategically significant location between Asian and European LNG markets, allowing Qatar to effectively act as a swing supplier between the two regions.[4] Qatar's plans for expansion did appear to push some higher cost producers out of the market, and in rapid fashion. Just weeks after Qatar's expansion announcement, Malaysia's proposed Pacific Northwest LNG terminal in Canada announced it would no longer pursue the project due to market conditions.[5]

All of Qatar's current trains are run in joint ventures with large foreign companies, and future trains are expected to take on the same form. In fact, many companies, including Shell, Total and ExxonMobil, which already operates ten of Qatar's LNG facilities, have expressed interest in being a part of Qatar's expansion, underlining the global interest in Qatar's energy markets despite the ongoing embargo, which is discussed further in this chapter. Qatar is also the primary shareholder in its own LNG shipping company. The company, Nakilat, holds around 15% of the total world LNG shipping capacity through its full or joint-ownership of over sixty vessels, which collectively cost more than US$11 billion.[6] The ships are on charter to Qatargas and RasGas. These companies are responsible for exporting Qatar's various energy products. In an effort to consolidate operations, Qatargas and RasGas were merged in early 2018, with the new unit taking the name of the former. The merger was projected by Qatari officials to produce US$550 million/year of cost savings.[7] These companies are managed according to world standards and therefore have costs in line with that of most other LNG carrier owners.

Long-term LNG prices have traditionally been based on the price of oil. The leading price index used in these long-term contracts in the Far East is the Japanese Crude Cocktail (JCC) in Tokyo, with a ceiling of around US$18/MMBtu and a floor of around US$4/MMBtu. The exact price indexing, ceiling and floors are provided in each contract with the buyers. The contracts are usually for a period calculated to match the loans provided by international lenders. The financing facilities for the LNG plants and the ships are extremely complex and their durations vary from seventeen years for ships, to complex arrangements of loans and bonds, which vary from fourteen to twenty-seven years, for plants. One could assume that on average financing will be for twenty years and thus contracts would be for the same duration. The banks lent on the basis of the expected cash flow of the projects and most loans were secured by the sale of natural gas to a given purchaser, usually a large well reputed Far Eastern buyer, like Tokyo Electric. Recently though, these long-term contracts have come under increasing pressure as purchasers fight for shorter-term contracts not indexed to oil. The effects of this pressure has already been felt, with India's Petronet reworking its 25-year agreement with RasGas in late 2015, cutting the price almost in half.[8]

Another major aspect of these long-term contacts has been destination clauses, which limit the buyers' ability to resell or change the final destination of the purchased cargo. These clauses have been instrumental in assisting Qatar maintain its stronghold on global LNG markets and limiting the growth of a spot, or secondary, market. Since 2016, these clauses have come under increasing pressure, with both Japanese and European Union officials launching official investigations into their legality. It is not unlikely that during the next round of contract negotiations, which for Japan should begin in the early 2020s, these clauses will be omitted.[9]

Trade and the Embargo

As the price of oil increased between 1998 and 2014 from US$12/bbl to US$120/bbl, the price of LNG went from floor to ceiling—all to Qatar's great benefit. On a production of 77 million t/y, this corresponded to an increase in gross income from US$15.6 billion per annum to US$71.8 billion per annum.[10] However, as oil prices declined from their peak in the summer of 2014, LNG prices in China and most of the Far East declined in tandem. In spite of the gyration of the price of oil and the subsequent impact on Qatar's overall income, Qatar has done well, with its gross income from LNG exports growing around 18% year on year to reach US$28 billion in 2017.[11] On the other hand, Qatar has large expenses. It needs to pay a share of the profits to its venture partners. Additionally, a large part of establishing its outsized global footprint has been through a very expensive foreign policy, including large gifts to the Muslim Brotherhood and to various groups in Syria, Lebanon, Yemen and Somalia. These gifts have undoubtedly been in the billions of dollars.

This larger footprint has brought about even more significant and costly problems with Qatar's immediate neighbors. Starting in June 2017, Saudi Arabia, the UAE, Bahrain and Egypt severed all diplomatic and economic ties with Qatar, demanding Qatar curb its diplomatic relations with Iran, cut ties with designated terrorist groups such as the Muslim Brotherhood, shut down the state-funded Al Jazeera news station, and pay reparations for problems allegedly caused by its policies. Qatar responded by saying such demands were an assault on its sovereignty. There has been extensive writing about the political impacts of this embargo, much of which is outside the scope of this work.[12] Inside the scope of this work though are the significant repercussions on trade and finance the embargo has had. The embargo had noted effects on key financial metrics like borrowing rates, with key interbank rates skyrocketing nearly 50% in the months following the embargo. To combat the effects of tighter liquidity and prevent further spikes in borrowing costs, the government dipped into its own reserves to prop up banks and state companies, injecting over US$26 billion into the domestic banking sector in the twelve months following the embargo.[13] While it is not immediately clear where the funds came from, Qatar Central Bank (QCB) data shows that at least US$10 billion was drawn from official foreign reserves in the six months following the embargo.[14] Substantially more was likely drawn from the country's sovereign wealth fund, the Qatar Investment Authority (QIA). While the QIA is secretive, liquidating QIA assets in order to shore up local finances in the wake of the embargo is within the realm of possibilities. This only further exacerbates the difficulty of gauging the SWF's current assets under management. Local Qatari banks have also tapped international markets at record levels in order to shore up their books, borrowing over US$7 billion in the first six months of 2018.

Despite these measures, Qatar's fiscal metrics for 2017, half of which was spent under the embargo, show that Qatar has found ways to survive. QCB data shows that the emirate's budget deficit for 2017, as a percent of GDP, fell by more than a third: from 9.2% in 2016 to 5.8% in 2017. As could be expected, the country also ran a significant trade surplus during this period due to a decline in imports from Saudi Arabia and the UAE, which had both previously been major trade partners. Overall, Qatar ran a trade surplus of US$38 billion in 2017, up 50% on 2016.[15] This surplus has helped Qatar rebuild its foreign reserves, which, including foreign currency deposits, had fallen around US$45 billion in the first half of 2017 to US$35 billion six months later. As of summer 2018, Qatar's foreign reserves were estimated to be back at around US$39 billion, in large part due to the sustained rally in LNG prices starting in late 2017.[16]

The trade surplus was driven primarily by two factors, both of which highlight the complexity of the embargo. Firstly, on the import side, there was a rapid development of new, alternate trade routes. There has been extensive discussion about Turkey, Oman and Iran's respective roles filling the gap created by the embargo, with their combined exports to Qatar jumping a substantive US$400 million year on year to reach US$640 million in Q4 2017.[17] Equally important though was trade with the US, as American exports to Qatar grew by over US$800 million, to reach US$2.1 billion, over this same time horizon. Where imports from Oman, Turkey and Iran made up 8% of total Qatari imports during Q4 2017, the US made up a whopping 22%.[18] In many regards, this underlined the solidification of the US's support for Qatar, despite pressure to do otherwise.

On the export side, the embargo had little to no impact on Qatar LNG exports. The country's key buyers have actually accelerated purchases since the embargo, with China taking a quarterly record of 2.92 million tons in Q1 2018.[19] Some of this was driven by a colder than average winter in 2018 and China's increasing reliance on natural gas for both power generation and space heating. That said, these export figures, as well as import trends, highlight Qatar's ability to successfully navigate the labyrinth the embargo has placed it in.

China has played an outsized role in this successful maneuvering. Where imports from the US to China jumped significantly in Q4 2017, longer-term trends show that this was a bumper quarter for US imports. In juxtaposition, Chinese imports to Qatar have shown steady, consistent growth since the embargo took hold, making China the leading source of imports into Qatar by late 2017, a position it took from the US.[20]

Qatar's burgeoning relationship with China is not new. The latter has grown dependent on Qatari LNG imports, having become one of, if not the, largest buyer of LNG in the world. Qatar recognized the country's importance well before the embargo, opening an offshore yuan center in Doha in 2015 and holding a 'Made in China Exhibition' in the capital annually since 2015.

The importance of China's growing role as an LNG importer cannot be overstated, specifically because Qatar's wealth is fully based on energy sales by state controlled companies, mainly QP, Industries Qatar and RasGas. These companies are managed by a highly professional cadre of Qatari and foreign employees. However, the boards and decision makers are all part of the royal family. In fact, it is interesting to note that the financial markets reflect the strong grip of the Al Thani on the economy. There are ten banks in Qatar, nine of which are chaired by a member of the Al Thani family. Most have numerous Al Thani board members. Similarly, most of the large companies traded on the stock exchange in Qatar are also chaired, and the boards populated, by members of the family and related clans.

Hence, it appears that the financial markets of Qatar are not truly markets but more of a switching center, where the royal family and relations receive the wealth from energy sales and then pass the funds through the financial institutions to firms and people, who de facto become quite dependent on maintaining strong, positive connections with the present leadership.

For visitors who traveled to Qatar in the 1970s and 1980s before the advent of large flows of cash from natural gas, the contrast on who controls the economy and the financial structure of the country is striking. In the second half of the 20th century, especially after Qatar's independence in 1971, economic power was with a few very powerful merchant families. Today the merchants still do well for themselves through the system of agencies, which guarantees them some income on imports of goods. However, the control of money flows within the country, as well as overseas investments, is almost exclusively held by the royal family and their affiliates.

The Banking Sector

There are ten banks in Qatar, five of which control over US$7 billion in assets each. However, one bank, the Qatar National Bank (QNB) is dominant. It controls more assets, loans and deposits than all the other banks put together. The QNB is owned 50% by the QIA, with the balance owned by the public. The public can buy and sell these shares on the Qatar stock exchange.

QNB is in fact the largest bank in the Middle East with deposits of over US$157 billion.[21] It has six affiliates and fifteen branches from Western Europe to Africa and the Far East. These units support Qatari investments overseas, as well as foreign firms involved in Qatar. QNB is the only bank not chaired by an Al Thani. The Chairman of the Board is the Minister of Finance, HE Ali Sharif Al Emadi, who is also a board member of the QIA. The other traditional banks are the Commercial Bank of Qatar, the Doha Bank and Al Ahli Bank. Smaller banks are the Al Khaliji Bank, and the International Bank of Qatar. Qatar also has three Shari'a-compliant banks, the Qatar Islamic Bank, Masraf Al Rayan and QIIB. All the banks are traded on the stock exchange. Collectively, these banks hold around US$220 billion in total deposits and US$350 billion in total assets, which while considerable, still makes the assets of Qatar's entire banking sector less than half the size of Scotiabank's assets and smaller than the market cap of the Saudi stock exchange.[22]

Along with these domestic banks, there are four active foreign banks in Qatar: HSBC and Standard Chartered, as could be expected in a former British protectorate, with the other two being UBL Bank, a Pakistani entity which deals primarily with the large number of Pakistani workers in Qatar, and Mashreq Bank, a branch of the Dubai's well-known Mashreq Bank, which is controlled by the Al Ghurair family, one of the best known merchant families in the Gulf.

The Capital Markets

The Qatar Stock Exchange (QSE) has a total capitalization of US$130 billion and offers a platform to trade forty-five companies, a large number considering Qatar's small size. The largest companies traded on the QSE are state controlled as the state uses the stock market to provide the broader Qatari population with a stake in the county's industrialization efforts.

For example, Qatar Petroleum (QP) merged three petrochemical companies it controlled under the umbrella of a holding company called Mesaieed Petrochemical Company (MPC). Mesaieed was established in 2013, and in 2014 merged the three chemical companies: Q-Chem I, Q-Chem II and Qatar Vinyl Company (QVC). Q-Chem I & II produces olefins, mainly ethylene, polyolefins and normal alfa olefins, while QVC produces caustic soda, ethylene dichloride and vinyl chlorine monomers and hydrochloric acid.[23] QP floated 26% of the shares of MPC to the public at large. Qataris were asked to request an allocation of shares. The flotation was extremely successful, five times oversold, and most requests had to be curtailed to satisfy the demand. Notably, despite curtailment, small requests for less than 750 shares were fully fulfilled. These smaller requests were put in primarily by individual Qatari citizens, as opposed to larger brokerages or investment companies, which tend to request significantly more shares. This underlined the state's intent to ensure that the broader population was given an opportunity to partake in the Qatar's growing wealth and is a similar strategy utilized elsewhere in the region, most famously by Saudi Arabia in its public offering of companies like SABIC. Ultimately, the MPC deal was closed with 199,000 shareholders, with about two-thirds of the Qatari population receiving shares in the company.

By the same token, QP regrouped four of the industrial firms it controlled into one firm called Industries Qatar (IQ). The four companies are very large downstream industries. QAFAC (Qatar Fuel Additive Co.), which makes and exports MTBE in a joint venture with LCI of Taiwan. QAPCO (Qatar Petrochemical Co.), which makes LDPE in JV with Total of France and QAFCO (Qatar Fertilizer Co.), a JV with the Norwegian fertilizer company which makes and exports urea and STEEL, which makes steel from imported iron ore. IQ is controlled 51% by QP and 49% by the public. As with MPC, IQ brings the benefits of industrialization to the public, but keeps the control of the companies with the state.

The exchange provides a detailed list of the companies that can be traded, but there are strict limitations on ownership of specific companies. For example, no one investor can legally hold more than 2% of either IQ or MPC, while no one investor can hold more than 5% of the Qatar National Bank. Of course these limits do not apply to the state, but indicates that the state wants to remain the controlling entity, while still sharing the benefits of the public firms with as many citizens as possible.

Unlike the banks, which are mostly chaired by Al Thani family members, the two industrial holding companies have a board and chairperson composed of non-royals. Hence, like in Saudi Arabia, the highly technical sector remains under the control of engineers and technocrats, thereby ensuring the quality and safety of production, which, indeed, is highly technical and difficult to successfully maintain.

There are other large notable companies whose shares are listed as well, including Oredoo the telecommunications company of Qatar, which has affiliates in Kuwait and Oman. It also trades shares of Nakilat, the LNG transport company, and Mannai Corp., a diversified trading company with sales of about US$1 billion. The company is chaired by an Al Thani, but the Vice Chairman is a member of the Al Mannai family, one of the main trading families of Qatar.

The Qatar Investment Authority

The QIA is the sovereign wealth fund of Qatar. Like most SWFs, it seeks to protect and grow the assets of its country. While the fund invests worldwide, it is by far one of the least transparent SWFs. It provides no information to the public at large, which naturally fuels speculation on the fund's value. What is quite sure is that the QIA owns Harrod's of London, very large pieces of real estate in New York, London, Paris, Spain, Hong Kong, and resorts in Italy. It owns 12.9% of the Agricultural Bank of China, a US$15 billion asset, and 19.5% of Rosneft of Russia. It owns large agricultural and food companies in Australia. It owns large chunks of Volkswagen of Germany, valued at Euro 10.6 billion in 2015. Many of these investments come through Qatar Holding which is controlled by QIA. In turn the QIA and Qatar Holdings own numerous holding companies in Cayman Islands and Luxembourg.

Yet, the overall secrecy of the fund makes computing the value of QIA's assets extremely difficult for any outsider. Indeed, reports in the press and various think tanks that estimate the QIA has assets of around US$350 billion may be true, but are just as likely to be quite off.[24] This discrepancy derives from a number of factors. Firstly, most of the QIA's investments are highly illiquid, including property and stakes in large companies, whose return remain secret and whose ability to divest is severely limited. QIA has also invested heavily within Qatar and many of these investments cannot be sold given the need to keep them within the control of the state. Additionally, one does not know how much leverage is incurred in each of the purchases or whether they were acquired for cash. Certainly, the financial engineering behind each of the purchases includes debt if only to limit taxes, especially in the case of real estate transactions outside the Gulf. However, this debt can come from holding companies that take QIA's funds through fiscal paradises and numerous nominees and trustees. Finally, as previously mentioned, Qatar's embargo by its neighbors has surely led to a significant drawdown in the SWF's assets. After all, these assets are intended for the prosperity of the country, and the embargo intends to dim that prosperity. Hence, in the absence of transparent reports, any estimate of QIA holdings is purely speculative.

It is somewhat unclear why the QIA seeks to hide its worth from the world and from its own people. After all, the money invested by QIA must have originated from the sale of oil and natural gas, which is the property of the state and therefore of the people of Qatar. On the other hand, providing detailed information to the citizens could open a Pandora's box of demands from the people and perhaps extensive criticism of how the money is managed.

Conclusion

It is hard not to see how Qatar is increasingly hemmed in from all sides. Regionally, it is literally embargoed by nearly all of its immediate neighbors. Globally, LNG markets, the same ones that have acted as the country's lifeblood for decades, are shifting in a manner that undercut Qatar's traditional business model. Qatar is fighting back though. In the face of the blockade, Qatar's energy exports were largely unchanged. Indeed, Qatari export revenues registered an annual increase of 18%, reaching US$67 billion in 2017, with natural gas exports contributing US$28 billion to total export receipts. Responding to tighter LNG dynamics, RasGas and QatarGas's merger was a clear effort at financial consolidation, and recently signed long-term contracts with Pakistan and Bangladesh, and the willingness to revise existing contracts with major players like PetroChina and Petronet, underline Qatar's agility. And when all else fails, Qatar has leaned on its low production costs, expansive infrastructure and strategic location to efficiently expand its production capacity in order to squeeze out other high cost producers.

This is not the first time Qatar has been able to hold its market position in light of trying conditions. In the wake of the 2009 financial crises, LNG demand in many of Qatar's European and American markets contracted, and was shortly followed by the US-shale boom, which further decimated Qatar's contracted volumes. Qatar acted nimbly though, shifting focus toward Asian markets, which it now dominates. Looking forward, Qatar will likely display more of this responsive positioning. Despite all this, while Qatar's financial strength and natural resources may be substantial, unless it creates some semblance of diversification, it will always struggle with an overdependence on a single revenue stream.

Notes

1. International Monetary Fund, *World Economic Outlook Database*, 2016.
2. Bassam Fattouh and Howard Rogers, "A More Flexible Future for Qatar's LNG," *About Energy*, March 1, 2018.
3. "Opec Members Unrestrained in Condensate Growth," *Middle East Economic Survey* 61, no. 16 (April 20, 2018).

4. Fattouh and Rogers, "A More Flexible Future for Qatar's LNG."
5. Natalie Obiko Pearson, Ryan Collins and Tim Loh, "A Worldwide Gas Glut Claims $27 Billion Victim in Canada," *Bloomberg*, July 26, 2017.
6. Nakilat, "Vessel Support Unit," Available at www.nakilat.com.qa/Page/Vessel.
7. "Qatar Petroleum Presses Ahead with Shakeup," *Middle East Economic Survey* 61, no. 1 (January 5, 2018).
8. Debjit Chakraborty and Rajesh Kumar Singh, "RasGas, Petronet Revise LNG Contract to Lower Indian Prices," *Bloomberg*, December 31, 2015.
9. Graham Vinter, Jeremy Wilson, William Park, Ike Morinaga and Peter Camesasca, "European Commission Launches New Antitrust Investigation into LNG Destination Clauses," *Inside Energy and Environment* (June 26, 2018). Available at https://www.insideenergyandenvironment.com/2018/06/european-commission-launches-new-antitrust-investigation-into-lng-destination-clauses/.
10. "Qatar Boosts 2013–14 Budget Expenditure," *Middle East Economic Survey* 56, no. 14 (April 5, 2013).
11. "Qatar Boosts Earnings," *Middle East Economic Survey* 61, no. 20 (May 18, 2018).
12. Kristian Ulrichsen, "How Qatar Weathered the Gulf Crisis," *Foreign Affairs*, June 11, 2018. Available at https://www.foreignaffairs.com/articles/middle-east/2018-06-11/how-qatar-weathered-gulf-crisis.
13. Arif Sharif, "The $26 Billion Reason Why Qatari Banks Are Enduring Embargo," *Bloomberg*, June 3, 2018.
14. Qatar Central Bank, *Monthly Statistics*, April 2018.
15. "Qatar Diversifies Trade Links Post-Embargo," *Middle East Economic Survey* 61, no. 21 (May 25, 2018).
16. Debasish Roy Chowdhury, "China a Pillar of Strength in Qatar's Fightback Against Arab Blockade," *South China Morning Post*, June 9, 2018.
17. Aya Batrawy, "Turkey, Iran Help Wealthy Qatar Thrive, 1 Year into Blockade," *Associated Press*, June 5, 2018; "Qatar Diversifies Trade Links Post-Embargo."
18. "Qatar Diversifies Trade Links Post-Embargo."
19. Ibid.
20. Batrawy, "Turkey, Iran Help Wealthy Qatar Thrive, 1 Year into Blockade."
21. Qatar National Bank, *Annual Report 2017*, 2017, p. 9.
22. Qatar Central Bank, *Monthly Statistics*, April 2018.
23. Normal Alfa Olefins used extensively among as polyethylene co-monomers, plasticizers, synthetic motor oils, lubricants, automotive additives, surfactants and paper sizing.
24. Mohammed Sergie, "The Tiny Gulf Country with a $335 Billion Global Empire," *Bloomberg*, January 11, 2017.

4.3 The Financial Markets of Kuwait

Introduction

Holding 7% of the world's oil reserves and a citizen population less than that of Dallas, Texas, Kuwait finds itself comfortably existing among the world's ultra-rich rentier states.[1] Yet, despite holding hydrocarbon reserves similar to Abu Dhabi, by most measures the Kuwaiti economy is relatively undiversified and underdeveloped compared to its regional peers.

It's historically strong oil-export driven current account masks an unsustainably large and under-productive public sector and a chronically small private sector. It is the lowest ranking GCC country in the World Bank's Ease of Doing Business, Starting a Business, Dealing with Construction Permits, Getting Electricity and Registering Property metrics.[2] Not surprisingly foreign direct investment into the Kuwaiti economy has chronically been among the lowest in the GCC.[3] Over the period of 2004 to 2012, inward FDI averaged between US$0.1 and US$0.2 billion, even less than that of the GCC's two poorest economies, Bahrain and Oman, which averaged US$0.8–1.9 billion and US$1.5–2.5 billion, respectively.[4]

This seemingly self-inflicted bearish market reality has stymied the country's efforts at becoming a financial hub and underlined its unfavorable business environment, past financial scandals and restricted royal autonomy in the realm of financial activity. Consequently, Kuwait's strength as an economic power is limited to that of its three largest, and most important, financial institutions the National Bank of Kuwait, The Kuwait Investment Authority and the Kuwait Finance House.

The National Assembly

Kuwait is unique for its relatively successful incorporation of both secular and Islamist political factions into what is widely considered the most democratic political structure in the region. The country's National Assembly can review government expenditures and has the power to draft, enact and veto legislation, rather than just act on legislation put forth by the government. While the parliament does not confirm cabinet members, it has the right to both publicly question ministers, known as interpellation, as well as the power to remove confidence in ministers effectively including the prime minister. This form of public grilling has taken on a life of its own. While, as of 2017, no minister has ever lost a vote of confidence, many have resigned immediately before a vote was taken and over forty have undergone interpellation since the Assembly's founding in 1962.

What truly makes the National Assembly so powerful though is its makeup. Historically, the two major constituencies which the al Sabah leaned on for support were the merchant class and the local tribes. While the latter were and remain the traditional allies of the royal family, the need to maintain the support of merchants largely dissipated in the early 1950s as oil wealth provided the royal family with financial independence. It was during this period that "merchants started to move to being customers of the state" and commoners became rich from government wealth transfers, in turn shifting the balance of power.[5] This is not to say that merchants lost all their power. Quite the contrary actually. Important merchant families, including Al Khurafi, Al Ghanim, Al Saqer and Al Marzoq, continued to hold senior positions of influence even after the discovery of oil. For example, Jasem Mohammed Al Khurafi was the president of the Parliament for twelve years, Abdulatef Thunaian Al Ghanim was the president of the first National Assembly, which drafted the Kuwaiti Constitution, and his brother Ali Thunaian Al Ghanim is the current Chairman of the Kuwait Chamber of Commerce and Industry while Talal Fahad Al Ghanim is the Chairman of the country's stock exchange. Conversely, instead of the combative and competitive hue that colored the merchant-royal relationship before the discovery of oil, since the 1950s, the merchant class have more often found themselves as partners of the al Sabah in the drive to catalyze industry and commerce in the country.

The second important constituency is that of the local tribes. It is important not to accidentally conflate bidun and tribal. The extensive literature on biduns in Kuwait refers to non-citizen Arab immigrants, many of whom came to Kuwait during the 1950s from Saudi Arabia looking for work during Kuwait's oil boom. These non-citizens do not have access to Kuwait's social welfare amenities and often cannot vote. Instead, the notion of the country's tribal population represents the largely non-merchant local population who has, over time, transitioned to urban life but still depend on the state for jobs and welfare. It is through the National Assembly that this segment of Kuwait's populace preserves the social welfare system that is often viewed as a birthright.

In a small country like Kuwait, were political parties are illegal, transnational tribes such as the Unaizah, Mutair, Dhafeer and Shammar play an important role in political mobilization. While not all tribal members are citizens with voting rights, both citizens and non-citizen constituencies play critical roles in the calculation of parliamentarians.[6] Throughout the last decade, many parliamentarians have taken on a role widely referred to as 'service deputies,' building popular support by providing constituents with access to government jobs, grants and other benefits.[7] These 'service deputies' make up a large contingent of the National Assembly often referred to the tribal current, representing much of Kuwait's middle class population. As of 2016, they held two out of every five parliamentary seats.[8]

Making up 25–30% of the population, Kuwait's Shi'a are another minority group within Kuwait that have used the National Parliament to have their concerns heard. Over numerous electoral cycles and policy issues, Kuwait's Shi'a-based political groups have allied with various Islamic Sunni groups and liberal parties, showing an ability for Shi'a-Sunni cooperation that is absent in other Gulf states.

The evolution of Kuwait's National Assembly has in turn placed checks on royal power that do not exist elsewhere. While Kuwait has many of the same labor and economic inequality challenges facing other Gulf countries, including Saudi Arabia, the key difference is that, through the National Assembly, the constitution of Kuwait provides for free elections that empower a parliament to hold the government publicly accountable. This is not to say that Kuwait is a perfect democracy, it most certainly is far from it, but compared to other countries that either lack real elections, have powerless elected officials or both, Kuwait's model is far ahead of the regional average.

Yet, as Michael Herb has explained, this nascent form of democracy has had significant economic implications.[9] Unlike the Al Maktoum or the Al Saud, the Al Sabah are not free to establish new economic zones or initiate major projects without parliamentary approval. The failed K-Dow project is the classic example of this conundrum. In 2008 the government approved an agreement with American petrochemical giant Dow Chemical to establish a large petrochemical complex in Kuwait. The project, K-Dow, had the ambitious aim of becoming the world's leading producer of petrochemicals and plastics.[10] Yet, as the deal was completed during a parliamentary recess, upon its return the National Assembly exercised its legal right to review the contract. Amidst accusations of profiteering, the Assembly forced the government to cancel the deal. In 2011, Dow closed a deal with Saudi Aramco to establish the plant in the Kingdom instead. To make matters even worse, in 2012, an international court ruled that Kuwait must pay Dow US$2.2 billion in compensation for canceling the deal. The controversy is often used by foreign and domestic private sector leaders as an example of how political concerns can often undermine economic common sense within Kuwait.

The Capital Markets

The history, form, and function of the Kuwaiti capital markets is bifurcated by the 1982 Souk Al Manakh crisis, which was covered extensively in Chapter 1 of this work. As discussed, the initial capital markets regulatory structure was devised by legislators who had little topical expertise and largely just mimicked the regulatory structure of foreign markets without consideration of unique domestic factors. It was the inefficiency of this regulatory structure, namely the lack of stringent regulation for private stock companies and companies incorporated abroad, coupled with the oil-driven easy money environment of the 1960s and 1970s and practice of post-dating checks, that inevitably led to the unofficial market's collapse.

Kuwait's modern stock exchange, the Kuwait Stock Exchange (KSE), and the Markets Committee (MC), the KSE's regulatory body, were established in 1983 in the wake of this crises as part of a capital markets overhaul that sought to remedy the market's root inefficiencies. Along with the MC and the KSE came the establishment of the Kuwaiti Clearing Committee (KCC), the first body mandated to match and verify financial holdings, accounts and transactions. By 1986, the KCC was responsible for all clearing and settling related to the KSE. The mere existence of a central regulatory body entrusted with settlement verification and empowered to prevent payment default was a significant improvement over the pre-Manakh environment. This said, the overall market reform efforts were still lacking. For example, through its inclusion of several government and KSE representatives, the MC was far from independent. Moreover, the KSE and MC lacked powers to adjust regulations according to the market's evolution, instead requiring that any changes be made through the formal, and largely reactionary, legislative process. Other notable deficiencies included a lack of regulations protecting minority shareholders or prohibiting insider trading and market manipulation, all issues that would prove catastrophic leading up to and during the 2008 financial crisis.[11]

Arguments have been made that these regulatory oversights were intentional, meant to leave loopholes for those merchant and political elite active in the capital markets. This theory is not far-fetched given the major role these elites had in fueling the rise of 'paper companies' and speculation during the Souk Al Manakh crisis.[12] Not only were many royal family members active players in the Souk Al Manakh, but the single largest player in the Souk Al Manakh was Sheikh Khalifah Al Abdullah al Sabah, who had signed US$23.4 billion in postdated checks. Indeed, market manipulation by influential elites is believed to have been integral to the Souk's explosive growth and eventual collapse. The hand of elite privilege was even present in the aftermath, when punishment for illegitimate activity was minimal and not applied to the royal family.[13]

In the twenty-five years that followed the crisis, aside from the two years of suspended trading due to the Iraqi invasion, strong commodity prices, relatively low barriers to entry, ample capital from the domestic banking sector, plus high rates of return from the regional property boom, all fueled a resurgence of the KSE. By 2002, the KSE was the second largest securities market in the Arab region.[14] Efforts to modernize the KSE played a key role in this boom, with the KSE being the first Gulf nation to introduce electronic trading, doing so in November 1995, later followed by the introduction of forward trading in October 1998, futures trading in August 2003 and online trading in November 2003.[15] Once again, the KSE was unable to enjoy the fruits of these efforts for long, this time due to the 2008 global financial crisis, in the wake of which the KSE's weighted index and price index declined 43% and 38%, respectively; subsequently sliding an additional 5% and 10% in 2009.[16]

Similar to efforts following the Souk Al Manakh crisis, after the 2008 global financial crisis the Kuwaiti government turned to regulatory overhaul to attempt and revitalize their capital markets. Key to these efforts was the 2010 Capital Markets Law which established the Capital Markets Authority, a truly independent regulatory body modeled around the US SEC and British FSA.[17] With the creation of the CMA, the regulatory and operational sides of the country's capital markets were separated for the first time. With this, Kuwait became the last GCC state to establish an independent capital market regulatory agency.

Another key aspect of the CML was the drive to privatize the KSE, which, finalized in late 2016, had been in the works since 2010. The KSE's new owner, Boursa Kuwait Securities Company (BKSE), a private, purpose-built firm, is the market's best hope for reviving what was once a thriving and innovative capital market. The one thing the BKSC did not change though is the stock market's intrinsic link to Kuwait's merchant elite. Talal Fahad al Ghunaim, part of the prominent merchant family that established the infamous Global Investment House, is the company's chairman, and Soliman Barrak al Marzouq, his own family well established in the retail and banking space, acts as one of BKSC's Non-Executive Directors.

Like many other regional stock markets, the BKSC's ultimate aim is to attract new foreign investors. Admittedly they are starting from a low bar, with only 13% of all trades transacted on KSE in 2016 done by foreigners, a metric that falls to 10.7% when not including other GCC citizens.[18] One method through which they hope to accomplish this is by adding new products to the bourse, including bonds, ETFs and sukuk, yet the official timeline for these introductions is unclear.

Other metrics betray the fact that merely introducing new products may do little to augment the declining interest in the stock market. For example, Kuwait's stock market turnover ratio, the value traded as a percentage of total market capitalization and a metric for market liquidity, fell to just 10% in 2016, from 19% in 2014 and a far cry from the 37% in 2007.[19] This compares bleakly to the United States, where, despite similar declines, the stock market turnover ratio still sat at 94% in 2016, as well as to regional peers Saudi Arabia and the UAE, who's turnover ratios were 77% and 23% in 2016, respectively.[20]

The 2014 commodity price crash has only added more headwinds to these efforts, which so far have failed to re-establish itself as a premier regional equities hub. Looking forward, the recent privatization of the KSE and the continued efforts at regulatory overhaul do highlight upside potential. For example, in 2018 FTSE announced that Kuwait would be included in the Secondary Emerging Markets list, making Kuwait the fourth country in the region (after Egypt, Qatar and the UAE) to achieve the ranking. The new market status, when fully implemented, is expected to lead to an inflow of foreign capital between US$100 million and US$700 million.[21]

The Banking Sector

The Commercial Banks

The formal banking industry in Kuwait began in 1943, when The Imperial Bank, now HSBC, received its banking license and began operations within the country. The bank monopolized the country's banking sector for the following decade, not only providing retail banking services to expatriates and conducting import finance, but also serving as the ruler's bank in lieu of an official central bank.[22]

This all changed in 1952 with the founding of the National Bank of Kuwait, considered the first private company in the region. The bank was founded by some of the leading merchant families in Kuwait, including the Al Kharafi, the Al Sagr, the Al Hamad and the Al Sayer, and rapidly took over the country's central banking functions, expanded its lending operations and opened new branches throughout the country. Today the bank is overwhelmingly the most dominant financial institution in the country, and leading figures from its founding merchant families still sit on NBK's board of directors and executive management.[23]

Through the 1970s, while the total number of conventional banks rose to five, competition amongst them was not fierce, with new banks generally arising when merchant or tribal groups desired their own financial institution. Once established, the main function of the banks was to finance merchant trading activities, with each bank generally relying on a unique customer base, which was often bound by kinship or friendship. Attempts at stealing competitors' customers were generally seen as socially unacceptable within the traditional standards of the period.[24]

These standards have not stood the test of time though and changed most dramatically following the 2004 amendment to the 1962 banking law allowing the establishment of branches of foreign banks within Kuwait.[25] Since then, twelve foreign banks have begun operations within the country. They join five conventional, five Islamic and two specialized Kuwaiti banks, for a total of twenty-four banks.[26] Local bankers have voiced concern over the effect of this proliferation, noting that foreign banks have taken to slashing prices, instigating fierce competition over the limited business opportunities in the country.[27]

Additionally, there is persistent concern over crowding out, with two specialized government-owned banks, the Kuwait Credit Bank and the Industrial Bank of Kuwait, providing medium and long-term business and residential financing at terms that commercial banks cannot compete with. This competitive atmosphere is further exacerbated by the large number of non-bank finance companies who compete with conventional banks in retail, auto and personal lending, as well as corporate services such as fleet finance, capital assets, and contracts.

Amidst all this, NBK still dominates the sector, holding over a third of Kuwait's total banking deposits and loans, respectively, in 2017 while the Kuwait Finance House holds another fifth of each.[28] This persistent dominance has been in no small part thanks to NBK's conservative behavior in the years leading up to the Souk Al Manakh fiasco.

Where most banks required some form of government assistance after the Souk's 1982 crash, NBK was the only bank to remain solvent. NBK also has the largest overseas presence of any Kuwaiti bank, with operations in leading financial centers such as London, Paris, Geneva, New York, Singapore and Shanghai, as well as the regional centers of Saudi Arabia, the UAE, Lebanon, Egypt, Iraq and Turkey. These international operations contribute 30% of the bank's bottom line.

Unlike Saudi Arabia and the United Arab Emirates, of the largest domestic banks in Kuwait, only one, the Burgan Bank, is controlled by the royal family or government-run institutions. Burgan Bank's largest shareholder, the Kuwait Projects Company (KIPCO) is effectively controlled by the royal family. The royal family's interest in Burgan Bank was driven by their desire to establish a banking institution of their own since all other major Kuwaiti banks were controlled by merchant families. Initially through Burgan Bank, and now through various other holding companies, the royal family also maintains controlling interest in the offshore Manama-based Bahrain Middle East Bank.

KIPCO's largest shareholder, Al Futtooh Holding Company (AFH), is owned by members of the Kuwaiti ruling family. AFH directly holds a 44.7% stake in KIPCO, and a larger 64.4% stake when its affiliates are taken into account. Since buying into KIPCO in 1988, AFH has repeatedly shown support for KIPCO, including increasing shareholding in times of crises such as the 2008 credit crunch, when its holdings in KIPCO grew by over 10 percentage points.[29] Further underlining this royal influence and support, KIPCO's chairman is Sheikh Hamad Sabah Al Ahmad Al Sabah. As a rule, KIPCO takes majority stakes in all of its companies and installs its own CEOs and board members, effectively extending royal influence across its entire portfolio.[30] Other major KIPCO holdings include United Gulf Bank, a major commercial bank in Bahrain, Gulf Insurance, one of the region's largest insurance companies, and OSN, one of the region's most successful cable networks.

Islamic Banks

Kuwait was the first country in the Gulf to establish a fully operational Islamic bank, the Kuwait Finance House. Established in 1977, the bank was able to quickly raise sizable deposits from within Kuwait, predominantly from the Muslim expatriate community. Since its founding it has not only grown into one of the largest Shari'a-compliant commercial banks in the world but has also consistently been on the forefront of Islamic finance, having pioneered specialized Islamic financial products for the construction sector, as well as consumer services such as Islamic Visa cards.[31] As of late 2016, KFH is the second largest bank in the country after NBK, holds a fifth of the country's deposits and issued a fifth of the country's loans.[32]

KFH has also been extensively active overseas. In fact, KFH was the first regional Islamic bank to expand beyond its own borders, establishing a Turkish subsidiary, the Kuveyt Turk Participation Bank, in 1989. It's expansion overseas started after a period of turbulence when, like the majority of its commercial peers, KFH found itself in financial trouble due to 1982 domestic equities market crash. In the years directly after its founding and in parallel with the Souk Al Manakh's meteoric rise, KFH primarily concentrated on the building and real estate sector, financing large real estate development projects against shares with rapidly rising value. This concentration into one sector was catastrophic for the bank. When the Souk crashed, not only did the backing equities lose their value, but so did the value of the real estate due to fire sale behavior. In the wake of this, the government was forced to take over the bank, recapitalizing it to the tune of US$10 billion and imposing strict regulations on its management.[33] Today, the Kuwaiti government collectively owns more than 40% of the bank's outstanding equity.

Due to the risk sharing nature of the bank, the real estate and equities crash resulted in zero returns for the bank's investment and saving deposits in 1984. Similarly, during the early 1990s, after the Iraqi invasion, KFH return rates were once again driven lower, hovering in the 4–5% range, and did not return to their pre-Souk el Manankh level until 2004, when they averaged 6–8%.[34]

During this period of low-domestic growth, KFH eschewed costly efforts to break into the hugely competitive wholesale markets, such as those in London, New York and Tokyo, and instead looked to build local banking operations in foreign markets that held significant potential for Islamic banking. This included opening branches in Bahrain, Oman, Bangladesh, Germany, Saudi Arabia and Jordan. Further east, Asia appeared as an area of special focus for the bank as early as 1995, when it attempted to extend into Indonesia and Malaysia but was unable to due to the Asian financial crisis and regulatory hurdles. Undeterred, in an effort to remain relevant, KFH opened a leasing company in Malaysia through a joint venture with local partners and the Islamic Development Bank.[35] A decade later, the efforts paid off and KFH was finally able to establish a stronghold in Asia in 2006 when it opened its Malaysian subsidiary, KFH Malaysia. KFH then leveraged KFH Malaysia to expand further into Singapore and Australia around 2008.[36] A similar process has been at play in China, with KFH using KFHM as a springboard to engage with China as early as 2006.[37] The largest example of this was in 2010, when KFHM capitalized on KFH's real estate investment expertise to finance a solid waste treatment facility in Qingdao, China. The strategy is likely to come full circle, with talk of KFH opening a branch in China escalating in 2017.

As of 2017, KFH has more than 430 branches across the world, helping it become the second largest purely Islamic bank in the world, after Saudi Arabia's Al Rajhi bank, which has 550 branches within Saudi Arabia alone. This expansive global growth led many to consider KFH the most successful Islamic bank when it comes to overseas expansion in any meaningful scale.

Amidst all this growth, KFH is still considered to be one of the most conservative Islamic banks when it comes to Shari'a compliance and the make-up of its lending portfolio. This conservative nature is best characterized in KFH's focus on protecting liquidity over profitability, which was a key aspect in the bank's ability to weather the 2008 financial crisis relatively unscathed compared to its domestic peers.

Sovereign Wealth Funds

Like it's Gulf peers, Kuwait has its own very large sovereign wealth fund. The precursor to the country's largest fund, the Kuwait Investment Authority, is the General Reserve Fund (GRF). Established in the 1960s as Kuwait was preparing independence from British protection, the GRF receives all government revenues and budget surpluses and effectively functions as the government's main treasury, receiving all revenues, including those from hydrocarbon exports and paying out all expenditures, including servicing public debt and government domestic equity investments. The exact mechanics behind this process are extremely obscure, allowing for a flexible use of fiscal reserves that enables short-term macro-stabilization and financing of government activities. Additionally, as a domestically focused fund, it holds stakes in Kuwaiti public enterprises such as the Kuwait Fund for Arab Economic Development and the Kuwait Petroleum Corporation.

Conversely, the GRF's peer, the Reserve Fund for Future Generations (RFFG) is a more traditional SWF that operates within a much stricter, internationally focused framework aimed at protecting and growing the government's long-term savings. Established through a 1976 Emiri decree, the RFFG initially received 50% of the GRF's assets, about US$3 billion at the time, and it has received at least 10% of governmental revenues annually, plus all profits earned from its assets and those of the GRF, since then.[38] In other words, whether or not the state's budget is in deficit or surplus, funds are placed into the RFFG before any state expenses or budget requirements. It did not take long for the RFFG to become Kuwait's largest holder of funds, managing assets valued at over US$60 billion by 1980.[39]

The fund is legally obligated to reinvest all of its profits every year and its assets can only be withdrawn from the fund with approval from the national parliament and the government. The collective effect of these restrictions has aided the RFFG in its exponential growth, with its foreign investments generating more income than Kuwait's direct oil sales as early as the 1980s. The fund generated US$6.3 billion in 1987 compared to the US$5.4 billion earned from oil in the wake of a global commodity price downturn.[40] This large capital accumulation led to the 1982 establishment of the Kuwaiti Investment Authority, an independent legal entity that replaced the Ministry of Finance as manager of both the GRF and the RFFG. The KIA was tasked with improving investment quality and operations at both funds, and is also mandated to manage any other funds entrusted to it by the Minister of Finance.

Among the funds that the KIA is supposed to oversee is the Kuwait Investment Office (KIO), which was established in 1961 and acted independently out of London. The KIO was the original manager of the RFFG's foreign investments. Even though the KIA was supposed to be in charge of KIO's investments, it's establishment did not change the way KIO was operating. KIO maintained most of its power and was seen as more experienced and successful than its new parent. Unable to control the KIO, the KIA instead just managed local investments in Kuwait, such as the funds passed onto domestic banks and investment companies.

Between its founding and the late 1990s, the leadership of the KIO has predominantly been appointed from within the royal family. Up until the late 1990s, while it was generally accepted that the KIO's funds were controlled by the al Sabah family, who actually approved investments proposed by the KIO's staff in London was less clear. Some of the KIO's most notable investments during its early years included minority stakes in major Western firms such as Mercedes-Benz, HOECHST, Henson and BP. This dynamic of secrecy and independence all changed in the wake of the Spanish Torras scandal, in which royal family members at the head of the KIO were implicated in the colossal mismanagement of millions from the country's SWFs. During the scandal, questionable investments, conducted through dubious strategies, were completed without the approval of the KIO's nominal regulator, the KIA, or the parliament, with the result being the disappearance of nearly US$1 billion out of US$5 billion of investments in Spanish conglomerate Groupo Torras.[41] When the name of the Emir's cousin, the very powerful former Minister of Oil Sheikh Ali Ali-Khalifa al Sabah was linked to the scandal, the Parliament and the Prime Minister (also a member of the royal family) took action to protect Kuwaiti investments from alleged mishandling by the KIO.

Since the Spanish scandal, parliamentary pressure for more public oversight has given birth to an intricate, non-public, inter-institutional oversight system in which the National Parliament plays a central role. This system not only limited royal influence over the KIO, instead bringing it firmly under the umbrella of the KIA, but also required the latter to provide annual closed door presentations on the full details of all funds under its management to the council of ministers and the national assembly.[42] While this bureaucratic system is often time consuming, weakening the efficiency of KIA's autonomous decision making, it has successfully minimized the risk of financial fraud.[43] More importantly, it led to a significant shift in power. Since the KIA was being supervised by the MoF, the ultimate management authority now rested with the Prime Minister, opposed to the KIO which was de facto directly under the authority of the Emir. In this sense, since 1994, the control of most of Kuwait's financial assets was taken away from the Emir and transferred to the Prime Minister. This evolution was in every way a massive palace coup. Since then, while the main protagonists, the Emir and the Prime Minister have died, the KIO has remained under the control of the KIA.

The total size of the funds the KIA manages are the topic of constant guesswork. This is because the public disclosure of any data or information about the KIA's portfolio or financial position is illegal, ostensibly to insulate the fund from political interference.[44] Because of this there is scant objective data on the fund's size, yet there is no dearth of educated guesswork. The latest estimates, published by major institutions including the International Monetary Fund and the Sovereign Wealth Fund Institute, peg the fund's total assets under management somewhere between US$530 and US$548 billion, broadly divided as two-thirds/one-third in the RFFG and the GRF, respectively, making it the fifth largest sovereign wealth fund in the world.[45]

From a portfolio perspective, the RFFG was set up to hold assets with long investment horizons in order to secure revenue flows in the future. The overwhelming bulk of its investments are held abroad, mostly in foreign capital markets.[46] From the 1950s to the 1970s, Kuwait's SWFs, be it the RFFG or GRF, held their assets almost solely in the UK. It wasn't until the late 1970s that the KIA grew significantly active in US equities. This concentration on two markets was deemed too risky, and new portfolios were created covering Germany, Switzerland, France, Belgium, the Netherlands and Japan and were handled by external managers. Simultaneously, the KIA's US investments grew increasingly speculative in nature, opposed to the quasi-index tracking they had utilized up until then. Throughout all this, ownership stakes were under ownership reporting thresholds, allowing for confidentiality of investment strategy. It wasn't until a decade later, in the late 1980s, that the KIA began investing in emerging markets. In time, this focus on emerging markets has taken on a much larger share of the fund's portfolios, with a heavy leaning toward Asian markets since 2005. This in turn has led to the creation of foreign investment organizations, such as the Kuwait China Investment Company, to help incubate these investments.[47]

Up to 99% of the KIA's assets are managed externally, but there is a drive to decrease that to as low as 94% in the near term.[48] Along with this external management, the KIA has repeatedly proven that it is a patient, often silent, long-term investor. For example, a shareholder in Daimler since 1969, the fund did not divest in Chrysler or Daimler after their merger and eventual spin off, despite more than sufficient financial rationale to do just that. More recently, this hard-nosed focus on long-term returns were disrupted by the 2008 financial crisis, when political pressure to alleviate domestic economic pain drove the KIA to sell some of its foreign assets held through the RFFG in order to stabilize the domestic economy and support local companies.[49] This included injecting US$418 million into Gulf Bank, Kuwait's fourth largest bank, after it suffered severe derivative trading losses, and another US$5.2 billion as part of a government effort to stabilize the stock market.

SWFs in Crisis: The KIO and the Gulf War

SWFs act as a savings fund for times of need. Across the GCC, these trying times are usually financial in nature, be it housing bubbles or threats of devaluation. In Kuwait, support for the domestic stock market and banking sector in 1982 act as examples of traditional SWF intervention. Yet, Kuwait's SWF has also been utilized for an entirely more existential threat. During the 1991 Iraqi invasion of Kuwait, as the primary Kuwaiti international financial institution, the KIO took on the role of financial lifeline for Kuwait's citizens and economy at a time when most domestic bank accounts were frozen and local infrastructure razed.

At that point, the KIO still operated independently and for the preceding two decades had been led by influential royals including Sheikh Ali Ali-Khalifa al Sabah, a cousin of the Emir and then Kuwait's finance minister and formerly the oil minister, and Sheikh Fahd Mohammed al Sabah, long-time chairman of KIO and also a cousin of the Emir. At the onset of the Iraqi invasion, Kuwaiti financial institutions across the world saw their bank accounts frozen because of threats that Iraq was seeking to transfer Kuwaiti assets into their possession. This limited Kuwait's ability to manage its financial assets and fund government activity at a critical juncture in Kuwait's history. The KIO, working with the Central Bank of England, was able to define itself as a London-based financial institutional, as opposed to Kuwaiti-based, in turn allowing its assets to remain liquid. With this ability, on August 2, 1990, the KIO was given control over all Kuwaiti assets held outside Kuwait, including those belonging to the RFFG.[50] Similar arrangements were made with the US Treasury.[51] These arrangements effectively allowed the KIO to act as the de facto central bank of Kuwait.

Of course, the KIO was always controlled by royal family members close to the Emir. During the occupation of Kuwait, this allowed the KIO to become the operational center of the Kuwaiti government even though the Emir himself took up residence in Saudi Arabia, with the senior royal family members not in Saudi Arabia working out of KIO's offices in London until the liberation. The KIO arranged for advances to be made to the Kuwaiti banks in exile for more than US$7 billion. The KIO also quickly compiled lists of all Kuwaitis who had managed to escape the country and began sending them a monthly stipend in order to provide some form of financial support. Without this support, many regular Kuwaiti's would have been unable to survive the period of Iraqi invasion despite being safely outside the country.

Along with these expenses, Kuwait experienced a sharp fall in oil production and exports while making large payments to cover operations Desert Shield and Desert Storm and financing the restoration of domestic infrastructure. All this led to a dramatic drawdown in country's sovereign wealth holdings, which fell by over 50% from their pre-war levels, from around US$113 billion to an estimated US$46.7 billion in 1995.[52] The bulk of this was spent in the seven months of the Iraqi occupation and expulsion, which cost nearly US$50 billion. According to claims filed with the United Nations, Kuwait liquidated US$50 billion from its RFFG for reconstruction and other expenses supporting the people of Kuwait, implying that the bulk of the finances used during this period came from the RFFG.[53] This is further substantiated by the fact that, at that time, the KIO managed many of the RFFG's assets. An additional US$17.7 billion was spent in the following four years, a quarter of which was on domestic debt forgiveness.

Conclusion

Compared to its peers, Kuwait's financial markets have remained largely static since the late 1980s. In many ways, this is a consequence of past failures, namely the Souk Al Manakh crash, but also because of the power of Kuwait's National Assembly. Admittedly, this legislative body has distinguished Kuwait politically amongst its regional peers, but the power enshrined in it has also placed checks on the monarchical power that has catalyzed development in otherwise lethargic markets elsewhere in the Gulf. This dynamic was clear in 2007 when Zain, then the largest listed company in Kuwait, decided move its headquarters to Bahrain despite the Kuwaiti government being its largest shareholder. Zain's decision to move was blamed on the National Assembly's inaction with regards to regulations in the telecommunications sector.[54] Whereas Kuwait strives to create financial markets like its neighbors in the UAE, the country lacks the ability to rapidly create the regulatory environment necessary to do just that. In many cases this may be for the better, but equally, it has limited Kuwait's agility in the face of dynamic and rapidly changing financial markets, of course to the great benefit of its neighbors.

In the face of these constraints, the largest and most dynamic actors in Kuwait's market have arisen out of the private sector. KFH and NBK are truly market leaders in their respective areas of practice, but unlike state-driven market leading firms from other Gulf states such as DP World and SABIC, they have been established by entrepreneurial Kuwaiti merchants. Ironically enough, moving forward this kind of private sector-led growth is what Saudi Arabia and the UAE strive to achieve.

Notes

1. The Organization of Petroleum Exporting Countries, *Annual Statistical Bulletin*, 2016; at the current production rate of 2.9 mbpd, Kuwait's oil reserves are expected to last around 100 years.
2. World Bank Group, *Doing Business 2017*. (Washington, D.C: World Bank Group, 2017).
3. World Bank Group, *World Development Indicators*. (Washington, DC, n.d.).
4. HSBC, *Middle East Economies: Picking Up the Pieces: Macro Middle East Economies, Q4*. (London: HSBC, 2012).
5. As quoted in Mary Ann Tetreault, "Autonomy, Necessity, and the Small State: Ruling Kuwait in the Twentieth Century," *International Organization* 45, no. 4 (1991): 578.
6. Scott Weiner, "The Politics of Kuwait's Bidoon Issue," *Carnegie Endowment for International Peace: Sada*, October 20, 2017.
7. Nathan Brown and Dina Bishara, "Kuwaitis Vote for a New Parliament . . . and Maybe a New Electoral System," *Carnegie Endowment for International Peace*, 2006.
8. Kenneth Katzman, *Kuwait: Governance, Security, and US Policy*. (Washington: Congressional Research Service, November 30, 2017), p. 3; Naser AlFozaie, "Tribalism in Kuwait: Impacts on the Parliament," (Master's thesis, Norwegian University of Life Sciences, 2016): 19–40.
9. For more on this see, Michael Herb, *The Wages of Oil: Parliaments and Economic Development in Kuwait and the UAE*. (Ithaca, NY: Cornell University Press, 2014).
10. Dow Chemical, "Dow and PIC of Kuwait Sign Binding Joint Venture Agreement to Launch K-Dow Petrochemicals," Dec 3, 2008. *Press Release*
11. International Monetary Fund, "Financial Sector Assessment Program: Kuwait," *International Monetary Fund, Country Report* no. 4/352 (Washington, DC, 2004), p. 4.
12. Fatemah Abdulla Al Shuraian, "Market Manipulation in Kuwait Stock Exchange: An Analysis of the Regulation of Market Manipulation Prior and Under Law no. 7 of 2010," (PhD. diss., University of Leicester School of Law, 2014), p. 43.
13. Jean-François Seznec, "The Politics of the Financial Mmarkets in Saudi Arabia, Kuwait and Bahrain," (PhD. diss., Yale University, May 1994), p. 237.
14. International Monetary Fund, "Financial Sector Assessment Program: Kuwait," *International Monetary Fund, Country Report* no. 04/352 (Washington, DC, 2004), p. 5; for a detailed discussion of these regulatory inefficiencies and market manipulation in Kuwait, see Fatemah Abdulla Al Shuraian, "Market Manipulation in Kuwait Stock Exchange: An Analysis of the Regulation of Market Manipulation Prior and under Law no. 7 of 2010," (PhD. diss., University of Leicester School of Law, 2014).
15. Oxford Business Group, "Transforming Kuwait's Capital Markets," *Oxford Business Group*, 2016.
16. Ibid.
17. Mark Thatcher, "Governing Markets in the Gulf States," in David Held and Kristian Ulrichsen, eds. *The Transformation of the Gulf: Politics, Economics and the Global Order* (Routledge 2013), p. 134.
18. Bourse Kuwait, *Annual Report, 2016*, p. 23.
19. Ibid.; Boursa Kuwait, *Monthly Report Details*, Various Months.
20. World Bank Group, *World Development Indicators*. (Washington, DC: World Bank Group, n.d.).

21. Chloe Domat, "Revamping Kuwait's Stock Exchange," *Global Finance*, February 15, 2018.
22. John R. Presley and Rodney Wilson, *Banking in the Arab Gulf*. (London: Macmillan Academic and Professional Ltd, 1991), p. 49.
23. Pete Moore, *Doing Business in the Middle East: Politics and Economic Crisis in Jordan and Kuwait* (Cambridge: Cambridge University Press, 2004), p. 45.
24. Presley and Wilson, *Banking in the Arab Gulf*, p. 51.
25. Central Bank of Kuwait, "Amendments to Central Bank Law," November 23, 2004. Available at www.cbk.gov.kw/en/assets/pdfs/23-feb-2004-stat-law-amend-10-5079-1.PDF.
26. Conventional banks include: market-leader National Bank of Kuwait, Commercial Bank of Kuwait, Gulf Bank, Al Ahli Bank of Kuwait, and Burgan Bank. Shari'a-compliant banks include Kuwait Finance House, Boubyan Bank, Kuwait International Bank, Al Ahli United Bank and Warba Bank. The foreign banks are BNP Paribas, HSBC, Citibank, First Abu Dhabi, Qatar National Bank, Doha Bank, Dubai-based Mashreq Bank, the Bank of Muscat, Riyadh-based Al Rajhi Bank, the Bank of Bahrain and Kuwait, the Industrial and Commercial Bank of China (ICBC) and Union National Bank. The government-owned Industrial Bank of Kuwait provides medium- and long-term financing to industrial companies and Kuwaiti citizens through customized financing packages.
27. Robert Hartley, "Competition Heating Up in Resurgent Kuwaiti Banking Sector," *The Banker*, January 4, 2014.; "Kuwait's Local Banks Compete to Face Foreign Banks," *Kuwait News Agency*, September 29, 2001.
28. Arzan Financial Group, "KSE Banking Quarterly Report (4Q 2016 Results)."
29. National Bank of Kuwait, *Investor Presentation*, October 2017.
30. Samuel Wendel, "Kuwait's Projects Company (KIPCO): A Three-Decade Transformation," *Forbes Middle East*, July 1, 2017.
31. Presley and Wilson, *Banking in the Arab Gulf*, p. 47.
32. Arzan Financial Group, "KSE Banking Quarterly Report (4Q 2016 Results)."
33. Jean-François Seznec. "The Politics of the financial markets in Saudi Arabia, Kuwait and Bahrain," (PhD. diss., Yale University. May 1994): 219.
34. May Y. Khamis, Abdullah Al-Hassan, and Nada Oulidi. The GCC banking sector: Topography and analysis. (No. 10–87. International Monetary Fund, 2010.): 10.
35. C Wright, 'Gulf banks set out to stage an Asian invasion', Global Capital, October 1, 2007.
36. "Kuwait Finance House: Company Profile," MarketLine, January 6, 2014: 5
37. "Kuwait Finance House to market China's first ever Islamic bond," Gulf News, September 9, 2006
38. Sara Bazoobandi. Political Economy of the Gulf Sovereign Wealth Funds: A Case Study of Iran, Kuwait, Saudi Arabia and the United Arab Emirates. (Routledge, 2012); authors calculations
39. Seznec, "The Politics of the Financial Markets in Saudi Arabia, Kuwait and Bahrain."
40. Sara Bazoobandi, *Political Economy of the Gulf Sovereign Wealth Funds: A Case Study of Iran, Kuwait, Saudi Arabia and the United Arab Emirates*. (London: Routledge, 2012).
41. Roger Cohen, "Missing Millions—Kuwait's Bad Bet—a Special Report: Big Wallets and Little Supervision," *The New York Times*, September 28, 1993.
42. Members of KIA's board are all appointed for an extendable 4-year period by the Council of Ministers. By law, the Board is chaired by the minister of finance and includes the minister of oil, the governor of the Central Bank of Kuwait, and the under-secretary of the Ministry of Finance, as well as five other Kuwaiti nationals from the private sector. The Chairman of KIA is officially responsible for submitting annual reports on activity and budgets to the government.

43. Bazoobandi, *Political Economy of the Gulf Sovereign Wealth Funds*, p. 53.
44. Kuwaiti Law No.47 of 1982, Clauses 5 and 8–9, bind the KIA to nondisclosure. Detailed data is provided to the Council of Ministers with strict restrictions on public access.
45. International Monetary Fund, "Kuwait: 2017 Article IV Consultation," *International Monetary Fund, IMF Country Report* no. 18/21, January 2018, p. 6.
46. Ugo Fasano-Filho, "Review of the Experience with Oil Stabilization and Savings Funds in Selected Countries. No. 0–112," *International Monetary Fund*, 2000.
47. Bazoobandi, *Political Economy of the Gulf Sovereign Wealth Funds*, p. 51.
48. Dominic Dudley, "How Kuwait Investment Authority Built a Solid Savings Nest," *Forbes Middle East*, October 12, 2017.
49. Khalid A. Alsweilem, Angela Cummine, Malan Rietveld and Katherine Tweedie, *A Comparative Study of Sovereign Investor Models: Sovereign Fund Profiles*. (Cambridge, MA: Harvard Kennedy School, Belfer Center for Science and International Affairs and Center for International Development at Harvard University, 2015), p. 66.
50. "Kuwaitis Move Quickly to Manage Finance from London," *Middle East Economic Digest* 33, no. 47 (August 27, 1990).
51. "US Treasury Clarifies Status of Kuwaiti Companies in the US," *Middle East Economic Digest* 34, no. 4 (October 29, 1990).
52. Yousef H. Al-Ebraheem, "Kuwait's Economic Travails," *Middle East Quarterly* 3, no. 3 (September 1996).
53. Timothy J. Feighery, Christopher S. Gibson and Trevor M. Rajah, eds. *War Reparations and the UN Compensation Commission: Designing Compensation after Conflict*. (Oxford: Oxford University Press, 2015), 359.
54. "Kuwait setback as Zain Opts for Bahrain," *Arabian Business*, September 19, 2007.

4.4 The Financial Markets of Oman

Introduction

Modern day Oman is very much the creation of its ruler, Sultan Qaboos bin Said Al Said. Since bloodlessly overthrowing his father, he has ended internal rebellion, modernized the economy and built a functioning government from scratch. In doing so, Qaboos built an economic and political balance dependent on his rule and the bargain he struck with merchant elites during the country's developmental period.

While the country has traditionally been considered one of the most stable in the region, concerns around Qaboos's health, ambiguity about royal succession and popular discontent with the sociopolitical status quo has brought this stability into question. These risks are only aggravated by the fact that Qaboos is widely considered the de facto minister of finance, defense and foreign affairs and that there have been limited efforts at succession planning.

Given the country's relatively limited natural resources and fiscal reserves, continued economic growth in Oman will be dependent on the government's ability to overhaul the investment climate, enhance the role of the private sector in job creation and expedite government privatizations.

Qaboos's Elite Bargain

Between 1932 and 1970, Oman was led by Sultan Said bin Taimur. Under his leadership, Oman was an indebted, undereducated, internationally isolated nation suffering from internal domestic unrest. Making matters worse, well into the 20th century, Oman had little in the way of a formal government. Where elsewhere in the region governments had developed some industry or extractive measure to generate revenues such as taxing merchants, before the discovery of hydrocarbons, the Omani state lacked a steady source of revenues outside of British loans. This is not to say that there were no taxes or fees in Oman prior to 1970s. Customs revenues, zakat collections, and British loans did find their way into the Omani treasury but were relatively minimal and were largely funneled to the private account of Taimur.[1]

In this sense, Sultan Qaboos's 1970 bloodless overthrow of his father did not give the young leader control over a state as much as it gave him control over a territory upon which a state could one day exist. Indeed, Qaboos had walked into a dire situation. At the time of his ascension, the country of 666,000 inhabitants only had three non-Qur'anic schools, no schools for girls, one hospital which held just twelve beds and lacked adequate housing, energy and road infrastructure.[2] This dramatic level of underdevelopment was worst inland in the Dhofar region, and is considered one of the primary reasons for the domestic rebellion there. Upon replacing his father, Qaboos focused on catalyzing development across health, education and infrastructure, igniting hope for progress in a country that felt left behind amidst a rapidly changing region.

Luckily, Qaboos's ascension coincided with key factors in global oil markets. Not only did Oman's domestic oil production rise considerably during the first two decades of his rule—so did oil prices due to the 1973–1974 oil embargo and the wave of nationalizations that followed. It was during this wave that Qaboos took the opportunity to purchase a majority (60%) stake in Petroleum Development Oman (PDO), the domestic oil company managing Omani oil assets, which until then had been majority owned by Shell. While Shell continued to play a dominant role in the company's management, Oman was now entitled to a much larger share of PDO's revenues. Under Taimur, Oman received only 50% oil profits, whereas today, as a result of the purchase, the government's total take is closer to 90%.[3]

Unlike Saudi, where a bureaucratic backbone already existed before the arrival of oil wealth, these energy rents enabled Oman to develop a government structure largely from scratch. This included the founding of new social programs and infrastructure, such as schools and hospitals, and developing an extensive road structure that catalyzed trade and mobility. These aims were best represented by successive 5-year development plans starting in September 1976. Broadly speaking, the first four of these plans focused on large-scale industrial projects ranging from state-funded fisheries, cement plants to refineries and social infrastructure development (roads, hospitals, schools and housing).

The establishment of roads was critical not only for transportation's sake, but also as an effort to integrate the coastal and interior populations. Unlike its regional 'city-state' peers, where an overwhelming proportion of the population live in urbanized cities, in Oman today more than a quarter of the population lives in rural areas.[4]

Whereas Oman's coastal region was cosmopolitan and oriented toward external trade with the Indian Ocean network, inland, rural territories were largely tribal and dependent on localized agriculture and husbandry trade.[5] The development of a road network tied the coastal region to the interior, not only catalyzing the growth of cities in the hinterland but also erasing this duality, integrating two historically divided and sometimes antagonistic populations.

Outside of managing resource wealth and financing infrastructure development, the royal family and the state itself largely kept its hands out of the private sector. This stands in stark contrast to regional peers like Dubai, often dubbed Dubai Inc., where vast swaths of the private sector are dominated by the royal family.

This provided a unique, and extremely lucrative, role for existing merchant elite. Where in countries like Qatar the royal family marginalized traditional merchant families, in Oman Qaboos turned to the existing power brokers for expertise and manpower, thus avoiding a statist economy, creating a *laissez faire* economic environment, and further empowering the existing commercial and tribal elite.[6]

This is not to say that royals were completely uninvolved in the private sector, some have successfully capitalized on their royal orientation. The three sons of former prime minister Sayyid Tariq bin Taimur, all of whom hold considerable domestic and international business interests, are interesting examples of this exception. One of the three, Sayyid Haitham, who has held leading positions in the Ministry of Foreign Affairs and currently acts as the Minister of National Heritage and Culture, is the chairman and primary shareholder of National Trading Company, a major Omani construction and trade firm. NTC was in charge of building two of the country's largest power plants (Manah and Sohar) and is the domestic agent for numerous multinational companies.[7] All three are considered to be leading candidates to succeed Qaboos, which, deriving from their extensive business dealings, could lead to a significant shift in the royal-elite bargain.

Even with these exceptions, business-savvy royals far from dominate Oman's business environment. Instead Oman's commercial activity is dominated by the elite families who were able to capitalize on Qaboos's development strategy during his early rule. This strategy, which depended on existing elites to drive economic growth, allowed historically powerful merchant families, such as the Zawawi, al Sultan, Zubair and al Harithi, to advocate for a system where their commercial dominance could not be questioned.

Key members of this merchant elite class held powerful political appointments and, deriving from their use of this power, were dubbed by the Central Intelligence Agency as the 'Muscat Mafia.' Among this group was, Qais Abdul-Munim al Zawawi, his brother Umar al Zawawi, and Muhammed al Zubayr. It is important to note that these men do not represent a specific ethnicity, but had diverse backgrounds ranging from Baluchi to Zanzibari and even Indian Hyderabadi, representing Oman's diverse trading-based coastal population and Qaboos's focus on co-opting powerful, and able, sociopolitical agents regardless of cultural factors.[8]

Key to the system this group of powerful politicians developed were laws governing distribution of foreign goods and horizontal and vertical commercial integration. While this legal environment allowed Qaboos to rapidly achieve his near-term development goals, namely by awarding infrastructure and industrial contracts to elites able to mobilize economic activity, it also prevented competition in the marketplace, allowed for the concentration of unrelated commercial activities into a few hands, leading to the proliferation of what would traditionally be considered serious conflicts of interest.[9]

Potentially the most notable early example of these elite's lucrative grip on power is Sayyid Hamad bin Hamood Al Bu Said, who had been Said bin Taimur's secretary and later became Qaboos's minister of diwan affairs. Sayyid Hamad bin Hamood capitalized on his positions not only to win numerous lucrative agency contracts but also to establish what are now two of Oman's largest companies, Oman Shapoorji Construction Company, which won contracts to build most of Oman's government buildings, and SABCO Group, an expansive company with interests ranging from finance to petrochemicals, mining and retail goods.[10]

Today, the majority of cabinet officials and senior government officials are either directly or indirectly involved in businesses that benefit from public contracts.[11] In fact, Sayyid Hamad B. Hamood's second son, Badr bin Hamad bin Hamood, is not only the Secretary General of the Ministry of Foreign Affairs, but was also the chairman of SABCO until 2000, when he passed the chairmanship to his brother due to public pressure. At least three more of Oman's largest business groups are thought to be controlled by the Minister of Justice and two special advisors to the Sultan, either personally or through their siblings.[12]

Through the mid-1990s, Oman's development goals, in many ways, benefited from this elite-bargain, which allowed for peace between old and new power centers and paved the way for rapid achievement of Qaboos's development goals. As Marc Valeri has noted, Qaboos allied, "with traditional Muscat merchant elites, who have been assured privileged access to the oil windfall through public contracts. In return, the merchant families have helped the ruler finance his nation-building endeavors."[13] In this sense, Qaboos used government contracts to support merchants with which the royal family had long-standing links, while simultaneously promoting additional families who had demonstrated loyalty to him personally. Valeri even suggests that some of these elites were given fixed percentages of Oman's oil revenue in order to ensure they had a personal stake in the country's successful development.[14]

The positive effects of this bargain can be found in the country's rapid development. By the early 1980s, Qaboos's efforts had led to the established of 28 new hospitals and 262 new schools.[15] Similarly, despite Oman's economic development beginning later than many of its regional peers, Oman is one of only thirteen countries in the world to grow at an average annual growth rate greater than 7% for twenty-five years or longer. Indeed, between 1965 and 2006 Oman saw its per capita income grow more than tenfold, similar to growth rates seen in economic power houses Singapore, Hong Kong and South Korea during the same period.[16]

The rapid development had a significant sociopolitical impact. By spreading roads, schools and hospitals where they had not existed before, Qaboos was able to create symbols of the Omani state, and in effect of himself, throughout the smallest towns. Simultaneously, like many of Oman's regional peers, oil revenues fueled the birth of a seemingly inexhaustible pool of public sector jobs throughout the intelligence, army, policy and state ministries. Proportional to population, Oman's armed forces was the largest in the region through the 1990s, with Oman justifying the military's size through the employment, training and education it provided the country's citizens. Unsurprisingly, Oman's military spending was exorbitant, averaging 17% of GDP between 1972 and 1988.[17]

Collectively these expenditures were a mechanism for income distribution, creating a salaried middle class that was able to enjoy a standard of living never before seen in Oman, in turn giving birth to a generation staunchly allied with Qaboos.

A New Challenge

By 1995, most of these foundational objectives (roads, schools, hospitals) had been achieved, and the next stage in development required transitioning toward a new economic model, one more in-line with traditional free market dynamics. This was highlighted by a now infamous 1994 World Bank report, which Oman itself had requested. The report identified a number of significant problems stifling Oman's development, including public monopolies, legally sanctioned monopolistic private trading and manufacturing systems, poor efficiency in the public sector and distortion-creating subsidies.[18]

Ironically, the issues that the report highlighted largely stemmed from the elite-bargain that Qaboos had struck. While the bargain with merchant elite and employment policies had helped take Oman from an underdeveloped nation to an emerging market, the structure built during this process has precluded and hindered more substantive development. This is clear through persistent un- and under-employment, with the World Bank estimating youth unemployment sitting well above 45% consistently since 1995.[19]

To his credit, Qaboos reacted positively to pressure for market and trade liberalization, moving the country toward lifting controls on foreign investment and expanding contacts with international organizations, even joining the World Trade Organization. As in the past, these new aims were best communicated through Oman's 5-year plans. Where between 1976 and 1995 these plans focused on infrastructure and social services, starting in 1995 Oman began implementing a reform strategy geared toward development in the liberal sense. These efforts were best encapsulated in the country's Vision 2020 (covering 1996–2020). Vision 2020 envisioned reforming Oman's legal environment to attract foreign investment, reducing the economy's dependence on public spending and oil revenues, shifting education policy toward technical and vocational training and expanding the tourism industry.

Follow through on these aims has been lacking at best. Objectives established in 1996 aimed to increase non-oil GDP from an average of 62.4% between 1991 and 1995 to 81% in 2020.[20] In reality, non-oil GDP has moved in the opposite direction, averaging 56% between 2011 and 2015, with Oman's ninth 5-year plan now envisioning non-oil GDP reaching 70% by 2020, a large reduction of its original goal.[21]

Similarly, despite over a decade of reform measures specifically aimed at easing Oman's business environment, including setting up one-stop shops for business registration, simplifying the taxation system and reducing compliance requirements for international commerce, the country's rank in the Ease of Doing Business index has actually deteriorated significantly, falling from 44th easiest country in 2012 to 71st in 2017.[22]

It is important to note that while these issues are not by any means unique to Oman, due to the sultanate's limited natural resources and small economy, they do mean that regular non-royal, non-elite Omanis have little opportunity in the classical capitalist sense. This is exacerbated by the fact that the Omani state does not have the financial leverage needed to finance these opportunities through endless public-sector employment like the UAE and Qatar do.

These tensions were primary drivers in Oman's experience during the Arab Spring starting early 2011, when it was one of two Arab countries to see significant popular mobilization. Yet, while the popular protests of the Arab Spring brought down leaders who many thought would die in power, in Oman, protests never threatened the existence of the regime. Instead they brought forth serious cracks in the ruling bargain, highlighting the potential for instability in what has been considered the most stable Gulf state.

Protests over economic conditions in Libya and Egypt quickly turned into demonstrations demanding the fall of autocratic leaders. Chants heard during Oman's protests, such as "The people want the reform of the regime," and "The people want the fall of corruption," underlined similar economic tensions. Markedly different though were the inclusion of protesters who were repeatedly quoted showing support for Qaboos, with statements like, "We love His Majesty, but there are problems we want to fix."[23] In this disparity, the lasting impact of Qaboos's change on Oman can be found, for while the people were expressing discontent with rising prices, a lack of jobs and spreading inequality, the anger was aimed directly toward the elite-royal bargain, not the royals themselves, as was the case in Bahrain.

Qaboos reacted to the protesters demands in late February, introducing a new monthly allowance for unemployed job seekers, the creation of 50,000 new jobs for Omanis, large increases in social security grants for needy families, increases in student allowances and increases in the private sector minimum wage. Yet, in a clear sign that this was not enough, just a week later protesters blockaded, looted and finally burned the Lulu Supermarket in Sohar.[24] Highlighting the protester's focus on corruption, the supermarket's building and land belonged to the powerful Minister of the Royal

Office and Oman's top security official, Ali Al Maamari.[25] Four days later, Ali Al Maamri was removed from his post. He had been a close confidant of Qaboos and a high-powered political official since 1976.[26]

It was at this point that Qaboos turned his focus squarely on corruption, dismissing one-third of his cabinet in the largest cabinet reshuffle since he took power. Many of those dismissed were thought to represent corrupt practices in the public eye.[27] Additionally, Qaboos dissolved the notoriously corrupt Ministry of National Economy. This did not appear to be enough though, as only a few weeks later protesters on March 21 handed a petition to Muscat's public prosecutor demanding immediate investigation of the finances of ministers and political officials.

Deriving from a combination of political concessions and security crackdown, Oman's experience with the Arab Spring lacked the critical mass seen in other countries. While there were some lasting institutional changes, including a restructuring of the judiciary and limited expansion of powers for the legislature, their real impacts are unclear. For example, Qaboos did expand the scope of the State Financial and Administrative Audit Institution (SFAAI), empowering it investigate suspicious cases. Since the jurisdictional change, over twenty people have been sentenced to prison terms ranging from one to twenty-three years, including Minister of National Economy Mohammed Al Khusaibi[28] Yet, the prosecutions have not included the most powerful of Oman's old economic elite.

This limited substantive change is important, as the sociopolitical pressure brought on by Oman's royal-elite bargain remain caustic. More than 56% of Omani nationals were under the age of 25 in 2017, a proportion that, due to Oman's chronically high birth rate, has remained stagnant for nearly a decade.[29] With Oman's population heavily geared toward the young, looking forward, if economic discontent continues, it is not unforeseen that the next wave of protesters will have less affinity for Qaboos, or his successor, as the major accomplishments of the state were achieved well before they could remember. Making matters more tenuous, Oman's limited finances make substantial expansion of social subsidies and largesse increasingly difficult, a factor that has been increasingly important since commodity prices began their steep descent in 2014.

Natural Resources and Diversification

Oman's oil reserves have always been understood to be limited and geologically difficult to extract. As of 2018, Oman's proved reserves stood at of 5.4 billion barrels of oil, compared to around 100 billion barrels in the UAE and Kuwait.[30] As noted earlier, deriving from these limited reserves, diversification efforts were always high on the reform list, yet did not show significant progress well into the 2000s. It was not until the wake of the 2014 commodity price crash when, like many of its peers, Oman's diversification efforts took a more serious tone. Yet, unlike its peers, the sultanate's financial reserves are counted in the tens of billions, opposed to hundreds of billions, and its oil reserves are estimated to last just another fifteen to twenty-five years at current rates of production, collectively making the matter even more pressing.[31]

In a testament to Oman's limited financial cushion, in the years following the oil price crash, Oman has had to lean heavily on international debt markets, with its debt to GDP ratio skyrocketing from under 5% in 2013 to over 45% in 2018.[32] Debt dependence is not new, nor unique, to the sultanate. During its initial developmental stages, between 1976 and 1995, the Omani government repeatedly found itself facing insufficient financial resources and responded by turning to international financial institutions or its neighbors. Throughout the 1970s, Saudi Arabia and Abu Dhabi repeatedly provided capital to cover budget deficits and during the 1980s, when the country's GDP averaged around US$8 billion, Oman borrowed at least US$1.4 billion from European commercial markets alone.[33]

Moving forward, a large part of Oman's diversification effort rests on the hope of international trade. Similar to Dubai, Oman aims to lean on its historical role as an Indian Ocean entrepôt. Key to this is the Duqm Special Economic Zone. The envisioned commercial zone is situated on the Arabian Sea near major shipping routes through the Red Sea to Asia and Africa, and is outside the crowded Strait of Hormuz, all major selling points. When completed Duqm will boast a shipping port, an airport, an oil refinery, a petrochemical complex and manufacturing facilities and has already attracted investment from Kuwait, the United Kingdom, China, India and South Korea.[34] The centerpiece of Duqm will still be hydrocarbons though, namely a 230,000 b/d export refinery, being built in conjunction with Kuwait's overseas refining company, Kuwait Petroleum International. The refinery is expected to cost US$7 billion and come online in 2023–2024.[35]

Iran is envisioned to be a major player in Duqm. In fact, Iran's publicly intended investments in Duqm are the largest from any foreign country.[36] Iran's role in Oman's diversification and economic development goes well beyond Duqm. Oman was the host of secret talks between the US and Iran that lead to the Joint Comprehensive Plan of Action (JCPOA), through which Iran agreed to monitoring of its nuclear activities in exchange for sanctions relief.[37] In parallel with these nuclear negotiations, Oman had held its own set of negotiations with Iran around economic integration and cooperation.

These negotiations were not the birth of a new Iranian-Omani relationship, but instead the extension of a long relationship of cooperation that reaches back to the 1970s when the Shah of Iranian helped Oman put down domestic uprisings in Dhofar.[38] Throughout the US-led Iranian embargo, Oman only chose to adhere to the sanctions pertaining to Iranian nuclear and ballistic missile programs, ignoring broader blanket sanctions. Moreover, economic activity between the two countries actually expanded during the period of sanctions, with Oman's annual bilateral trade with Iran growing by 70% between 2012 and 2013, later breaching the US$1 billion mark in 2015.[39]

Where the 2013 parallel negotiations focused on the development of a US$60 billion undersea natural gas pipeline, which would take Iranian gas to Oman, where it would be liquefied and exported, Iran's activity at Duqm has focused on the establishment of a US$200 million car manufacturing hub in partnership with the Iranian Khodor Industrial Group, the region's largest auto manufacturer.[40]

Yet, starting in 2017, natural gas discoveries, tepid demand growth and limited LNG export capacity have significantly reduced Oman's need for natural gas imports, diminishing the urgency of the Iran-Oman pipeline.[41] Even more troublesome, with the transition of Donald Trump into the White House, American foreign policy has dramatically turned against Iran, stalling progress on these projects and putting pressure on Oman's foreign policy and diversification efforts.

The tourism sector acts as another avenue of diversification that Oman has focused on. The Omani government targets tourism making up 6% of the country's GDP by 2040. Oman's tourism sector has shown healthy growth recently, growing from 2% in 2012 to 3.2% of GDP in 2017.[42] Helping drive this growth was the Omani Sovereign Wealth Fund's decision to boost investments at home following Oman's Arab Spring protests in an attempt to generate local employment and economic growth. By shifting its focus back home, where investments centered on tourism, mining and fisheries, the fund reduced its proportion of overseas assets to domestic assets to 50:50 from 70:30.[43] The fund is estimated to hold assets of around US$7 billion, while the larger Omani SWF, the State General Reserve Fund, is estimated to have US$20 billion in assets under management.[44]

Yet, even with this investment boost, tourism still only makes up a small portion of the domestic workforce. In fact, while the tourism sector is estimated to make up 3.4% of Oman's total employment, Omani nationals make up only 6% of the employees in hotels and restaurants, a key part of the tourism sector, highlighting the limited impact that boosting the tourism sector will have for the common Omani national.[45]

The Banking Sector

Like most other public functions before the ascension of Qaboos, until the mid-1970s there existed no regulator for the banking sector. For many reasons, there was no need for one as the number of banks were minimal and their activities limited. Yet, with the discovery of oil wealth came the expectations for significant development. It was partially driven by these expectations that the modern Omani banking sector came to life in 1974 through the Banking Law of 1974 and its establishment of the Central Bank of Oman.

Presently, the sector has sixteen conventional banks, seven of which are locally incorporated and nine foreign, in addition to two Islamic banks. By all regulatory measures, these banks comply with international standards, with the implementation of Basel III and the ninth International Financial Reporting Standard both expected in 2018.[46] While between the 1970s and 1990s the banking sector was heavily controlled by foreign banks, since the mid-1990s, the domestic banks have taken over an overwhelming share of the sector, with foreign banks proportion of total commercial banking assets falling precipitously from 15% in 2007 to around 6% in 2017. Currently, foreign banks are focused on corporate business niches, such as trade finance, rather than the retail market.[47]

Bank Muscat is Oman's largest bank, with around 35% market share by assets as of 2017, more than three times larger than the second largest Omani bank.[48] As a testament to the country's small economy, Bank Muscat is also the largest company listed on Oman's securities exchange, the Muscat Securities Market (MSM).[49] The Omani Royal Court holds a direct 24% stake in Bank Muscat, but through various public pension and insurance funds, effectively owns over 40% of the bank.[50] This trend of government ownership is not limited to Bank Muscat, with government or quasi-government entities owning around a quarter of the next two largest banks.[51]

Oman's Islamic banking sector is young relative to the region, having only launched in 2013, nearly forty years later than regional peers, when the CBO licensed what is still the country's only two Shari'a-compliant banks—Al Izz Islamic Bank and Bank Nizwa. Slow development of the domestic Islamic banking sector has been blamed on the sector's strict regulatory environment relative to other GCC states.[52]

Oman's limited natural resources have also reverberated into the private sector, where lack of domestic capital has led to constrained equities and banking sectors. In fact, Oman's recent turn to international debt markets was in part a byproduct of concerns about domestic liquidity. The Omani state is arguably the most important depositor to domestic banks, itself providing over a third of the sector's deposits.[53] In the wake of the 2008 financial crises there were significant concerns that the government would draw on those deposits to fund its fiscal deficit. Doing so would have created a serious liquidity crunch for local banks. Aware of this dynamic, the government instead turned toward international lenders, issuing US$11.5 billion via bonds and sukuk in 2016 and 2017 and then started 2018 with its largest issuance ever, a massive US$6.5 billion bond in January, equating to over 10% of its GDP.[54] Over 93% of the January issuance was allocated to non-Middle East investors.[55] The debt issuance took the country's debt to GDP ratio from under 5% in 2013 to over 45% in 2018.[56]

Moving forward, international markets have only so much appetite for Omani debt, a dynamic that could be detrimental for domestic banks. In August 2017 this led rating agencies to downgrade the long-term local and foreign currency deposit ratings of Oman's six largest banks.[57]

Despite this, key indicators, including capital adequacy ratios and non-performing loans remain healthy, averaging around 17% and 2% sector wide in 2018, respectively. Accordingly, aside from the regionally common dependence on government deposits, Oman's banking sector is generally considered to be stable.[58] The health of Oman's banking sector was highlighted during the 2008 crisis, when the Omani Central Bank's strict prudential measures limited domestic bank's exposure to toxic assets afflicting banks globally.[59]

Additionally positive, Oman's banking sector has seen its depth grow, with the domestic credit provision to GDP ratio growing from around 40% in 2008, then among the lowest in the Gulf region, to 70% in 2017, well within range of its regional peers.[60]

The trouble though is that the Omani banking sector must not just be stable, but also attractive, given the country's need to draw in foreign investment. In this regard, the Omani banking sector underperformed, with foreign deposits and long-term bonds making up less than 5% of the banking sector's aggregate deposits as of late 2016.[61] The sector is also limited by its size. Oman's largest bank, Bank Muscat, holding assets of just over US$28 billion, is around a third the size of Kuwait's largest bank, the National Bank of Kuwait.[62]

The Capital Markets

Oman's modern capital market, the Muscat Securities Exchange, was founded in 1989 by government decree due the need to regulate the country's growing number of joint stock companies. The MSM started humbly, operating from the basement of the Ministry of Commerce and Industry. At the time of its founding, it was only the third exchange in the region, after the Kuwaiti and Bahraini stock markets. In the decade that followed, the MSM saw more than 135 listings, brought together 118,000 distinct investors, and was considered "the best kept secret in the Gulf" by global bankers.[63] This rapid growth came to a screeching halt in 1998, when external market factors, namely the Asian financial crisis and low oil prices, combined with a lack of domestic capital market regulations, led to a market crash, with the MSM losing more than 50% of its capitalization.[64]

While the crash acted as the impetus for full scale regulatory modernization of the exchange, including the establishment of the Capital Markets Authority and the Muscat Clearing and Depository Company, in many ways the exchange has never really recovered. Today it is one of the smaller exchanges in the region, larger only than Bahrain's capital markets. As of mid-2018 it had around 120 listed stocks, many of which represent small companies with limited trading volume, split into three main sectors (financial, services and industrial) and further refined into a larger set of 23 sub-sectors, which cover segments such as banking, insurance, cement, chemicals, telecommunications, tourism, logistics, oil and gas, education and real estate.

Despite being small, the market has exhibited healthy growth, with an average annual growth rate of 6% between 2013 and 2017.[65] Even with this growth though, significant problems persist. Like the banking sector, the MSM is supposed to act as a catalyst for foreign activity, but as of 2018 only 10% of MSM's market activity was conducted by foreign, non-GCC, nationals.[66] Foreign participation has oscillated between 25% and 30% since 2008.

There even exist issues with the domestic market participants, who are overwhelming dominated by institutions such as pension funds that adopt a buy-and-hold strategy. This long-term investment strategy has been a major contributing factor in the MSM's chronic illiquidity over the last decade. Oman attempted to remedy this issue through the establishment of a designated market maker, the Oman Investment Stability Fund, in 2009. While having limited success, the stability fund has created another issue, that of government ownership of domestic companies, therefore limiting private, let alone foreign, participation and threatening crowding out behavior.

This is not the only area where there has been reform mismatch. The growth of the domestic capital markets has come into conflict with necessary market reforms such as cuts in domestic fuel subsidies and revisions to corporate tax policies, both of which were cited as contributors to poor MSM performance in 2017.[67] Even worse, these corporate tax changes, as of 2018, had not translated to any material increase in non-oil revenues for the government.[68]

Looking forward, privatizations and local listings are central to revitalizing the MSM. Yet, despite significant efforts by the government to steer local firms toward public listing, overall market conditions and illiquidity have acted as a deterrent to IPOs, with the few IPOs that have taken place being either government privatizations or the result of new legal mandates requiring public listing. In fact, the MSM itself, a government owned-company, is rumored to be next in line for privatization.[69]

Conclusion

It is hard not to be impressed by Oman's transformation. While the country's financial and banking sectors are still relatively small by most metrics, they have developed from zero in less than half a century. That said, the formula which allowed for this development, one based on the bargain Sultan Qaboos struck with leading merchant families during the country's developmental period, appears to have run its course. As the popular protests of 2011 show, the real or perceived corruption this bargain incubated undermined the same equation that initially drove Oman into its current developmental phase. Moving forward, while rebounding natural gas production has allowed for some recovery in the country's finances, constrained export infrastructure limits the upside from these hydrocarbon reserves. Accordingly, like Dubai, Oman will need to turn to more traditional market strategies in order to attract investment and financial flows.

The events of 2018 have shown that Iran will likely be a large factor in these efforts. For example, in March 2018, Oman and Iran signed a number of significant agreements on banking cooperation and re-export trade.[70] While many agreements are signed in the Gulf without significant action afterward, Iran finds its traditional conduit for financial and trade flows, Dubai, increasingly aligning its foreign policy with that of Abu Dhabi, who has become even more fixated on what the Arab Gulf states see as Iran's hegemonic efforts in the region. Oman appears to be attempting to capitalize on this space through measures like its Duqm industrial zone, the maintenance of its relatively non-aligned stance despite pressure to do otherwise, and agreements like those from March. Like most of its Gulf peers, Oman's population is heavily geared toward the young. Consequently, if a new model for growth is not developed, it is possible that the next wave of protesters will have less affinity for Qaboos, or more likely his successor, as the major progress that the Sultan was once praised for becomes an achievement of a past age.

Notes

1. Abdel Razzaq Takriti, *Monsoon Revolution Republicans, Sultans, and Empires in Oman, 1965—1976*. (London: Oxford University Press, 2013).
2. Robert E. Looney, "The Omani and the Bahraini Paths to Development: Rare and Contrasting Oil-Based Economic Success Stories," in Augustin K. Fosu, ed. *Achieving Development Success: Strategies and Lessons from the Developing World*. (Oxford: Oxford University Press, 2013), p. 19.
3. Sarah G. Phillips and Jennifer S. Hunt, " 'Without Sultan Qaboos, We Would Be Yemen': The Renaissance Narrative and the Political Settlement in Oman," *Journal of International Development* 29, no. 5 (2017): 645–660.
4. Mohamed A. Ramady, *Political, Economic and Financial Country Risk*. (New York, NY: Springer, 2013), p. 162.
5. Kawee Jarach and Mark Speece, "Arab Gulf Cities: Competing Identities of Cosmopolitanism vs. Localism," *CUI '13, Proceedings of the International Contemporary Urban Issues Conference* (Istanbul: DAKAM Publishing, November 2013).
6. Calvin H. Allen and W. Lynn Rigsbee II, *Oman under Qaboos: From Coup to Constitution, 1970–1996*. (London: Routledge, 2014), p. 113.
7. Marc Valeri, "Oman and the Succession of Sultan Qaboos," *Hurst Publishers*, December 3, 2014.
8. Central Intelligence Agency: Directorate of Intelligence, "Oman: Domestic Forces and the Succession [REDACTED]," *Intelligence Assessment*, March 1985. Declassified May 2011.
9. Allen and Rigsbee II, *Oman under Qaboos*, pp. 114–117.
10. Ibid.
11. Bertelsmann Stiftung, *Oman Country Report*. (Gütersloh: Bertelsmann Stiftung, 2016).
12. Bertelsmann Stiftung, *Oman Country Report*. (Gütersloh: Bertelsmann Stiftung, 2018).
13. Marc Valeri, "Simmering Unrest and Succession Challenges in Oman," *Carnegie Endowment for International Peace*, January 2015, p. 7.
14. Marc Valeri, *Oman: Politics and Society in the Qaboos State*. (London: Hurst, 2009), p. 102.
15. Mandana E. Limbert, *In the Time of Oil : Piety, Memory, and Social Life in an Omani Town*. (Stanford, CA: Stanford University Press, 2010).
16. Michael Spence, "The Growth Report: Strategies for Sustained Growth and Inclusive Development," *Commission on Growth and Development Final Report*. (Washington, DC: World Bank, 2008), p. 20.

17. Afshin Molavi, "Oman's Economy: Back on Track," *Middle East Policy Council* V, no. 4 (1998).
18. World Bank Group, "Sultanate of Oman Sustainable Growth and Economic Diversification," *World Bank Report* no. 12199-OM, May 31, 1994.
19. World Bank Group, *World Development Indicators*. (Washington, DC: World Bank, n.d.).
20. Antoine Mansour, "Planning for Economic Diversification in Oman," *Omani Economic Association*, Undated.
21. Government of Oman, *The National Program for Enhancing Economic Diversification, TANFEED Handbook*, July 2017.
22. World Bank Group, *Doing Business Economy Profile 2017: Oman*. (Washington, DC: World Bank Group, 2017).
23. Thomas Fuller, "Rallies in Oman Steer Clear of Criticism of Its Leader," *The New York Times*, March 1, 2011.
24. Saleh al Shaibany, "Lulu Supermarket Set Ablaze by Oman Protesters," *The National*, March 1, 2011.
25. Marc Valeri, "Simmering Unrest and Succession Challenges in Oman," p. 9.
26. Central Intelligence Agency: Directorate of Intelligence, "Oman: Domestic Forces and the Succession [REDACTED]," *Intelligence Assessment*, March 1985. Declassified May 2011.
27. Bertelsmann Stiftung, *Oman Country Report*, (Gütersloh: Bertelsmann Stiftung, 2018).
28. Reuters Staff, "After Popular Protests, Oman Starts to Pursue Graft," *Reuters*, March 23, 2014.
29. Government of Oman National Center for Statistics, *Oman Statistical Yearbook 2017*, 79.
30. British Petroleum Company, *BP Statistical Review of World Energy*. (London: British Petroleum Company, 2017).
31. Anita Yadav, "Sultanate of Oman Update," *Emirates NBD Credit Note*, January 10, 2018.
32. "Oman Looks to Foreign Firms and Downstream to Combat Economic Woes," *Middle East Economic Survey* 61, no. 12 (March 23, 2018).
33. Allen and Rigsbee II, *Oman under Qaboos*, pp. 104–107.
34. Andrew Torchia and Fatma Alarimi, "Oman Builds Industrial Outpost in Desert to Escape Oil Trap," *Reuters*, April 20, 2016.
35. "Oman Eyes Coal Power," *Middle East Economic Survey* 61, no. 15 (April 13, 2018).
36. Torchia and Alarimi, "Oman Builds Industrial Outpost in Desert to Escape Oil Trap."
37. Jay Solomon, "Will the Trump Administration Force Oman to Choose Sides?" *Washington Institute for Near East Policy*, January 9, 2018.
38. Maryam Al-Bolushi, "The Effect of Omani-Iranian Relations on the Security of the Gulf Cooperation Council Countries after the Arab Spring," *Contemporary Arab Affairs* 9, no. 3 (2016): 383–399.
39. Yakir Gillis, "Oman: Iran's Best Friend in the Gulf," *Financial Times*, April 11, 2016.
40. Ibid.
41. "Oman: Khazzan Boosts LNG Exports to Record Levels," *Middle East Economic Survey* 61, no. 18 (May 4, 2018).
42. "Travel and Tourism Economic Impact 2018 Oman," *World Travel and Tourism Council*, March 2018.
43. Mohamed A. Ramady, *Political, Economic and Financial Country Risk*. (New York, NY: Springer, 2013), p. 166.
44. Mark Cobley, "Oman's Sovereign Wealth Fund Makes Bold Emerging Markets Call," *Financial News*, May 8, 2018.

45. "Travel and Tourism Economic Impact 2018 Oman," *World Travel and Tourism Council*, March 2018; Government of Oman National Center for Statistics, *Oman Statistical Yearbook 2017*, 116; Author's Calculations.
46. Imran Azad, Mohd Faiyaz and A. H. M. Saifullah Sadi, "Growth of Banking sector in Sultanate of Oman: An Analysis," *International Journal of Finance and Policy Analysis* 3 (2011): 91–100. Oxford Business Group, *The Report: Oman 2018* (London: Oxford Business Group, 2018).
47. Oxford Business Group, *The Report: Oman 2016*. (London: Oxford Business Group, 2016).
48. Bank Muscat, *Investor Presentation December 2017*, December 2017.
49. Oxford Business Group, *The Report: Oman 2018*. (London: Oxford Business Group, 2018).
50. Bank Muscat, *Major Shareholders*. Available at www.bankmuscat.com/en-us/InvestorRelation/si/Pages/MajorShareholders.aspx.
51. Ananthakrishnan Prasad and Pierluigi Bologna, *Oman: Banking Sector Resilience*, No. 10–61 (Washington D.C.: International Monetary Fund, 2010), p. 6.
52. Mohamed A. Ramady, *Political, Economic and Financial Country Risk*. (New York, NY: Springer, 2013), p. 166.
53. Central Bank of Oman, *Annual Report 2016*, 89.
54. Anita Yadav, "Sultanate of Oman Update," *Emirates NBD Credit Note*, January 10, 2018.
55. "Gulf Bonds in 2018 Another Bumper Year?" *Middle East Economic Survey* 61, no. 13 (March 30, 2018).
56. Anita Yadav. "Sultanate of Oman Update," Emirates NBD Credit Note, January 10, 2018.
57. Oxford Business Group, *The Report: Oman 2018*. (London: Oxford Business Group, 2018).
58. Ibid.
59. Ananthakrishnan Prasad and Pierluigi Bologna, *Oman : Banking Sector Resilience*, No. 10–61. (Washington, DC: International Monetary Fund, 2010), pp. 6–10.
60. World Bank Group, *World Development Indicators*. (Washington, DC: World Bank, n.d.).
61. Central Bank of Oman, *Annual Report 2016*, p. 90.
62. Morningstar Data.
63. Abdullah Salem Al Salmi, "Capital Market Developments in Oman," *Business Today*, October 31, 2010; Afshin Molavi, "Oman's Economy: Back on Track," *Middle East Policy Council* V, no. 4 (1998).
64. Salmi, "Capital Market Developments in Oman."
65. Muscat Securities Exchange, *Annual Report*, Various Years; Authors Calculations.
66. Muscat Securities Exchange, *Annual Report*, 2017.
67. Oxford Business Group, *The Report: Oman 2018*. (London: Oxford Business Group, 2018).
68. Anita Yadav, "Sultanate of Oman Update," *Emirates NBD Credit Note*, January 10, 2018.
69. Oxford Business Group, *The Report*.
70. "Oman to Become a Re-Export Hub / Iran and Oman Expand Banking Relationships," *Central Bank of the Islamic Republic of Iran*, March 18, 2018.

5 The Gulf States in Global Financial Markets

Introduction

The Gulf has always been linked to the global economy in some manner. Throughout the 18th and 19th centuries, maritime trade linked regional entrepôts trading everything from frankincense to pearls across ports stretching from North Africa to Western India. These trade links fueled the growth of powerful merchant families across the region, many of which form the commercial elite discussed earlier in this work. Yet, over the last half century, the region's most commented upon contribution to the global economy has undoubtedly been oil. Admittedly, this contribution is not insignificant. The GCC's share of global oil production nearly doubled from around 15% in 1960 to over 27% in 1970; a level it holds once again in 2017 after having fallen back to the teens in the 1980s.[1] Yet equally, if not more, important are the capital gains this oil wealth generated and how this wealth has transformed the Gulf states' position in the global economy.

The transformation was not linear nor immediate. Between 1970 and 1980, capital accrued to the Gulf states from hydrocarbon rents rose from US$5.2 billion to US$158 billion, the equivalent of roughly US$500 billion in 2018.[2] During the most recent oil boom between 2000 and 2008, estimates of oil rent accumulation range from US$800 billion to US$1.2 trillion. While these are both vast sums of money, they were not treated the same. Where the former was either squandered extravagantly, or funneled into low-risk, low-return investments in the Western world, the latter found itself increasingly funneled to higher-risk asset classes across the developing world. This chapter will trace this transformation, first discussing the investment strategies employed during each of these phases, with a heavy focus on the rise of sovereign wealth funds during the latter phase. Finally, the Western response to these new financial power brokers will be explored, as will the shift in tone that came with the 2008 crisis and recent trends toward south-south investment.

Phase 1: 1960–1985

The Gulf state's accumulation of wealth through hydrocarbon sales can be viewed in two periods—from 1960 to 1985 and from 1995 to the present.

During the first phase of wealth accumulation, oil rents were generally not used to generate the maximum potential returns in domestic or financial investments. This is not to devalue the significant developments in domestic health, education, energy and housing infrastructure during this period, but instead to say that, relatively speaking, irresponsible levels of the newfound wealth were squandered on low-value initiatives and reckless spending. As Steffen Hertog has noted, Saudi Arabian state income experienced a compound annual growth of 57% between 1969 and 1976, while the same rate for state expenditure was 55%, meaning, "almost all the additional income in this period of oil price increases was spent immediately."[3] Moreover, even the public works projects that contributed to these spending habits were far from cost-effective, with one 1975 estimate finding that a public works project would cost up to three times as much in Saudi Arabia as it would in California.[4] By contrast, from 2002 to 2008, the growth rate of state income was 31%, while expenditure growth was 14%, underlining the shift toward more prudent spending and saving habits. The profligate spending during the first phase of wealth accumulation gave way to the Gulf States' inability to weather the oil price crash of the late 1980s, when many of the Gulf States debt levels rose to near or above 100% of GDP.

With respect to international markets, through to the mid-1980s, the Gulf States played a passive, limited role in global political economy that primarily focused on keeping the international economy supplied with hydrocarbons. A large portion of the revenues generated by these oil exports found their way back to western economies, namely the United States and the United Kingdom, through investments in government securities. High-profile investments in real estate and corporate stock did occur during this period, but made up a smaller portion of the overall investment portfolio.

To some degree, this focus on Western markets was at the behest of Western advisors. As the late Mary Ann Tétreault has said, "oil exporters were disdained as *nouveaux riches* and urged to recycle their windfalls in the importers' economies for the sake of global economic balance and stability."[5] Unsurprisingly, this focus on treasuries proved critical to the currencies of both the US and the UK. For the latter, the rise of GCC economic prowess came just as the British pound was facing its harshest headwinds. The Gulf States, primarily Kuwait, was foundational in the UK's ability to maintain the value of the sterling. In fact, going into the 1960s, it was estimated that Gulf holdings made up around one-quarter of the UK's total gold and foreign reserve assets.[6] This dependence continued until the UK's massive devaluation in 1967, which sank the value of the Gulf's holdings and led them to diversify their foreign treasury holdings.

It was not long before the Gulf States took on an instrumental role in the strength of another currency, the US$. The growth of 'petrodollars,' the denomination of oil contracts in US$ which were then invested or held in the US financial system, in effect propped up the American economy just as its global dominance was under threat in the post-Bretton Woods period.[7]

For the Gulf States, this was exchanged for an American security umbrella during a time of turbulent conflict in the region, including the Iranian Revolution, the Iran-Iraq war and the Soviet incursion into Afghanistan.

Between the early 1970s and 1982, the GCC state's combined holdings of short- and long-term US Treasuries grew from US$2.2 billion to US$42 billion, or the equivalent of around US$107 in 2018 inflation-adjusted dollars. The growth took the Arab state's total share of foreign-held Treasury securities from under 2% to a peak of nearly 30% in 1982 (See Figure 5.1). When viewed from this perspective, the notion that the petrodollar was fundamental to both the Sterling and the US$ is clearly not understated.

This exponential growth occurred in tandem with the precipitous rise in global oil prices, which rose from under US$5/bbl in the early 1970s to nearly US$40/bbl in early 1980s. By 1983 though, the bubble popped, and oil prices plummeted to as low as US$10/bbl. Keeping in tandem with global oil revenues, GCC states' foreign Treasury holdings nearly halved, falling to just over US$22 billion in 1987, from US$42 billion just five years prior. This fall took the Gulf States' share of foreign held US Treasuries from fell nearly 30% in 1982, to below the 5%-mark by 1991.

The correlation between oil revenues and Gulf Treasury holdings is not in and of itself surprising. Surplus oil revenues have to be invested somewhere, and US debt traditionally has been considered one of the safest investment options. Surplus oil revenues in the 1970s and 1980s thus took on the role of a backstop to the US Dollar, which had just been taken off the gold standard and was prone to significant volatility. Decades later, with the rise in global oil prices in the mid-2000s, total US Treasury holdings by Gulf States ballooned once again, growing from US$50 billion in 2005 to over US$250 billion in 2017. The bulk of this was overwhelmingly held by Saudi Arabia who, as of early 2018, held US$151 billion in short and long-term US Treasuries. What is notable though is, even with this massive growth in Treasury holdings, the GCC states collectively have not held more than 5% of total outstanding foreign-held Treasuries since 1992, despite having the liquidity to do so.

While it should be noted that these numbers are likely somewhat understated given that the GCC states have increasingly purchased US debt through private financial intermediaries, transactions that would not be reflected in official US Department of the Treasury foreign holdings data, the transformation in the Gulf state's role in the US economy is undeniable. Where in the 1970s the petro-states clearly acted as the backstop to the US$, since the turn of the century, this role has been increasingly taken on by other actors, namely China and Japan, whose visible portion of US Treasury holdings have collectively been between 42% and 49% since 2000, all while the GCC state's collectively have not made up more than 5%. In tandem with this shift, there has been a significant transformation in the form and direction of investments the Arab Gulf States' have made with their surplus oil revenues.

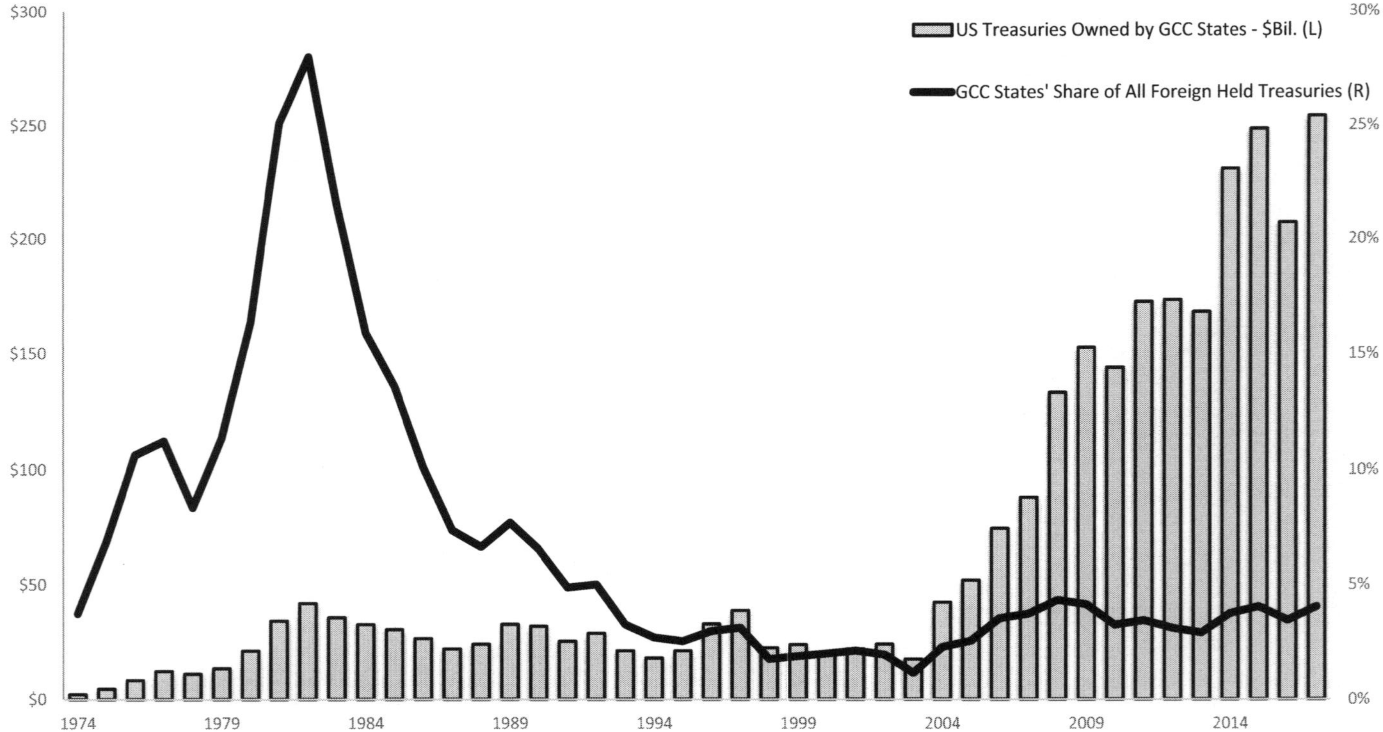

1982

- Oil Price: US$38 (US$99/bbl in 2018 US$)
- US Treasuries Owned GCC States: US$42 bill. ($107 bill. in 2018 US$)
- Percent of all Foreign Held Treasuries: 28%

2014

- Oil Price: US$96/bbl
- US Treasuries Owned GCC States: US$231
- Percent of all Foreign Held Treasuries: 4%

Figure 5.1 GCC States' Holdings of US Treasuries

Source: OPEC, EIA, US Dept. of the Treasury

Phase 2: 1985–Present

Just like in the 1970s and 80s, the oil price boom of the early 2000s fueled significant capital accumulation, with the six GCC states collectively acquiring an average of US$270 billion annually between 2003 and 2008, for a total of around US$1.6 trillion from oil exports after taking production costs into consideration.[8] After further considerations for total military spending based on data from the SIPRI Military Expenditure Database and estimates on sums diverted to royal diwans, the authors estimate as much as US$1.25 trillion remained for regular budgetary expenditures (military spending is generally not included in the standard budgetary expenses of GCC states).[9] Assuming that 70% of US$1.25 trillion went to budgetary expenditures, an assumption that is in line with trends seen in official SAMA data, that would leave nearly US$375 billion available for broader investment during those six years alone, not taking into consideration any sort of accrued investment returns. This exponential growth in capital also came when the GCC states had already paid down the significant domestic and external debt they had built up following the oil price crash in the late 1980s. In the case of Saudi Arabia, debt to GDP levels that were over 100% in the late 1990s fell to almost zero, effectively providing a larger pool of capital for investment.

Unlike the wealth accumulation in the two decades leading up to the 1986 bust cycle, these accrued revenues were used more strategically, with the Gulf states taking on an active, engaged and most importantly, less risk-averse, role in the global economy. Opposed to the prior phase in wealth accumulation where safe, low-risk corporate and sovereign bonds were the focus, this second phase, from the late eighties to present, has been underpinned by the placement of funds in a wider array of assets, ranging from real estate to high technology across a wider geography including Asia and the Middle East. These investments regularly take the form of partnerships, either with other funds or with foreign corporations, and represent the Gulf states' desire to actively diversify revenue streams and in some cases foster technology transfer. This new policy priority overtook the prior oil-for-security dogma that had guided capital outflows and led to the heavy focus on government treasuries during the prior phase.

The growth of international financial clout and activism is best exemplified by the growth of the region's SWFs, who saw their assets quadruple in the decade leading up to 2008, when they reached an estimated US$883 billion, the majority of this coming from surplus oil revenues.[10] For Abu Dhabi, the dominant SWF is the Abu Dhabi Investment Authority. In Kuwait, the leader is the Kuwait Investment Authority. In Saudi Arabia, it is the Public Investment Fund. In Qatar it is Qatar Investment Authority, as well as Qatar Holding, which is controlled by QIA. In-depth discussions around the organization, size and history of these SWFs are included in the countries' respective chapters.

The growth of these funds provided an avenue for the Gulf countries to play a more dynamic, active role in global financial markets, and in many ways embodied a new era in the GCC's global engagement. The dominance of the petrodollar system, whereby oil revenues kept foreign and central banks capitalized and the US dominant, has given way to more diversified Gulf capital outflows, where more of the region's accrued oil rents are aimed at public and private equity markets not only in Western markets, but also in the broader developing world, in turn building the economic prestige and power of the Gulf states and their economic elite.

This change was not wholly well received in the US, with the concerns most clearly articulated by Former Treasury Secretary Larry Summers, who in 2007 explained,

> The logic of the capitalist system depends on shareholders causing companies to . . . maximize the value of their shares. It is far from obvious that this will over time be the only motivation of governments as shareholders. They may want to see their national companies compete effectively, or to extract technology or to achieve influence.[11]

The best example of these concerns was the firestorm raised over the 2006 prospect of Dubai Ports World's acquisition of P&O, a British company that operated six major ports in the eastern United States. As Kristian Ulrichsen states, "The DP World case caught the Gulf States in the crossfire of a populist xenophobic domestic backlash against perceived geopolitical swings against US interests."[12] The concerns were not limited to the US, with similar concerns arising in New Zealand and Sweden in 2007, following Dubai's offers to buy the Auckland International Airport and the Swedish stock exchange OMX, respectively. While Dubai eventually backed out of the former purchase, it's purchase into OMX was successfully transformed into key stakes in Nasdaq and the London Stock Exchange through a series of swaps, despite opposition from US Senator Charles E. Schumer.[13] Bourse Dubai has sold down both holdings since, liquidating part of its Nasdaq holdings at a loss in order to meet debt obligations in 2010.[14]

2008: Shifting Tones

Western animosity toward the Gulf's rising role in international finance appeared to shift considerably in the wake of the 2008 crisis. In fact, what ensued in the wake of the financial collapse was reminiscent of the financial-shuttle diplomacy the US undertook in the 1970s when it was looking to find support for the USD. In the more recent iteration, US Treasury Secretary Henry Paulson traveled to Saudi Arabia, the UAE and Qatar in May 2008, followed by his successor Timothy Geithner in July 2009, with both arguing for dollar-supporting policies despite the fact that, at the time, additional investments in treasuries were not the most attractive investments available.

US pressure was especially heavy on Saudi Arabia ahead of the winter 2008–2009 G20 meetings, when the US was publicly calling for an additional US$500 billion to be put into the IMF. Similarly, in November 2008, British Prime Minister Gordon Brown traveled to the UAE, Saudi Arabia and Qatar, asking for substantial injections into the IMF's coffers. These overtures came just two years after the visceral reaction to DP World's attempted port acquisition and represented a shift in policymakers stance, which now actively sought to draw, rather than fend off, capital from the Gulf.

The shift in tone was not limited to the United States, but also applied to politicians across Europe who had called for regulating SWF investment shortly before the crisis, including Peer Steinbrück, then Germany's federal finance minister.[15] Just a few months into the 2008 credit crunch, Peer Steinbrück notably changed his tune, saying ahead of a trip to the GCC where he met leadership from the KIA and ADIA that, "sovereign wealth funds are welcome in Germany. . . . Their commitment contributes to value creation and employment . . . and to stabilization in times of financial market turbulence."[16] Italy's Silvio Berlusconi made a similar about face.[17]

The notable exception from this trend was France, which had actively advocated for increased cooperation with Gulf SWFs, including QIA and Mubadala, in the years before and after 2008.[18] SWF investments in France during this period even extended into strategic sectors, most notably Qatar's investments in Lagardère in 2006 and EADS, both strategic firms in defense and high technology. As of 2017 Qatar is the largest single shareholder in Lagardère in terms of both share capital and voting rights.[19] Oddly enough, France's tone shifted in the opposite direction in 2008, with French president Nicolas Sarkozy promising to protect innocent French managers from 'extremely aggressive' sovereign investments.[20] At the time of the statement, no publicly disclosed SWF investments into French companies had been spurred by the financial crisis.

It is important to note that the Gulf states were not unaffected by the crisis, the region's SWFs were estimated to see possible losses of over US$200 billion, GCC stock markets saw their market capitalizations halved and Dubai's property market implosion required Abu Dhabi's bailout. Yet, the regional block still sat on considerable liquid assets at a time when the global economy was in need, and assets across the globe were at rock bottom prices.

That said, the GCC states initially rebuffed overtures to bailout the global economy, and in doing so reiterated their demand for greater representation and respect. They wanted to be viewed as an equal participant in the development of global financial architecture, not just a piggy bank. These desires were not hidden, in fact, at the time the UAE's Central Bank Governor Sultan Nasser Al Suweidi put it very bluntly, stating, the GCC, "will not be providing funds without extra voice and extra recognition."[21] Similar sentiment was expressed by Saudi Arabia and Qatar.

Despite initial hesitancy, the overtures were eventually successful, with the Gulf states proving to be a vital source of liquidity for Western financial institutions. Abu Dhabi's ADIA famously bought into Citigroup, a deal that would eventually sour. Qatar's QIA bought into Barclays and Credit Suisse in 2008, and later saved troubled banks KBC and Dexia of Belgium and Luxembourg, respectively, in 2011. Kuwait's KIA invested heavily in Citigroup and Merrill Lynch; investments that received significant backlash in Kuwait. In total, Gulf SWFs completed over US$33 billion in acquisitions of Western companies in 2007 and early 2008 alone.[22] The SWFs were not the only Gulf entities to pour money into financial institutions. In January, The Olayan Group, one of Saudi Arabia's biggest private, family-owned conglomerates, took part in a massive US$6.6 billion capital infusion into Merrill Lynch. The Olayan Group already held stakes in JPMorganChase and Credit Suisse.[23] In November of the same year, Saudi Prince Alwaleed bin Talal spent nearly US$400 million of his fortune to raise his share of Citigroup from 4% to 5%.[24]

It is important to note that these infusions of capital came at a time of pessimism and risk-avoidance across most markets. The SWFs purchased these stakes when their credit default swap spreads were at historically high levels and their stock prices at particularly low levels, in turn suggesting this capital infusion allowed the banks to continue their operation. This is substantiated by the general trend of stock price appreciation after the respective deals' announcements.[25]

The differences between political and economic motivations throughout these investments are unclear, but their size is undeniable. Estimates by Richard Youngs show that GCC SWFs provided a third of the emergency financing made available by European governments in the autumn of 2008.[26] This newfound international clout was not lost on the Saudis, who successfully used it to limit the redistribution of IMF voting shares to developing countries in 2010, a maneuver aimed at protecting its own voting rights.

The aforementioned investments were not welcomed by everyone, with many questioning the funds' motives, including then Senator Hillary Clinton who, in January 2008 said, "We need to have a lot more control over what they [sovereign wealth funds] do and how they do it."[27] These kind of public blowbacks are not new. In fact, Kuwait learned its lesson early after being forced to divest part of its holdings in British Petroleum by the Thatcher government in 1988.

The only conclusion that can be reached is that Western policy makers often assume Arab funds have ulterior motives that endanger national interests and ultimately desire to force changes in foreign policy and domestic culture. These concerns, which are seemingly set aside in times of need, are largely unwarranted. Despite the breadth of investments, on the whole SWF investments have not shown any overt political malicious intent or forward-leaning assertion of financial prowess. Instead, SWF investments have overwhelmingly highlighted the group's focus on domestic diversification and economic reform, both considerations that have only grown in priority since 2014. Indeed, SWFs, like other financial actors, seek to maximize returns. By and large, these SWFs are staffed by elite finance professionals. In fact, as discussed in previous chapters, Western finance professionals make up a significant portion of their leadership and mid-level staff. Accordingly, like any other rational investment vehicle, the respective funds' leadership are primarily concerned with growing, or at least maintaining, the value of their assets, guarding the security of their assets, and having a voice in the companies within which they hold stakes. Ulterior political considerations are not traditionally a part of these calculations.

Indeed, when GCC states want to affect a political outcome through financial investment, they rarely do so through SWFs. There is little need for this. The GCC states are anything but coy with their ability to influence political outcomes with money. This was clear in Saudi Arabia's intervention to save the Lebanese banking sector after Israel's 2006 invasion, and the subsequent financial backing of select parties in the 2009 Lebanese elections. More recently, the starkest example of the Gulf states employing capital to affect favorable political outcomes has been the UAE and Saudi Arabia's ardent support of Egypt's Abdel Fattah al Sisi with direct budget injections, bilateral aid and fuel products.

In fact, the larger strategic threat to the United States would be the concerted focus of investments *away* from Western markets. As shown, in times of need, GCC investment funds have provided European and American markets with a critical source of liquidity. If these funds were to decide that the cost of heavily weighting Western markets in their portfolios was net negative, be it for financial or political considerations, another systemic crash could prove significantly harder to recover from. This is especially critical given the new dual-role of the SWFs which has them not only saving for future generations, but also catalyzing domestic economies through targeted investment. Generally speaking, targeted publicly financed investment aimed at spurring domestic growth is not new, but the fervor with which some of the funds have recently turned toward it is. Key examples of this fervor can be found in the recent activities of PIF and Mubadala. All things considered, this new focus reduces the pool of available funds for US investment. This inward focus has only accelerated since the 2014 commodity slump, and it will likely continue given the breadth and ambition of recent domestic reform agendas and pressing labor market concerns.

Lasting Change

Opposition to Arab investment in the early 2000s came just as the Gulf states were already shifting their investment focus away from low-risk assets in developed, Western countries and toward riskier assets in emerging and developing markets across Asia and the Middle East. Where 46% of the GCC's overseas investments took the form of bank deposits in 2001, by

2006 this number fell to just 28%. Concurrently, the dispersion of these investments shifted as well, with investments in MENA growing to equal those in the United States and Europe.[28] Overall, these SWFs have a much larger tolerance for emerging market risk than somewhat comparable western peers. For example, while ADIA gives emerging markets a weighting between 15% and 25% in its portfolio, US pension funds on average put just 5% of their assets in emerging markets.[29] These trends make the Gulf SWF assets not only one of the largest pools of assets in the world, but also one of the most extensively diversified across geographies and relatively riskier assets.

It is not hard to assume that the pivot away from Western markets was fueled, and eventually solidified, by the controversy that ensued in the lead up to and following the 2008 financial crisis. Recent SWF activity has only substantiated this. For example, KIA began increasing its exposure to equities and alternative assets around 2005, with equities taking up as much half its portfolio by 2008. It is largely believed that the KIA parred back its equities position in the wake of the 2008 crash, but as of 2018 had refocused on emerging markets, with KIA CEO Farouk Bastaki stating in 2018 that Kuwait "is moving to increase its investments in emerging markets. This does not mean abandoning developed markets, but . . . a reduction in some investments in them." As the fund's chairman said just months prior "I have no choice . . . the alpha is there."[30] Similarly, in its 2016 annual review, ADIA made it clear that its focus area would be emerging markets, stating that the SWF expects around a third of global growth "coming from China and India alone."[31]

Even with the secrecy of these funds, public information makes their emerging market focus clear. For example, ADIA, along with KIA, acted as anchor investors in the IPO of Indian insurer SBI Life in September 2017. Just one month later, ADIA committed US$1 billion to India's The National Investment and Infrastructure Fund. It was the first international investor to commit to the fund.[32] Abu Dhabi is also extremely active in China, where Mubadala has joined with the China Development Bank Capital and China's State Administration of Foreign Exchange to launch the UAE-China Joint Investment Cooperation Fund in 2015. The fund will target mutually strategic sectors such as conventional and renewable energy, infrastructure and technology and advanced manufacturing, according to comments by UAE Minister of State Sultan Al Jaber.[33]

Real estate investments, which have always been a mainstay in Gulf SWF portfolios, have also recently focused on emerging markets. In 2015, ADIA made the largest Asian real estate investment by a SWF when it acquired three hotels in Hong Kong for US$2.4 billion, then the largest real estate investment by an SWF in Asia. It wasn't long though before the deal was dethroned, with QIA purchasing Singapore's Asia Square Tower 1 from BlackRock Inc. for US$2.5 billion in June 2017.[34]

The holdout to diversification during the 90s and early 2000s was Saudi Arabia, with the Saudi Arabian Monetary Authority still believed to hold as much as 80% of its assets in currency and bonds, a tactic that kept it relatively unscathed during the 2008 market crash. As of April 2018, if 80% of its holdings were held in low-risk assets, this would equate to around US$400 billion, down from an all-time high of US$600 billion in 2014.[35] That said, the increasingly powerful Public Investment Fund, under the direction of Mohammed bin Salman, has taken an aggressive approach to diversification. The fund has set targeted annual returns of 8 to 9% between 2025 and 2030 from a base of about 3% in 2017.[36] While the PIF is largely focused on investments within Saudi Arabia, it aims to invest a quarter of its total portfolio in foreign markets by 2020. Presently, the PIF has about US$220 billion in assets under managements.[37] At that level, recent investments have already breached the 25% mark, with the fund committing US$20 billion to an infrastructure fund with Blackstone and US$45 billion to a tech-focused fund with SoftBank. In more consumer-facing deals, PIF made a US$3.5 billion investment in Uber, as well as a US$1 billion cash infusion in Virgin's space companies. PIF's international investment decisions have not always been a success though. For example, Blackstone reportedly had to offer steep discounts in order to attract investors to the Saudi-backed infrastructure fund.[38] More notably, the US$70 billion valuation used to purchase the 5% stake in Uber in 2016 was written down by over 30% in a subsequent major Uber-share purchase by none other than Softbank, PIF's partner in the unrelated tech-fund, who purchased 15% of Uber at a valuation of US$48 billion, instantly writing down the market value of PIF's stake in Uber.[39]

Moving forward, the PIF is set to inherit the windfall of assets from two key sources. Firstly, proceeds from the planned flotation of Saudi Aramco and other privatizations, as well as the savings from subsidy and public-sector spending cuts, are to be transferred to the PIF. Secondly, as Mohammed Al Tuwaijri, the kingdom's Minister of Economy and Planning, said in March 2018, any excess oil revenues after meeting state budgetary needs would be funneled to the PIF, more in line with how other Gulf state SWFs receive funding.[40] This will not only dramatically boost the wealth held by PIF, potentially making a quarter of its asset as large as US$250 billion, but also effectively undercut the role of SAMA, which has been the traditional recipient of surplus oil revenues.

With this in mind, PIF still aims to earn around between 6.5% and 8% from its international investments, rates of return that developed-nation sovereign debt will never reach in the current interest rate environment. This underlines the strong likelihood that the PIF will move into riskier assets, which raise the potential for larger returns but also big losses at what is poised to be the kingdom's financial buffer. As part of this movement into riskier assets, the PIF is more likely to move aggressively into emerging market public and private equity.[41] Highlighting the likelihood that much of this will be pointed away from US markets is the passage of the Justice Against Sponsors of Terrorism Act (JASTA), which came into force in late 2016 and allows 9/11 first responders and families of victims to sue the Saudi government for complicity in the attacks. While the justification for this law is not within the scope of this work, its effect on Saudi investment dynamics is. Nowhere is this clearer than in the considerations for Saudi Aramco's public listing, which saw US exchanges nixed as a potential location for the IPO by Aramco officials due to concerns that JASTA would open the firm-up to unacceptable legal vulnerabilities.

Interestingly, one of the investments specifically included in PIF forward looking documents is a US$10 billion investment fund with Russia's SWF, the Russian Direct Investment Fund, for investments in Russia, a significant development in geo-economic relations given the tenuous history between the two countries. This thawing of relations with Russia, one bolstered by agreements over oil production, could be considered emblematic of the shift in investment focus away from Western markets. Deriving from the size of their economies, America and Europe will always play a large role in the calculations of Gulf state SWFs. Yet, viewed from a broader perspective, the position from which the Arab States interact with these economies, often through their respective SWFs, has shifted in tone, with the American and European markets taking on the form of clientele who increasingly have to compete with emerging or developing markets for the SWFs' attention.

Looking East: Energy Investments in Asia and Southeast Asia

The shift in capital flows away from Western capital markets occurred simultaneous with the broader growth of south-south trade and investment (See Figure 5.2). Europe and North America's total share of exports from the GCC fell from nearly 40% in 1990 to around 19% in 2013, while India and China grew from around 2% to 3% each to around 12% each over the same time horizon.[42] These trade flows have been driven by rapid industrialization and growth in these emerging market economies and have given way to significant private and public investments. This eastward shift may even impact the Saudi Aramco IPO, with Saudi Arabian Oil Minister Khalid Al Falih noting in June 2018 that the pending decision on where to list shares in the country's state-owned oil giant will be influenced by what he called oil demand's shift to the east.

Along with SWF investments, a large portion of the Gulf's investment in China, India and Southeast Asia are focused on downstream energy markets and led by Gulf state's national oil companies. In doing so, the GCC is flexing its financial muscle in an area it knows well and has a comparative advantage in. The heavy focus on expanding participation in downstream activity throughout developing markets began in earnest in the late 1980s,

Figure 5.2 **GCC States Participation in Global Agreements**

GCC states' accession to global governance institutions also picked up notably during the second phase of oil wealth accumulation. Saudi Arabia was the last GCC country to join the World Trade Organization, doing so in December 2005 after fifteen years of grueling accession talks. With that, all six GCC states were members of not only the WTO, but also the World Intellectual Property Organization, the Trade-Related Aspects of Intellectual Property Rights and the Greater Arab Free Trade Area. These memberships are significant in the fact that they represent a step toward bringing domestic economic standards in line with international norms, in turn providing more clout to GCC member states' aspirations for global leadership. Unfortunately, broader free trade agreements negotiated on behalf of the GCC as a single unit have largely come up short due to divergent intra-GCC policy objectives and regulatory environments, the stalled unification of the GCC into a true customs union, as well as a lack of definitive supranational authority. This drive toward global leadership is better encapsulated by the GCC states' active engagement in inter-regional organizations, such as the Asia Cooperation Dialogue, the Indian Ocean Naval Symposium and GCC-Association of Southeast Asian Nations (ASEAN) secretariat-to-secretariat initiatives.

and at the time was identified by the US intelligence community as having the potential to give the GCC states "significant control over selected segments of foreign petroleum markets."[43] In reality though, instead of providing one-sided control of foreign markets, what has developed are interdependencies between developing markets thirsty for hydrocarbons, and GCC states in need of a home for their raw materials. This creates a situation where all parties have a vested interest in ensuring that commercial and financial transactions remain unhindered by political considerations.

The strength of these interdependencies was on demonstration during King Salman's February 2017, month-long trip through the Southeast Asia and South Asia. Accompanied by 1,500 princes, government officials and business leaders, the whirlwind trip took the King to Brunei, Japan, China, the Maldives, Indonesia and Malaysia. The length of King Salman's Asia tour, and the time devoted to meeting with heads of state, underlines how seriously the Kingdom assesses Asia's investment potential.

Throughout the tour, numerous energy and economic agreements were finalized. In China, Salman and President Xi Jinping signed a memorandum of understanding to explore US$65 billion worth of joint ventures between Chinese and Saudi firms involving sectors ranging from energy and renewables to space. These included an agreement between Sinopec and SABIC, which already jointly run a chemical complex in Tianjin, to develop petrochemical projects in both China and Saudi Arabia, as well as a memorandum of understanding between Aramco and China's North Industries Group

Corp to explore building refining and chemical plants in China.[44] In Japan, a string of deals included an undertaking by Toyota Motor Corp to study the possibility of making vehicles in Saudi Arabia. In Indonesia, Saudi Arabia signed an agreement to develop a US$6 billion refinery joint venture in central Java between the two countries' state-owned oil companies, Pertamina and Saudi Aramco.[45] In Malaysia, Aramco made a US$7 billion investment in a joint venture with Malaysia's state oil company Petronas for a project known as Refinery and Petrochemicals Integrated Development, or RAPID, in Malaysia's southern state of Johor. Where other projects were only proposed, RAPID is in advanced stages of construction and on track to come online in 2019. The project will include a 300,000 bbl/day refinery, which can produce fuels that meet Euro 5 emissions standards, as well as provide feedstock for a connected petrochemical plant.[46] As part of the finalized agreement, Aramco will hold a 50% ownership interest in RAPID ventures and provide as much as 70% of the refinery's feedstock requirements, while Petronas and its affiliates will supply natural gas, power and other utilities.[47] The RAPID project acts as a cornerstone example for how Saudi Arabia is looking East, not only to firm-up alliances but to also effectively invest in ways that captures market share for its oil production. Saudi's extension into these markets is central to the Kingdom's plans to raise its refining capacity to between 8 million and 10 million b/d, from some 5 million b/d in 2018, and double its petrochemicals production, by 2030.[48]

Similar dynamics are at play in India, where Saudi Arabia committed US$44 billion for the 1.2 million b/d refinery in Ratnagiri on India's west coast in 2018. Unsurprisingly, a supply deal with Saudi Aramco is a condition for final investment.[49] While India's relationship with the Gulf has long been driven by commercial interests, India's rise toward the top of the global hierarchy has made these economic linkages increasingly acute. Since 2015, the total portion of Indian oil demand met through imports has breached the 80% mark, with over 20% of these coming from Saudi Arabia, and over 50% of all oil and gas imports coming from the GCC more broadly.[50] Combined, the GCC states were India's largest trading partner in 2014–2015 with trade valued at US$137.7 billion, having grown from US$5.5 billion in 2001.[51] The impact of these import dependencies were felt in 2018, when rebounding oil indices drove higher domestic gasoline prices and fueled public discontent.[52]

Due to these obvious repercussions on hydrocarbon imports, India and China, as well as their regional peers, have increasingly looked to hedge the import-dependency by investing in their own upstream assets. In fact, through strategic, often non-operating, investments and partnerships across the Middle East, China National Petroleum Company has turned itself into one of the leading foreign oil companies active in the region. Estimates pin CNPC's net oil entitlements from the Middle East as high as 350,000 b/d, compared to BP's 330,000 b/d and Total's 384,000 b/d—the latter being the region's largest IOC as measured by net oil entitlements.[53] CNPC's regional oil output does not come only from GCC states though, with roughly equal volumes coming from Abu Dhabi and Iraq. While Iraq has made up the bulk of CNPC's equity oil since 2014, deals struck in 2017 have made Abu Dhabi a central part of CNPC's MENA portfolio.

The dependencies are a two-way street. Indian food products, technical expertise, industrial products and low-wage labor are driving forces of most Gulf economies. As of 2016, the Gulf hosted 7 million Indians, up from 5 million in 2008, earning remittances of around US$40 billion annually.[54] Additionally, the Gulf states have an overwhelming dependence on imported food products, importing 90% of their food products from other countries on average, much of which come from Asian, Southeast Asian and African states.[55] Just as India and China have looked to hedge their energy dependence by investing in foreign energy assets, many GCC states have taken it upon themselves to secure access to arable, fertile land abroad in order to hedge their dependence on foreign grain imports.

It is important to note the relationship between Arab Gulf states and India is undoubtedly more expansive than just energy, labor and food. India's regional ambitions across the Indian Ocean, coupled with the GCC state's strategic location, make cooperation paramount to the former's national security. To some India observers, deepening cleavages in the Middle Eastern political environment requires, "increased Indian engagement with the GCC to directly protect Delhi's interests and gain influence with GCC governments."[56] Recognition of these needs can be seen in Prime Minister Narendra Modi's 'Link West' initiatives, the development of which was equally spurred by overtures by the UAE.[57]

Conclusion

Through the selective channeling of their accumulated wealth, the likes of Saudi Arabia and the UAE have become a significant, and often sought after, actor in global financial markets. This shift cannot be understated, for it comes after repeated instances of their investments being meet with resistance, if not xenophobia, in Western, developed markets. Ironically, as these concerns have receded, the Arab states have aggressively turned their investment focus toward Asian and African markets. In most cases, these regions have been much more receptive of the investment, even when they come with overtly political or military objectives. Yet, the cases of dual-purposed investments are the exception rather than the rule. The Arab Gulf states' investment vehicles remain primarily return-focused entities. This is underlined by the overwhelming amount of SWF capital that is externally managed. In this regard, Western concerns of politically charged investments from the Gulf, in the opinion of these authors, are exaggerated, if not baseless. The real concern for Western financial markets is the naturally occurring shift toward developing, and formally developing, markets. This shift in investment focus fosters and incubates new channels of political interdependency that, in times of crises, may leave Western markets without the support from Arab capital they had in 2008.

Notes

1. British Petroleum Company, *BP Statistical Review of World Energy*. (London: British Petroleum Company, 2017).
2. Kristian Ulrichsen, *The Gulf States in International Political Economy*. (New York, NY: Palgrave Macmillan, 2016), pp. 26–27.
3. Steffen Hertog, "Gulf Economies: The Current Crisis and Lessons of the 1980s," *Carnegie Endowment for International Peace*, Sada, July 7, 2009.
4. Rover Owen, "The Arab Economies in the 1970s," *MERIP Reports* 100, no. 101 (1981): 3–13.
5. Mary Ann Tétreault, "Gulf Arab States' Investment of Oil Revenues," in Matteo Legrenzi and Bessma Momani, eds. *Shifting Geo-Economic Power of the Gulf*. (London: Routledge, 2011), pp. 25–30.
6. Ulrichsen, *The Gulf States*, pp. 26–27.
7. See David E. Spiro, *The Hidden Hand of American Hegemony*. (Ithaca, NY: Cornell University Press, 1999).
8. Bessma Momani, 'Shifting Gulf Arab Investment into the Mashreq: Underlying Political Economy Rationales?' in Matteo Legrenzi and Bessma Momani, eds. *Shifting Geo-Economic Power of the Gulf* (London: Routledge, 2011), p. 168.
9. Authors calculations based on modeled estimates presented in Jean-François Seznec, "The Sovereign Wealth Funds of the Persian Gulf," in Mehran Kamrava, ed. *The Political Economy of the Persian Gulf* (Oxford: Oxford University Press, 2012), pp. 69–93.
10. Rachel Ziemba and Anton Malkin, 'The GCC's International Investment Dynamics: The Role of Sovereign Wealth Funds,' in Matteo Legrenzi and Bessma Momani, eds. *Shifting Geo-Economic Power of the Gulf* (London: Routledge, 2011), p. 116.
11. Lawrence Summers, "Funds That Shake Capitalist Logic," *Financial Times*, July 29, 2007.
12. Ulrichsen, *The Gulf States*, 121.
13. Joseph B. Treaster. "Dubai to Buy Large Stake in Nasdaq," *The New York Times*, September 20, 2007.
14. Simeon Kerr, Telis Demos and Andrew Ward, "Borse Dubai in Nasdaq OMX Sell-Off," *Financial Times*, December 16, 2010.
15. Mark Thatcher, "National Policies Towards Sovereign Wealth Funds in Europe: A Comparison of France, Germany and Italy," *London School of Economics and Politics Kuwait Programme on Development, Governance and Globalisation in the Gulf States* (April 2013): 7–10.
16. Reuters Staff. "Sovereign funds welcome in Germany," *Reuters*, May 9, 2008.
17. Thatcher, "National Policies Towards Sovereign Wealth Funds in Europe," p. 7.
18. Ibid.
19. Reuters Staff, "Lagardere's Top Investor Qatar Wins Voting Rights Loyalty Reward," *Reuters*, May 3, 2017.
20. "The Invasion of the Sovereign-Wealth Funds," *The Economist*, January 17, 2008.
21. Reuters Staff, "UAE Central Bank Chief Says Dollar Peg Stays," *Reuters*, November 21, 2008.
22. Tayyeb Shabbir, "Role of the Middle Eastern Sovereign Wealth Funds in the Current Global Financial Crisis," *Topics in Middle Eastern and North African Economies* 11 (2009).

23. David Enrich, Robin Sidel and Susanne Craig, "World Rides to Wall Street's Rescue," *Wall Street Journal*, January 16, 2008.
24. James Doran, "Saudi Prince Comes to Rescue of Citigroup," *The Guardian*, November 20, 2008.
25. Shabbir, "Role of the Middle Eastern Sovereign Wealth Funds in the Current Global Financial Crisis."
26. Richard Youngs, "Impasse in Euro-Gulf Relations," FRIDE, Working Paper No. 80, 2009.
27. "The Invasion of the Sovereign-Wealth Funds."
28. Floreince Eid, "The New Face of Arab Investment," in John Nugee and Paola Subacchi, eds. *The Gulf Region: A New Hub of Global Financial Power*. (London: Royal Institute of International Affairs, 2008), pp. 70–72.
29. Oxford Business Group, *The Report: Abu Dhabi 2017*. (Oxford Business Group, 2017), p. 34; Charles McGrath, "Pension Funds Broaden EM Allocations, Still Boom or Bust," *Pensions & Investments*, May 17, 2018.
30. Ahmed Hagagy, "Kuwait Investment Authority Plans to Increase Investment in Emerging Markets," *Reuters*, May 2, 2018; Jess Delaney, "Kuwait's Sovereign Wealth Fund Is Hungry for (Private) Deals," *Institutional Investor*, February 1, 2017.
31. Abu Dhabi Investment Authority, *2016 Review: A Legacy in Motion* (Abu Dhabi: ADIA, 2016), p. 7.
32. "National Investment and Infrastructure Fund Inks Pact Worth $1 b with Abu Dhabi Investment Authority," *The Hindu Business Line*, October 16, 2017.
33. "UAE, China to Increase $10b Joint Investment Fund," *Thomson Reuters Zawya*, April 12, 2016.
34. "Revealed: Qatar Investment Authority's Investments across the World," *Arabian Business*, May 17, 2017.
35. Saudi Arabian Monetary Authority, *Monthly Statistical Bulletin*, April 2018.
36. Sarah Algethami, "How Saudi Arabia Is Building Its $2 Trillion Fund," *Bloomberg*, October 22, 2017.
37. Public Investment Fund, *The Public Investment Fund Program (2018–2020)*, 2017.
38. Mark Vandevelde, "Blackstone Offers Discounts on Saudi-Backed Infrastructure Fund," *Financial Times*, June 10, 2018.
39. Leslie Hook, "Saudi Wealth Fund Takes $3.5bn Uber Stake," *Financial Times*, June 1, 2016; Heather Somerville, "SoftBank Is Now Uber's Largest Shareholder as Deal Closes," *Reuters*, January 18, 2018.
40. Simeon Kerr and Anjili Raval, "Oil Cash Set to Boost Saudi Arabia's Sovereign Wealth Fund," *Financial Times*, March 9, 2018.
41. Public Investment Fund, *The Public Investment Fund Program (2018–2020)*.
42. Economist Intelligence Unit, *GCC Trade and Investment Flows*. (London: The Economist Intelligence Unit, 2014).
43. Central Intelligence Agency, "The Gulf States: Changing Trade Patterns [REDACTED]," December 1988. Declassified, October 2012.
44. Ben Blanchard, "China, Saudi Arabia Eye $65 Billion in Deals as King Visits," *Reuters*, March 16, 2017.
45. Reuters Staff, "Saudi Arabia Spends Money to Make Money in Foreign Investment Drive," *Reuters*, March 22, 2017.
46. Matthew Martin, Elffie Chew and Archana Narayanan, "Saudi Aramco and Petronas Are Close to Raising $8 Billion Loan," *Bloomberg*, February 6, 2018.
47. Robert Breisford, "Aramco, Petronas Form Joint Ventures for Malaysia's RAPID Project," *Oil and Gas Journal*, March 29, 2018.
48. Rania El Gamal, "Saudi Aramco Eyes Partnerships as It Expands Refining, Petrochems," *Reuters*, June 12, 2018.

49. "Saudi Aramco to Invest $44b in Giant India Oil Refinery," *Gulf News*, April 12, 2018.
50. Kadira Pethiyagoda, "India-GCC Relations: Delhi's Strategic Opportunity," Brookings Doha Center Analysis Paper Number 18, February 2017: 7.
51. Ibid.
52. Amy Kazmin, "Oil Price Rise Puts Heat on Narendra Modi's Government," *Financial Times*, May 22, 2018.
53. "The Dragon Rises in the Middle East," *Middle East Economic Survey* 61, no. 2 (May 25, 2018).
54. Pethiyagoda, "India-GCC Relations: Delhi's Strategic Opportunity."
55. Sharif M. Taha. "Kingdom Imports 80% of Food Products," *Arab News*, April 19, 2014.
56. Kadira Pethiyagoda, "India-GCC Relations: Delhi's Strategic Opportunity" Brookings Doha Center Analysis Paper Number 18, February 2017.
57. Pramit Pal Chaudhuri, "Think West to Go West: Origins and Implications of India's West Asia Policy Under Modi (Part II)," *Middle East Institute*, October 24, 2017.

6 Case Studies

Introduction

As has been detailed throughout this text, financial markets across the Arab Gulf States have unique specificities that require a more detailed analysis in order to understand how and why political and financial leadership take the decisions they do. Through four case studies, this chapter delves into these specificities, and how particular events and financial tools have, and will continue to, influence the evolution of the region's financial markets.

The first case study unpacks the potential for the privatization of Saudi Aramco, offering a simple back-of-the-envelope valuation based on the basic premise that Saudi Aramco is managed more like an international oil company than a national oil company. More importantly, the chapter discusses in detail the motivations behind the privatization, its implications and challenges that may stand in its way.

The second case study focuses on the fallout from the bankruptcy of The International Banking Cooperation (TIBC), a Bahrain offshore banking unit. The case study is an investigation into regulatory arbitrage by unscrupulous investors and how foreign banks and service companies failed to prevent the affair.

The third case study evaluates Dubai's evolving role in regional trade, reviewing how financially lucrative gold trading with India in the 1970s foreshadowed similarly lucrative trade with Iran over the last two decades, subsequently offering a theoretical model for how Iranian leadership may set up companies in Dubai to transfer money from Tehran to the emirate.

The final case study details how banks have had great success by working the very traditional banking instruments of documentary credits to facilitate the implementation of hundreds of billions worth of major infrastructure projects since the 1970s.

These case studies strive to elucidate the interaction between the financial institutions and power structures covered throughout the preceding chapters in order to provide a clearer picture of the region's financial markets from a functional level.

6.1 The Saudi Aramco Privatization

Introduction

In 2016, the Crown Prince of Saudi Arabia stunned the world of energy and finance by announcing that Saudi Aramco would be privatized and that 5% of its shares would be floated in a public offering open to investors worldwide. The mega-oil company has not only financed the Kingdom's budget for decades, but, aided by Aramco's opaque financial practices, has also, either directly or indirectly, supported much of the royal family's expenditures.[1] Much has been said and written about the privatization of Aramco, and by all accounts, the privatization has the potential to be historic. Listing shares locally would provide a liquidity boost to domestic capital markets, listing shares globally would open the Kingdom to foreign investment to an unparalleled degree, and share revenue would feed into Saudi's sovereign wealth fund, which seeks to replace oil as the main source of government revenue.

However, cash generation is not the only, and perhaps not even the primary, motive behind the privatization. One of the key references in all of the Crown Prince and various Ministers' speeches and statements referencing Vision 2030 is the fact that the economy should be transparent. In light of this, the privatization should be viewed as a keystone to achieving this aspect of modernization. Indeed, how could the Kingdom's leadership transform the economy if the country's main asset, one that has provided for the country for the past seventy years, is managed secretly and to the outsized benefit of certain segments of society without the knowledge of the rest. It is in this sense that imbedded in the Aramco IPO lies numerous objectives and obstacles, which the Kingdom will have to face if it is to succeed in its ambitious reform strategy.

Valuation

In announcing the intended IPO, Mohammed bin Salman (MbS), then Deputy Crown Prince, noted that the value of the company would be around US$2 trillion, which would make it the largest company in the world and, through a flotation of just 5%, the largest share issuance in history. Ever since, this valuation has been criticized and termed unrealistic by many analysts and investment companies. On the other hand, since no figure has been published on the actual profits of the company, all estimates are based on speculative assumptions of cash flows, costs and distributions to the government.

Since MbS's announcement though, Saudi Aramco has allowed information surrounding the structure and finances of the company to leak in bits and drabs. For instance, while there were no publicly disclosed laws or regulations specifying that Aramco pays or paid the Kingdom of Saudi Arabia a royalty on its production or exports, it had always been generally accepted that some such mechanism existed. In the wake of the Aramco initial public offering announcement, this mechanism became clearer. Leaked accounting statements, written to an IFRS standard, show that since January 2017, Aramco has paid a royalty set at a marginal rate of 20% that applies when oil prices rise as high as US$70/bbl, increases to 40% when oil is priced between US$70 and US$100, and increases further to 50% when oil prices breach the US$100/bbl-mark. Royalties are levied against total production of crude oil and natural gas liquids. Prior to January 2017, a fixed royalty of 20% had been set against just exported volumes. Along with these royalties, Saudi Aramco also pays 50% income tax on its net profits.[2] Apparently, this tax had been as high as 75%, but, to make the privatization more attractive, the percentage has been reduced to 50%, more in line with other countries' practices.

The leak containing this information was published by Bloomberg on April 13, 2018, and included actual sales and profit figures for the first half of 2017, which has allowed for more precise estimates of what Aramco's income would be at various oil price levels, and ultimately a simple valuation of the company (See Figure 6.1). For the first half of 2017, Bloomberg disclosed that the company had netted US$33.8 billion after paying the state a total of US$39.9 billion in income taxes and US$18.5 billion in royalties.[3] Hence, one can safely assume that income before tax and operating expenses was about US$74 billion. Assuming operating expenses at 15% of sales would imply a total sales figure in the region of US$106 billion for the first half of 2017. Seeing as the OPEC Reference Basket averaged US$48.62/bbl throughout the first half of 2017, it would be fair to estimate that Saudi Aramco's income was achieved at a US$50/bbl level. In the second half of 2017, however, prices increased to an average of US$55/bbl, or an increase of 12% over the first half of the year. Assuming flat production levels, which are corroborated by Saudi production data, it would be safe to assume that revenue in the second half of 2017 was 112% of revenue from the first half of 2017.[4] This would take total revenue throughout 2017 to around US$225 billion. Looking at 2018, the OPEC Reference Basket averaged US$68/bbl for the first half of the year, which if held consistent for the remainder of 2018, along with the conservative estimate of flat production, would provide revenues before royalties and taxes of nearly US$300 billion.

Figure 6.1 Saudi Aramco Valuation Utilizing P/E Ratios

(USD Billion)	1H 2017	2H 2017	Full Year 2017	1H 2018	Full Year 2018
Avg Oil Prod. ('000 BPD)	*9,942*	*9,977*	*9,960*	*9,923*	-
Revenue	$106.03	$118.75	$224.78	$149.50	$299.00
COGS (15%)	$13.83	$15.49	$29.32	$19.50	$39.00
Royalties	$18.50	$20.72	$39.22	$26.09	$52.17
EBITD	$73.70	$ 82.54	$156.24	$103.92	$207.83
Tax	$39.90	$44.69	$84.59	$56.26	$112.52
Net Income	**$33.80**	**$37.86**	**$71.66**	**$47.66**	**$95.32**
Rough Valuation Using Trailing P/E			**$1,741.88**		**$2,317.04**
Rough Valuation Using Forward P/E			**$1,330.14**		**$1,769.34**

Daily Trailing P/E and Forward P/E Multiples
February 2013 to February 2018

	Trailing P/E	Forward P/E
ExxonMobil	19.84	20.57
Chevron	31.89	29.25
BP	**	16.62
Shell	24.36	14.40
Total	21.14	11.97
Average of Averages	**24.31**	**18.56**

** *Interruption in Daily Data Makes It Anomalous*

OPEC Price Basket	
1H 2017	$ 48.62
2H 2017	$ 54.62
1H 2018	$ 68.40

Source: JODI

Assumptions

1. Baseline Royalties, Tax and Net Income for 1H 2017 Sourced from Bloomberg April 13, 2018 and utilized as baseline for growth in subsequent years. Growth calculated using JODI production data and OPEC Oil Price Basket historical data.

2. Flat production volumes assumed across all periods, consistent with JODI production data and application of OPEC production agreement. For Full Year 2018, production assumed constant, despite room for upside given changes to OPEC agreement.

3. Revenue for 2H 2017 calculated as 112% of revenue for 1H 2017, based on growth in oil prices as seen through OPEC Oil Price Basket. Revenue for 1H 2018 calculated as 141% of revenue for 1H 2017 through identical calculation.

To complete the valuation, we turned to the old rule of thumb of multiplying earnings by the price-to-earnings (P/E) ratios of similar companies. As explained later, we chose to employ the P/E ratios of global supermajor oil companies, opposed to national oil companies. We took the P/E ratio published every day for Chevron, BP, Shell and Total and computed an average of their trailing and forward P/E ratios. The trailing P/E uses recent share prices and company earnings, while forward P/E ratios are based on projected future earnings and performance as estimated by analysts. In the case of the supermajor oil companies, the forward P/E tended to be lower on average than the trailing P/E, probably because analysts want to show a certain conservatism in their expectations. The table included in this text shows that the average daily trailing P/E for the past five years is about 24.3, while the forward is about 18.6. If we apply these multiples to Saudi Aramco's expected after tax earnings, the rough valuation of the company will be between US$1.7 trillion and US$2.3 trillion using the trailing P/E and US$1.3 trillion and US$1.8 trillion for the forward P/E, for an overall average of around US$1.8 trillion.[5] Since July 2017 prices have consistently remained above US$65/bbl, implying that a valuation of around US$2 trillion will remain possible for some time.

Our admittedly very simple valuation is based on using the multiple of earnings, which markets apply to major international oil companies (IOCs). The reasoning behind this approach is that Saudi Aramco is in fact much more like an IOC than a national oil company (NOC). The focus at Aramco today has moved from just production of oil to the refining and conversion of oil across all downstream sectors, ranging from petrochemicals to refined products. The company has announced that it will refine over 10 million b/d within a few years. It is already refining 5.4 million b/d and is expected to invest in new large refineries in India, Indonesia and Malaysia as well as increase capacity at its plants in China.[6] This capacity is not merely for the purpose of producing middle distillates like gasoline, diesel and kerosene as average refineries do. Saudi's future refineries are designed to maximize higher-value products from low-value, bottom of the barrel, feedstocks. These refineries are also designed to integrate the conversion of natural gas liquids and naphtha into the on-site refining stream, allowing for the production of a wide variety of advanced chemicals. Even the company's older refineries are being refurbished to accomplish the same task, an upgrade that comes at great upfront expense, underlining Aramco's resolve in its long-term downstream push. Naturally the crude oil used in these downstream ventures give Saudi Arabia a base load for its crude production. More importantly, these refining ventures will allow for Saudi Arabia's crude production to increase three to ten times in value.

Adding value to the crude implies very large capital investments. Saudi Aramco is planning US$414 billion worth of new plants and refining capacity over the next ten years.[7] It has already started advanced chemical production in the US$20 billion SADARA joint venture with Dow Chemical and is supporting numerous downstream producers to further refine SADARA's output, both on its own, such as through the Aramco-Total JV SATORP, and at the adjacent PlasChem Park industrial zone. PlasChem Park has a direct connection to SADARA, which will integrate the latter's ethylene oxide and propylene oxide production into the operations of industrial firms including US-based Harcros Chemicals and Haliburton and Germany's Ilco Chemikalien, in turn establishing a locked-in market for SADARA's higher-value refined products.[8] In other words, just like ExxonMobil or Chevron, Saudi Aramco is now a fully integrated energy and chemical company with value-creating operations across the entire carbon chain, hence making it comparable in earning capacity and financial multiples to leading IOCs.

In another sign of this push toward downstream activity, Bloomberg announced in late July 2018 that Saudi Aramco was in talks to buy a stake in SABIC, the large petrochemical company of Saudi Arabia.[9] Today SABIC is the fifth largest chemical company in the world in sales and the first in terms of capitalization. Both companies would see some advantages to rationalizing their operations. This would primarily come through Saudi Aramco adding numerous advanced chemical lines to its production and refining operations, potentially increasing its line of value-adding products by US$40 billion/y. This would take Aramco one step closer to resembling the ExxonMobil or Shell Oils of the world, validating the multiples mentioned earlier.

It is not entirely clear from the statements whether Saudi Aramco will buy the entire company. It did mention that the 30% of SABIC that is publicly held will remain so. Perhaps, it could imply that Saudi Aramco will buy the 70% of SABIC's shares that are owned by PIF. At today's market rate this would amount to a capitalization of around US$70 billion. If, as discussed previously, Saudi Aramco's value is about US$2 trillion, Saudi Aramco could exchange about 3.5% of its shares for the whole 70% of SABIC. If PIF receives shares of Saudi Aramco in payment, it would equate to a 3.5% direct investment in Saudi Aramco and increase PIF's investments to around US$320 billion. In fact, this would make PIF the largest shareholder in Saudi Aramco after the Ministry of Energy, possibly even getting PIF a seat on the board. Alternatively, if PIF were to accept cash, it would provide it with the liquidity it seeks to make further outside investments, just as if it had received the cash from the IPO. It would make more business sense for Saudi Aramco to conserve its cash for its own projects and provide shares to PIF, effectively providing both with some of the advantages they seek.

From a purely business standpoint, if Saudi Aramco were to take over SABIC, it would most likely have to divest itself of SABIC's non-core assets, including fertilizers or metals, as well as many low-margin commodity-type chemicals. However, such divestment or restructuring would likely lead to numerous jobs losses and perhaps substantial opposition to the deal. In any case, a merger of Saudi Aramco and SABIC would be a major endeavor and would likely delay the IPO for considerable time.

Transparency through Privatization

When the IPO was announced, it was not clear where Saudi Aramco's shares would be sold, nor was it clear who owned the shares ahead of the IPO, or even what the actual legal status of the company was. Some of this has now been clarified. The company was registered as a corporation in late 2017 and the shares are owned by the Ministry of Energy.[10] It was also confirmed that the proceeds of the 5% share sale, approximately US$100 billion if MbS's valuation holds true, would go to PIF, who would then use the money to invest in various industries with the ultimate objective of diversifying the Saudi economy. Of course, this financial sum is considerable and would require a major expansion of the PIF's financial management capacity. As of September 2017, the PIF managed somewhere between US$220 and US$240 billion.[11]

As was noted in the chapter on Saudi Arabia's financial markets, the PIF is now managed independently from the Ministry of Finance. However, it is still extremely opaque. It does not publish figures on the size and results of its investments. Thus, rumors tend to be the norm, just as they are for other SWFs in the Gulf, like ADIA or QIA, which are equally or even more opaque. Hence it is ironic, that one of the main objectives behind the privatization of Saudi Aramco is to show to the Saudi citizenry that Saudi Aramco, the main asset of the Kingdom, is now transparent. In fact, the privatization is the keystone to MbS's efforts at modernizing the economy, to which transparency is paramount. Selling a small portion of Saudi Aramco is certainly meant to raise money to diversify investments, but in great part it also seeks to provide transparency to the larger population on what the company does, how it does it and how much money it makes. In this sense, it undoubtedly wants to show that Saudi Aramco is a well-managed company and confirm to Saudis that it is managed better than the leading NOCs and at par with the major international companies like ExxonMobil, Chevron, BP, Shell or Total. Equally important though, it is meant to take away the ability of some groups in the country to take funds out of the Saudi Aramco income for their own benefit or the benefit of a select few.

It is not a secret that each prince and princess receives an allowance, which directly or indirectly comes from Saudi Aramco. Once Saudi Aramco becomes a publicly traded company it will have to publish detailed audited statements and reports on its governance. This would allow the public to pinpoint how money is earned and how much of it is transferred to the state, where it could be used for everyone's benefit. Most in the Kingdom would not begrudge the fact that the Al Saud family provides leadership and stability, but many would want to know how much money is used to that effect. It is very much in the interest of Saudi Aramco to either disclose what the amount of these payments have been and are, or merely show that it is not involved in them. In the latter scenario, then it would likely be the case that the payments are made by the Ministry of Finance, which receives Aramco's tax and royalty payments. Once it is made clear that payments to the royal family come from the Ministry of Finance, the Ministry would eventually have to disclose, in whole or in part, the size of these payments. In other words, the privatization will act as an integral step toward more financial and political transparency in the Kingdom. This will effectively put certain limits on how much, and in what form, the Saudi state and royal family use the land's oil rent.

Many in the royal family may oppose the very notion of transparency, but, as MbS likely recognizes, it is critical at this time of reform in the Kingdom. Simultaneous with preparations for the Saudi Aramco IPO, there have been numerous revisions to Saudi Arabia's traditional social welfare system. A value-added tax has been levied across the Kingdom and energy subsidies have been reduced substantially. These changes come at a significant cost to the Saudi public. With the Aramco IPO, the government wants to show how the major asset of the kingdom is developed in a transparent way so everyone knows what that asset is earning and where the money is going. With the public at large asked to make financial sacrifices, such as higher energy costs and a value-added tax, the public should know the royal family is limiting its indulgences as well. This dynamic is critical for the Kingdom's citizens, young and old alike, to believe that everyone is benefiting from, and contributing to, the Kingdom's modernization.

To IPO, But Where?

Where the shares will be floated has been the subject of numerous articles in the press and is not yet decided. HE the Minister of Energy has said that the company has checked all the boxes needed to start the privatization procedure. However, the state still needs to make the political decision on where and when to float.

Regardless of where the shares are eventually offered, floating shares on most stock exchanges require companies, large and small, to provide quite extensive information and disclosures. This is a tall order for Saudi Aramco, which has not had to provide any financial information despite being one of the largest oil producers and exporters for over half a century. Indeed, any memorandum presented to potential shareholders would have to disclose among many other things:

- Details, such as duration and restrictions, of the lease agreements with the state allowing Saudi Aramco to explore, drill, extract and sell crude oil and natural gas in the Kingdom.[12]
- Valuation of the leases according to standard international practice.
- Audited statements of the company and all its affiliates and investments.
- Actual payments to the state of royalties and income taxes, and guarantees by the state that the percentages of royalties and income taxes will not change.

- Financial details on all the company's subsidiaries both in the Kingdom and overseas, including joint venture partners.
- Forward looking statements on expected financial results.
- Details on the governance of the company by the Board of Directors and Supreme Council for Saudi Aramco.[13]
- Guarantees, to a satisfactory degree, that potential shareholders, even minority ones, would have their interests considered in Company decisions—a major requirement of the main stock exchanges.

Some of the world's largest and most important market places have been competing to host the listing. London in particular has changed some of its rules to allow the listing to take place there. In particular, London changed the rule that requires firms to have at least 20% of their shares tradable, not just 5% as would be the case of Saudi Aramco. The New York Stock Exchange can safely say that it is the largest market in the world and could easily absorb a float of US$100 billion, even though it would be the largest ever. Hong Kong can claim that it is favored by most large Chinese investors. Ultimately, regardless of which foreign exchange is included in the IPO, Saudi Aramco would have to place a substantial amount of the float in Saudi Arabia's own capital market, the Tadawul. In fact, considering the political ramifications and pressure that will be placed on Saudi Aramco and key leadership in the Kingdom through the float, it may be much simpler and faster to float on the Tadawul. Of course, a US$100 billion issuance would amount to about 20% of the total valuation of the Tadawul. However, it would also allow the market to be seen as a truly international one. In this regard, the CMA has already changed many of the rules allowing medium size and large brokerage firms and investment banks to trade on the Tadawul, thus de facto opening itself up to foreign investments. On the other hand, the capitalization of the market might have to include the entire value of Saudi Aramco, which would increase it from over US$500 billion today to US$2.5 trillion, with Saudi Aramco's valuation providing 80% of the value.

An issue that could come up in floating on the Tadawul is the practice in the Gulf of issuing shares at a set price and then allocating shares according to demand. In other words, if a company offers 1 million shares at SAR 10/share, and demand indicated in writing by potential investors is for 2 million shares, the investors will receive ½ of the shares they signed up for, still at SAR 10/share. Should the demand for Saudi Aramco shares exceed the amount offered, the number of shares allocated would be less than required at the given par value. In reverse, however, if the demand is less than what is offered, Saudi Aramco would receive less for the issue. On other major stock exchanges, the demand and supply of shares would be arbitrated by changes in price. If demand is high, the price increases and vice versa. The practice of the set price for share would be difficult to change in Saudi Arabia, as all the firms traded on the Tadawul were issued in the manner discussed. Further, all dividends are shown by the companies as a percentage of the par value, which makes it convenient for small shareholders to see what return they get on their investment.

Another important issue for foreign investors potentially interested in investing through an IPO on the Tadawul is the currency of issue. Of course, for the past three decades the Saudi Riyal has been linked to the dollar at SAR3.75 per US$1, but this could be changed at any time. Naturally, the Saudi government has no intention of changing the value of its currency, and it is not in the interest of the country when most of its income and expenses are in dollars. On the other hand, foreign investors may feel that the currency risk associated with a minor currency which they cannot truly hedge is unattractive. Hence, it would seem that the IPO would have to be in US$, which has never been done in the Kingdom. There are no rules against such issuance, but it would require Saudi Aramco manage the company in US Dollars, which it probably does already de facto since most of its income and major expenses are also in dollars.

Conclusion

Saudi Aramco's IPO is one of many privatization schemes advanced by the leadership. Privatization is being considered for grain imports, the postal service, water distribution, power generation and healthcare. Mohamed Al Tuwaijri, then Vice Minister for Economy and Planning, announced a plan to privatize US$200 billion of businesses besides Saudi Aramco.[14] Of course, the purpose is to raise funds to cover deficits and to limit bureaucracy, but also to make the economy more efficient, transparent and reactive. In this regard, delays in the IPO could rightly be seen as a byproduct of the difficulty that comes with this form of change. If the IPO were never to happen, as many have speculated, it will overwhelmingly be because the country has been unable to progress through the challenges aforementioned. Listing requires transparency, and transparency brings with it additional scrutiny; scrutiny that has the tendency to disrupt sitting balances of power.

Moreover, as far as broader transparency goes, the current proposal for the privatization may be for naught given the proceeds are destined to end up in an opaque fund, such as the PIF. This final destination for the cash windfall that is supposed to jolt forward transparency and development seems to contradict the original purpose of the privatization. Perhaps, PIF will open itself to some public scrutiny, but as of now it has not happened. Yet, while the drive to achieve broader transparency may not be accomplished, the secondary goal of spreading the wealth across a broader swath of the population may. A smaller flotation, potentially of just 1%, conducted solely on the Tadawul, would not only bypass issues of liquidity that a Tadawul-floatation would otherwise face, but would also provide the broader public a piece of the Kingdom's wealth, just as the privatization of SABIC did some years ago. All this said, as of late 2018, the urgency to achieve these privatization plans has admittedly abated. The notion of transforming the economy from a lumbering state controlled group of companies to a modern and efficient machine implies that the labor market will be liberalized, with hiring and firing easily arranged and regulations simplified or abandoned. These changes come with costs, and the current leadership is rethinking whether it is a good idea to take the risk of throwing thousands of people out of work for the sake of efficiency. Furthermore, with the price of oil increasing, the urgency to make up the deficits by privatizing state-owned companies has declined substantially. In many ways, the urgent need to reform and diversify the Saudi economy is being impaired by the very improvement in oil revenue; revenues which the reforms themselves seek to de-emphasize.

Notes

1. Jean-François Seznec, "Saudi Energy Changes: The End of the Rentier state," *The Atlantic Council Policy Brief*, March 24, 2016.
2. "The Aramco Accounts: Inside the World's Most Profitable Company," *Bloomberg*, April 13, 2018.
3. Javier Blas, "Aramco Accounts Show Scale of Challenge Facing Crown Prince," *Bloomberg*, April 13, 2018.
4. The JODI Oil World Database.
5. Jean-François Seznec, "Saudi Aramco's Downstream Push Will Increase Its Value," *Atlantic Council Blog*, March 19, 2018.
6. For more on this see Chapter 5 of this work.
7. Reem Shamseddine and Rania El Gama, "Saudi Aramco Lifts Spending Plans to $414 bln over Next Decade," *Reuters*, December 12, 2017.
8. "Aramco Downstream Strategy: Plastic Fantastic as Sadara Park Ramps Up," *Middle East Economic Survey* 61, no. 24 (June 15, 2018).
9. Summer Said, "Saudi Aramco in Talks to Buy Stake in Petrochemical Firm," *Wall Street Journal*, July 19, 2018.
10. This was disclosed by a high ranking Saudi participant in a conference in Washington, DC in 2018. The conference was held under Chatham House rules.
11. Public Investment Fund, *The Public Investment Fund Program (2018–2020)*, 2017, p. 12.
12. One would expect the leases to have a long tenor, perhaps fifty years or more. In any case the duration would greatly impact the expected long term cash flow of the company.
13. The Supreme Council for Saudi Aramco is chaired by MbS and defines and implements oil policy in the Kingdom.
14. Tom Arnold, Saeed Azhar and Katie Paul, "Saudi Arabia's $300 billion 'sale of the century' Is Moving at a Snail's Pace," December 1, 2017.

6.2 Name Lending and the TIBC Bankruptcy

Introduction

In the 1980s, in an effort to bypass Kuwait's financial regulatory authorities, Kuwaiti investors used the burgeoning Bahraini banking markets to establish banks solely for the purpose of floating shares on Kuwait's parallel market, the Souk Al Manakh. In a parallel form, in the early part of the 21st century, some Gulf investors took advantage of Bahrain's financial markets to bypass Saudi Arabia's banking regulations. In both cases, individuals capitalized on regulatory inefficiencies and financial practices prevalent in the region such as name lending to generate outsized financial gains which were not discovered until financial crises were already at hand.

Background

The case of the International Bank (TIBC), allegedly owned by a scion of the Saudi merchant class, the Al Gosaibi family of Al Khobar, is a poignant example of this latter regulatory arbitrage. The case was not only covered widely in regional press, but also garnered wide coverage in the West. The global press's interest was driven by the sheer size of the affair, and the numerous legal actions stemming from its fallout and was bolstered by leaks of confidential reports that provided a glimpse into a case of high finance gone wrong.

Summarizing the TIBC scandal is challenging considering the scandal itself spans ten jurisdictions stretching from the Gulf to New York and California- all with different laws and financial regulations. The case finds its roots with the Ahmed Hamad Al Gosaibi & Brothers (AHAB) investment company in Saudi Arabia known as the Exchange. This firm was basically a money-changing operation with no banking license or banking authority.[1] The Exchange was managed by one of AHAB's business relations, Mr. Ma'an Al Sanea, a Kuwaiti citizen married to one of the Al Gosaibi daughters. In 2003, after years of running the Exchange, Mr. Al Sanea proceeded to establish an offshore banking unit in Bahrain called TIBC, which obtained an Offshore Banking Unit license, accomplishing the feat principally on the basis of the name Al Gosaibi (See Figure 6.2). This use of the Gosaibi name was not new for Sanea. In fact, he used it extensively, building an empire on leverage even before shifting operations to Bahrain. Most of the loans gathered in this pursuit were provided to Sanea unsecured, with the lenders simply handing over the money and relying on the strength of the Gosabi name as their security.

Figure 6.2 **Name Lending: A Primer**

At the most basic level, name lending refers to the practice of lending on the basis of personal reputation rather than financial fundamentals. Prior to the 1980s in the Gulf, most companies and merchants did not publish audited statements. Hence, financial institutions would be very conservative in their approach to new business, keeping their funds for their existing clients and families whom they had known for a long-time and whose reputation was well established. In other words, the banks could lend safely on the basis of the name of the person and of his/her family. During the enormous economic growth of the Gulf economies since the 1970s, demand for bank services grew exponentially and the practice of name lending continued, albeit on a lesser scale as more sophisticated and audited financials became available.

The growth of certain family's wealth was staggering and thus there was widespread willingness by banks to lend to the rich, or those perceived to be rich for whatever reason (profitable trading agencies, real estate holdings, shares in foreign companies, etc.). Dealing in perception, allowed banks to rapidly issue loans and documentary credits, unimpeded by time consuming paper work and appropriate credit analysis. It also helped the banks avoid delving into the private affairs of merchants or other powerful families. This practice of name lending, which goes back centuries and was the foundation for all banking transactions since the Middle Ages, has continued in the Gulf but is declining rapidly and is being replaced by standard credit analysis, even for the biggest names. Nowadays, if any financial institution claims that the reputation of a borrower is sufficient to disburse funds, it should act as a red light for other banks and regulators alike.

It should also be pointed out that name lending is fairly common in sophisticated banks worldwide. In some cases, banks may lower their standards if they want to participate in loans to a well-known developer, even if the developer has had some bankruptcies in the past, as was the case in loans to the Trump organization. In some cases, loans may be extended by major banks on the basis of knowing how wealthy a person or group is, without too many details. In all cases, however, as more information is available and bank secrecy worldwide is declining, name lending is becoming a thing of the past.

TIBC initially moved to Bahrain's offshore marketplace to evade the regulatory remit of the Saudi Arabian Monetary Authority (SAMA). At the time, SAMA had extensively ramped up its regulatory controls on money exchanges due to US pressure to clamp down on potential sources of illicit finance in the wake of 9/11. As uncovered in a lengthy New Yorker article by Nicholas Schmidle, Sanea and the bank management had explicitly discussed the benefits of opening a bank in Bahrain, writing in an internal memo that establishing the new business in Bahrain would "increase the level of comfort that international banks would have in dealing with us. . . . The advantage of this is that a number of banks we deal with could raise their limits to us substantially."[2]

Using the Al Gosaibi name, TIBC raised funds from Saudi depositors and international financial institutions. It was not long before Al Saena opened another bank in the Bahrain offshore market, Awal Bank, using the same process. Awal Bank was used primarily to raise more funds which could be passed to TIBC. The bank then proceeded to market loans to Saudi borrowers, which were approved in Bahrain by TIBC, but disbursed out of the Exchange in Al Khobar. Of course, this practice was illegal in Saudi Arabia as the Exchange was not licensed as a bank. Nonetheless, between its founding in 2003 and its downfall in 2009, TIBC lent billions to more than a hundred customers, ranging from textile merchants to car dealers. The key to the entire affair is that most of these loans were not real. The loans were made to individuals or establishments that either did not exist or, if they did exist, had no knowledge of the transactions. Instead, the billions passed on to the Exchange by TIBC and Awal were allegedly credited to a company owned and controlled by Mr. Al Sanea.

At the time of its collapse, TIBC was the fourth largest wholesale bank in Bahrain. Yet its loan book was entirely a product of Al Sanea's fraud.[3] Eventually, Sanea's companies were unable to repay the banks who had lent them money. The defaults began in May 2009 when TIBC missed a payment to the Dubai-based Mashreq Bank, which filed a suit in response. At the same time, TIBC, and Sanea's related Awal Bank, were believed to be indebted to over sixty other banks. Among these were some of the most prominent names in banking, including Citigroup, Standard Chartered and BNP Paribas, the last of which was reportedly Sanea's largest foreign lender. Regionally, over thirty GCC banks were owed nearly US$10 billion at the time of default.[4]

The Central Bank of Bahrain (CBB) took over both Awal and TIBC and hired Trowers and Hamlin, a liquidation firm from London, to recoup some of the funds for payment to the creditors; The CBB also sued the auditors of TIBC in Bahrain for the amount of the losses. In the meantime, AHAB sued Al Sanea in Saudi Arabia and the CEO of TIBC, Mr. Glenn Steward, in California. Mr. Stewart was already under criminal investigation by the CBB and forbidden to leave Bahrain but managed to escape the island and returned to the US, which has no extradition treaty with Bahrain. Alongside all this, international banks that had funded TIBC and Awal began suing AHAB in various global financial centers. AHAB claimed they were taken advantage of by Al Sanea, and knew nothing of the inflated loans, a claim that a Cayman Islands court would rule as false almost a decade later. Altogether, lawsuits in Bahrain pinned the losses at around US$2 billion, while subsequent estimates put the total losses at a much higher US$20 billion.

Regulatory, Personality or Practice: Who Is at Fault?

In the aftermath of TIBC's demise, leading bankers in the region pointed blame at the CBB, including Kuwait Finance House General Manager Abdulhakeem Y. Al Khayyat, who asserted to US officials that "a competent central bank should have seen it coming."[5] These concerns were not totally unwarranted. TIBC was licensed to operate in Bahrain, but was only able to receive this license because the name of the main shareholders was from the Al Gosaibi family. However, the senior members of the family never attended any of the board meetings or credit committee meetings. They even claimed that they were not aware of the banking application to the CBB, that they did not take any part in the management of the bank, and that their signatures were forged. In the aftermath, it even came out that one of the credit applications TIBC submitted was 'signed' by an older, senior member of the family, while in fact the senior member was on his deathbed in a hospital in Europe.[6] For all intents and purposes, the CBB was hoodwinked into approving banking licenses through Al Sanea's use of the Al Gosaibi name. The same pattern had happened in the 1980s when the Bahrain Monetary Authority (BMA), the CBB's predecessor, would license banks started by Kuwaiti merchants, who used borrowed money to fund the capital and depended on their name to bypass most formal regulatory checks.

In a region where name lending and familial reputation is critical in the arena of business, it is quite unusual that the CBB approved banking licenses to one of the region's most prominent families without even contacting senior members of the family. In the absence of in-depth research prior to licensing, it would have been legitimate to see the CBB significantly more involved in the operations of these banks. It appears that the CBB (and the BMA) wanted to believe that the banks would somehow grow into successful and solid institutions. It could be argued that the CBB had a conflict of interest. On the one hand, the Bahraini authorities wished to develop the country's financial markets by accelerating the number of the banks established in Bahrain. On the other hand, it was still required to regulate each of these banks thoroughly, a very demanding task for the Bahraini regulatory authorities, who have relatively limited means in relation to the size and growth rate of the country's banking sector. Of course, by and large, the Bahraini financial authorities have been successful in creating a respected market and did attract numerous quality institutions. The managers of the CBB have always had a top reputation in managing the wholesale (formerly offshore) markets. However, as has been shown, some institutions did slip through the cracks.

SAMA also bears some responsibility. Indeed, the Saudi central bank should have known that a minor money-changer in Al Khobar, albeit one owned by an important family, was actually channeling loans from Bahraini banks in violation of SAMA's regulations. Saudi Arabian authorities did end up ring fencing the Saudi portion of the scandal, thereby limiting the impact on the reputation of the family in the country and protecting, as best as possible, the Saudi banks involved. In the months following May 2009, SAMA acted rapidly, freezing all of Al Sanea's assets, and before the end of 2009 had extended the freeze order to cover assets of other Al Gosaibi family members. This freeze should not be taken lightly. At the time, Sanea was reportedly the second wealthiest man in the Kingdom and had close ties with then-Emir of the Eastern Province, Prince Mohammed bin Fahd, making an order of this magnitude likely cleared by then-King Abdullah himself.

The Saudi government established a Royal Commission to facilitate the restructuring of Sanea's companies. The commission forced Al Sanea and AHAB to liquidate numerous Saudi assets to pay back Saudi banks with outstanding claims. Many of these banks accepted between a 10% and 15% haircut on their debt repayments.[7] SAMA also arranged or approved settlements between the local Saudi banks and AHAB. AHAB transferred some of their properties to Saudi banks to settle outstanding debts, including the transfer of one of AHAB's most valuable assets, an ultramodern aluminum can plant, which provides cans to soft drink bottlers in the Kingdom. Amidst all of this though, SAMA's focus was solely on domestic institutions. SAMA leadership insisted TIBC and Awal were headquartered in Bahrain and thus outside SAMA's jurisdiction. SAMA and the Royal Commission refused to address the claims of any foreign creditors, allowing international creditors to find no recourse in Saudi Arabia.

The foreign banks, many of which lost the bulk of their loans to TIBC and Awal, had lent to the two banks on the basis of the Al Gosaibi name. "Name lending" is indeed a specialty of the region and goes back many generations. Despite this, banks with long histories of practicing in the Gulf should have known better and actually checked with the "names" before lending billions. Relatedly, regulatory authorities across the Gulf, including SAMA, could require banks to obtain and scrutinize financial statements before approving loans instead of leaving the responsibility in the hands of the auditors or the banks themselves. While the latter, more limited, form of oversight is in-line with most central banking practices globally, the extent to which name lending is utilized, and often abused, in the Gulf should warrant further action.

The blame did not lie with the regulators and Al Sanea alone. Leading foreign banks also had a role in the regulatory lapse. To put things in context, the Exchange, whose legitimate function was to assist low-paid foreign workers transfer their modest earnings home, was estimated to see only US$60 million in actual remittance or currency exchange annually.[8] Despite this, Bank of America New York granted Sanea's request for a correspondent account with a transactional limit of US$15 billion annually, which it regularly exceeded. These sums are even more stunning when taking into consideration that not all remittances involve USD and that all remittances leaving Saudi Arabia in 2008 amounted to US$21 billion.[9] The numbers just did not add up, and in hindsight should have ignited internal reviews of Sanea's practices. Thus, the error does not lie only on the CBB, but also on US and Saudi regulators who allowed for such a laissez-faire attitude to persist across the market.

Similarly, the international auditors of all the banks discussed here do not seem to have subjected the TIBC or Awal to very intensive reviews. Auditors are not responsible to stop systematic fraud but can make it difficult to pull it off successfully. Had the auditors just checked some of the 'borrowers' and questioned some of the documents and signatures, the fraud could have been discovered earlier.

In the case of TIBC, the bank's management should have recognized that not all was right. Yet, they did not inform the auditors or the CBB that something could have been amiss. This inaction should be viewed in consideration of the fact that most employees of TIBC and Awal were expatriates eager to preserve their jobs and that any complaints would have been met with ruthless punishments. Certainly, any employee losing his or her job in Bahrain would have found it difficult to find another job in the region or even in their own country of origin, consequences that guaranteed misplaced but real loyalty.

The flashy personalities involved in top management seem to always play a role in limiting scrutiny by central banks, auditors and top tier management. As seen in the New Yorker article, Mr. Stewart, who introduced himself to the region as an Arabic speaking expert on Islamic finance, benefited greatly from his association with Ma'an Al Sanea. He claimed, since his escape from Bahrain, that he was merely a well-paid slave to the Al Gosaibis and to Al Sanea.[10] This may have been the case. However, he had to know that the borrowers in Saudi Arabia were fictitious and that the money was subverted by Al Manea to his own company. If he did not know, which is technically possible, it would have been his role to check on them from time to time by direct visit to Saudi Arabia, a practice that any 'suitcase banker' in the offshore market of Bahrain undertook regularly.

Conclusion

When the Al Sanea/AHAB empire collapsed in 2009, it had defrauded more than 100 banks, taking out more than 12,500 loans during a 9-year period, worth more than US$120 billion that resulted in a cash of flow over US$330 billion over a decade.[11] In 2018, a Cayman Islands court ruled the AHAB had in fact known of Al Sanea's fraudulent activity. The ruling does take numerous international banks a step closer to finally finding reimbursement for their loans, but it does not change the facts of the case. The Gosaibi/Sanea affair amounts to a regulatory arbitrage, one in which Sanaa capitalized on the weak intrastate regulatory controls to exploit Bahrain's offshore market for his own benefit in Saudi Arabia. By dispersing the loans through the Exchange, and not directly from TIBC, Al Sanea was able to keep regulatory authorities one step removed from each transaction. To Bahraini authorities, TIBC was lending to an accredited institution. In Saudi Arabia, the Exchange was not regulated as a bank, thus there was no oversight role to be played. Tellingly, the affair was not dissimilar from events that transpired between Bahrain and Kuwait around the Souk Al Manakh crash, and thus highlights the inability, or unwillingness, of regulatory authorities in the region to establish stringent cross-border controls despite obvious signs and history of malfeasance.

While the Royal Commission and SAMA did act rapidly, at the time their real power to take conventional action in cases like this was limited. The freezing of Al Gosaibi and Al Sanea assets and the focus on domestic institutions was an effort to contain the fallout and restore investor confidence. In many ways, it was also all that could be done. There was no bankruptcy code that SAMA could lean on for an organized liquidation of a systemically important, internationally significant bank. Moreover, while SAMA did maintain regular dialogue with other central banks in the region, including the CBB, there was, and remains, limited formal cooperation arrangements in place, hindering the ability to effectively regulate anything cross-border in nature. In fact, at the time, other Gulf governments including the UAE, Oman and Bahrain reportedly expressed frustration that creditors from their own countries were excluded from the initial restructuring.

These limitations have only grown in significance since the implosion of TIBC. This was clear in 2018 through the collapse of Dubai-based Abraaj. Once the leading emerging market private equity firm, unscrupulous accounting practices and financial shell games led to its effective bankruptcy, and in turn set Middle Eastern private equity back years. To be sure, there are efforts at reforming the system. Both the UAE and Saudi passed formal bankruptcy laws in 2017 and 2018, respectively, and the Gosaibi case may prove to be the first significant use of the latter. That said, heavy handed tactics are often still the only recourse in the region. Al Sanea himself is a prime example. In 2017, he was arrested in what would be the first arrest in a wide- ranging crackdown on corrupt officials and businessmen across the Kingdom. The arrests and the new bankruptcy laws are both significant parts of Mohamed bin Salman's efforts to modernize the Saudi economy at any cost.

Just as the Souk Al Manakh still hinders the growth of Kuwait's capital markets, the Gosaibi affair is still a topic of discussion in Saudi business circles. These blemishes on the region's financial history require substantive reform in order for their negative effects to dissipate. The Gulf's financial markets are increasingly linked with global markets, and with this growth comes increasing need for merchant family networks and Gulf corporations that are historically opaque to incorporate western transparency and accountability norms. If for nothing else, these norms act as the cost to play in Western markets, and while institutions like SAMA and the CBB can protect their domestic constituencies in times of crises, without a formalized supranational regulatory structure, the economies of the Gulf will always face limits when aspiring to reach the stature of their Western peers.

Notes

1. More on money changers in Saudi Arabia can be found in Chapter 1 and Chapter 3.
2. Nicholas Schmidle, "The Kings of the Desert," *The New Yorker*, April 13, 2015.
3. Testimony of Eric L. Lewis to the United States House of Representatives Committee on Financial Service Subcommittee on Oversight and Investigations, "Hearing: A Review of Current and Evolving Trends in Terrorism Financing," September 28, 2010. Available at https://financialservices.house.gov/media/file/hearings/111/lewis092810.pdf.
4. Wael Kamal Eid, "Mapping the Risks and Risk Management Practices in Islamic Banking, Durham theses, Durham University," (PhD. diss., Durham University School of Government and International Affairs, September 2011): 130.
5. "Bahrain Central Bank Criticized for Financial Sector Woes," *The Telegraph*, February 18, 2011.
6. Schmidle, "The Kings of the Desert."
7. Robert J. Shapiro, "The Importance of International Standards in Managing Defaults in Islamic Finance: Saudi Arabia and the Saad Group's Sukuk Default," *Sonecon*, May 2013.
8. Testimony of Eric L. Lewis to the United States House of Representatives Committee on Financial Service Subcommittee on Oversight and Investigations, "Hearing: A Review of Current and Evolving Trends in Terrorism Financing."
9. Ibid.
10. Schmidle, "The Kings of the Desert."
11. "A Judge Blames Many Parties in the Gulf's Biggest-Ever Corporate Scandal," *The Economist*, June 9, 2018; Simeon Kerr, "Cayman Court Finds Saudi Companies Complicit in $126bn Fraud," *Financial Times*, June 1, 2018.

6.3 Dubai as a Financial Safe Haven

Introduction

Dubai's growth as a regional entrepôt has been intrinsically linked to dynamics in Iran for over a century. The number of Iranian merchants and blue-collar workers calling Dubai home has consistently swelled as Persian ports fell out of favor, Iran's leadership grew unendurable or the local Iranian economy fell deeper into disarray. In recent years as Tehran's isolation has intensified, Dubai's relatively liberal regulatory environment, state-of-the-art port infrastructure and massive Iranian diaspora have made the Arab emirate Iran's most significant link to the broader global economy. This relationship has proven to be extremely lucrative not only to Iranian officials, but also to Dubai's banks, as well as Iranian businessmen in Dubai. This case study delves into these relationships, their benefits and how they may evolve in the near term, highlighting how Dubai's perfectly legitimate framework for trade and business has allowed the emirate to benefit from restrictive trade regulations imposed by other countries.

Indian Gold Smuggling

Iran is not the only economy to which Dubai has provided a back door. In the 1970s, a favorite financial transaction involving India would foreshadow similar practices that took place years later involving Iran. In the early part of the 1970s, merchants realized that there was a great opportunity for profit if they could arrange to sell gold in India. At the time, the Indian government had placed huge taxes on the sale of gold. Indian tradition of gold dowries and marriage ceremonies with gold-laden brides has created strong demand for gold bullion and 21- to 24-carat gold jewelry in India. The trade in gold continues to this day and is a major activity in India and in the Gulf where most gold traders and craftsmen are Indian. In the 1970s, the ability to sell gold, bypassing India's customs and treasury regulations was seen as a major source of revenue by Dubai's merchants.

Banks were quick to offer their services to the trade. At the time, most of the banks in Dubai were headquartered right on the banks of the Creek, the body of water that was the heart of old Dubai and the traditional old harbor for all the trading dhows. A well-established merchant, who owned and operated a number of dhows for importing and exporting of goods, would have good relations with a number of banks, and may even own a portion of the capital of some. The banks in turn could have traditional relations with gold bullion suppliers like Swiss Bank Corporation or Credit Suisse. In fact, the Swiss banks often leased vault space from Dubai banks in order to warehouse kilos of gold.

The merchant could buy the gold from the Swiss banks, and to do so would often borrow money from the bank where the gold was stored. The merchant would then transfer the gold to his dhow moored in the Creek, across the street from the bank. The dhows looked quite ancient, made of teak wood, but upon close inspection would be powered by the most advanced and powerful engines available. These dhows could likely overpower any Indian patrol boat if necessary. Thus the gold would be sent to India and sold to local Indian traders, who could provide the gold to their clients at a great profit to themselves and to the Dubai traders, while still giving their Indian clients an extremely competitive price, all at the expense of the Indian treasury.

Dubai's banks did well by these transactions. They would make profit on the rental space leased to the Swiss banks. They would also earn interest on the loan to the merchants. Finally, the banks could also establish broader business relations with this merchant for other trades, including establishing letters of credits, letters of guarantees, holding deposits and conducting foreign exchange transactions, among other things. While India's demand for gold has only grown, the smuggling of gold by dhow has declined as Indian tariffs have declined and other forms of gold smuggling have evolved to meet demand.

Iranian Trade Links

In the 1980s, the trade of gold to India was supplemented by smuggling of goods to Iran and, to a lesser degree, to Iraq. In the case of the latter, some trading took place between Dubai and Iraq when Baghdad was embargoed by Western powers and the United Nations after the Gulf War. In the case of Iran, the trade has been considerably more expansive. During the Iran-Iraq war, Dubai acted as a conduit for goods, a dynamic that was ironic given Abu Dhabi's support for Iraq. Similarly, after the Iranian Revolution, when Iran was subject of US sanctions, trading blossomed between Dubai and the Iranian coast a mere 100 miles away. One could sit on the deck of restaurants on the Creek and watch the heavily laden dhows leave for Iran. Since the turn of the century, as Iran has increasingly found itself hemmed in by Western sanctions, this trade has taken on an even more significant role.

It is telltale that there are an estimated 400,000 Iranian citizens living in Dubai, more than the native population, and there are over 8,000

Iranian-owned companies operating in the emirate. The vast majority of these companies are completely legitimate and operated by the plethora of Iranian expats who have lived in Dubai for some time, many of whom do not hold the Iranian regime in high regard. There have even been numerous professional associations established to assist and serve these businesses, including the Iranian Business Council—Dubai.

One of the largest activities these businesses conduct is simply the re-export of goods, with everything from consumer goods to heavy industrial equipment regularly findings its way to Dubai's ports from all over the world just to subsequently navigate the short six-hour sail to Iranian ports. This re-export trade benefits traders and banks just as the Indian gold trade did. The price differentials between global markets and Iranian markets create a lucrative spread for willing traders, and the banks continue to benefit handsomely by servicing the traders with loans, letters of credits, letters of guarantees and other financial intermediation.

While there has been plenty of discussion around the tightening of export and banking controls since the ratcheting up of sanctions against Iran in the 2000s, the re-export of goods from the UAE to Iran has actually grown considerably as new sanctions have been put in place. According to data from the United Nations Comtrade Database, the total value of re-exports from the UAE to Iran grew from around US$4.6 billion in 2008 when United Nations sanctions on Iran went into effect, to over US$16 billion in 2014, the last full year before Iran and Western countries signed a nuclear non-proliferation agreement. Since then, re-exports have fallen in value consistently every year, hitting US$8.3 billion in 2016 (See Figure 6.3).[1] This decreasing trend in re-exports appears to align with the loosening of sanctions in the wake of the 2015 Joint Comprehensive Plan of Action, which lifted numerous nuclear related sanctions on Iran and generally eased the environment in which Iranian companies sought to do business. In theory, this change in environment would have provided Iranian leadership with the opportunity to conduct more of their business through traditional international trade, opposed to the dependence on re-export through Dubai's ports.

Whereas trade conducted out of Dubai is legitimate from Dubai's stand point, it is not always legitimate under other countries' rules. Deriving from the Iranian government's strong control over the domestic economy, some of the trade between Dubai and Iran is bound to be tied to sanctioned individuals and organizations or involve contraband of some sort. In this regard, it is easy to see how Iranian officials, especially those associated with the Islamic Revolutionary Guard Corps (IRGC) or who can benefit from their business and government connections, can capitalize on Dubai's regulatory environment and trade patterns to establish a steady conduit of supply for a broad range of goods, one in which they can also personally profit if they so choose. For example, an official could pass an order to a company in Dubai, who in turn would find the required equipment, repackage it in new containers and ship it to Iran. Naturally, the company in Dubai would have to be

Figure 6.3 Dubai-Iran Re-Exports and the Sanctions Regime

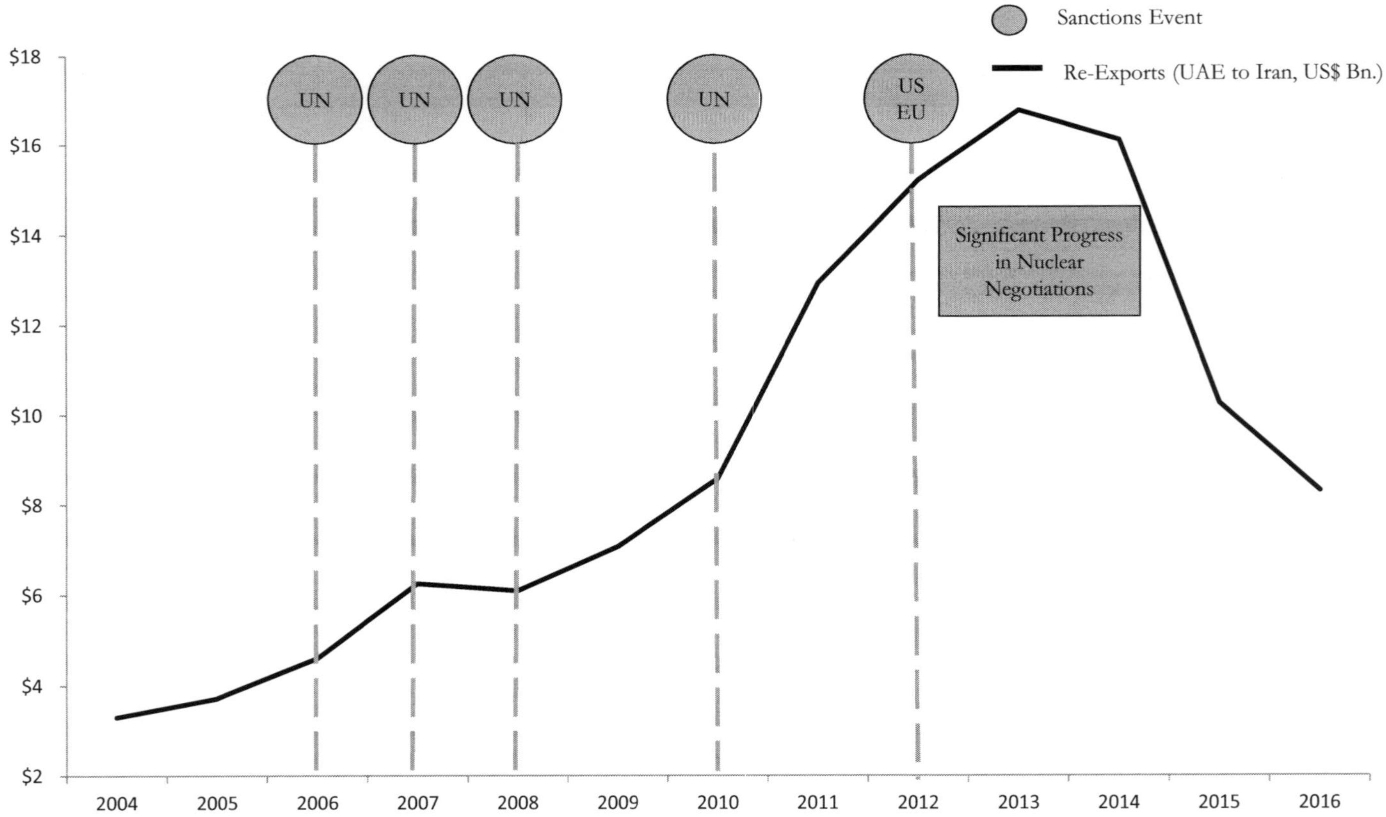

Source: United Nations Comtrade Database

trusted by the official, so in most cases the company used would be owned by the official's wife, son, daughter, relative or trusted confidante. A letter of credit could be opened for the perfectly bona fide transaction, approved by a bank in Iran and ultimately by the Central Bank of Iran so that payment could be made in US dollars to the company in Dubai. In turn the company in Dubai could issue a back-to-back letter of credit in favor of the seller anywhere in the world. In a variation of this transaction, the company in Dubai would take a profit margin, potentially by buying the equipment in the world market at X dollars and reselling it the Iranian buyer at three times X. This would, in theory, leave 2X profits in the account of the Dubai firm, which again is owned indirectly by the Iranian official either outright or through a JV with associates in Dubai (See Figure 6.4). These profits could then be split accordingly, with the added possibility of entering the global economy.

Again, banks greatly benefit from such trade. They charge a confirming fee for the letter of credit, an opening fee for the back-to-back letter of credit and a payment fee when paying the sellers. They also receive the money from Iran and keep it as deposits in Dubai. It is in this last point that Dubai also finds significant benefit. This accumulation of deposits in Dubai's banks must be used to profit in some manner. Usually, banks with large dollar deposits will place the funds in financial institutions in London

Figure 6.4 Iranian-Dubai Trade Schematic

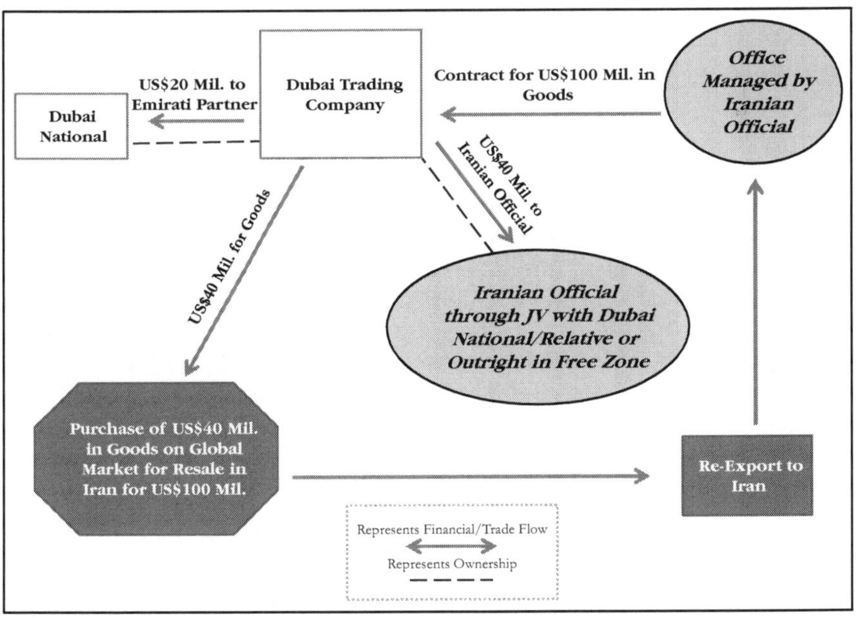

©The Lafayette Group LLC 2017

or New York where they can accrue a higher rate of return. However, under the international Know Your Customer rules, banks cannot transfer funds to other banks without disclosing the source of the payments. If these re-export-fueled deposits were transferred to foreign institutions, all of which maintain strong relationships with US banks, the funds would quickly be blocked by the US Treasury. Hence, the banks in Dubai are stuck with the deposits, which have to be used locally. This has the advantage of providing substantial liquidity to Dubai's financial markets. This liquidity has played a large part in the ability for Dubai to finance enormous domestic infrastructure and real estate projects, a situation that has benefited companies like Dubai World. In fact, this deep liquidity may have been a source of funding for the real estate boom that took place in Dubai until the financial crisis of 2008/2009.

All of this is not say that Dubai has not taken any action to enforce sanctions against Iran. There have been repeated instances where UAE authorities have cracked down on individuals and entities explicitly sanctioned by US authorities or suspected of smuggling illicit material to Iran.[2] These efforts have increased noticeably since 2008, in lock step with Abu Dhabi's increasing leverage over Dubai in the wake of the latter's 2009 debt crises. This role has been an important consideration as Abu Dhabi's leadership has grown closer to Saudi Arabia since 2015, and this broader Saudi-UAE relationship has become even more fixated on what the Arab Gulf states see as Iran's hegemonic efforts in the region.

These dynamics, coupled with the re-initiation of unilateral sanctions by the United States during the Trump administration has led Iran to shift some of its financial and trade relationships away from the UAE. While still evolving, the largest GCC beneficiary of this movement appears to be Oman. Iranian-Omani relations have deep historical precedent, which provides fertile ground for deeper economic cooperation. This has already begun. For example, in March 2018, Oman and Iran signed a number of significant agreements with the core element being closer banking cooperation, including the acceptance of Iranian bank guarantees by Omani banks, the possibility of transactions in local currencies, and the potential for growth in re-export trade.[3]

Even without Iran, Dubai will continue to be a haven for funds. Geopolitical hot spots in the region do pop up often and Dubai ends up being the recipient of funds from these areas. Pakistan is known in Dubai to be a source of funds with transactions very similar to the ones described earlier for Iran. The Kurdish territories, Afghanistan and some African states are also a source of income through similar means. Again, the banks are the recipient of the funds sent from these countries and can be the intermediary to the purchase of freehold properties by foreigners wanting to have a toehold outside their own troubled countries.

Notes

1. United Nations International Trade Statistics Database.
2. Simeon Kerr and Harvey Morris, "N Korean Arms for Iran' Seized by UAE," *Financial Times*, August 28, 2009; Lesley Wroughton, "U.S., UAE Crack Down on Network for Smuggling Funds to Elite Iran Group," *Reuters*, May 10, 2018.
3. "Oman to Become a Re-Export Hub / Iran and Oman Expand Banking Relationships," *Central Bank of the Islamic Republic of Iran*, March 18, 2018.

6.4 Documentary Credits

Introduction

Since the 1970s, one of the primary areas of business for international and domestic banks in the Gulf has been the issuance of documentary credits for very large government infrastructure projects including roads, harbors, schools and airports. Such documents include letters of credits, performance bonds, bid bonds, advance payment guarantees and facilities related to these credits such as short-term loans.

The Mechanics

A theoretical example will show how important these credits have been to the banks in the region (See Table 6.5). Let's assume that contracting company XYZ bids and obtains a contract of US$200 million. Large contracts such as these in Saudi Arabia are denominated in US dollars.

- To bid, XYZ has to provide a sealed bid accompanied by a bid bond of 1% of the bid. This bid bond is usually issued by the banks overnight, just before the sealed bid is due. The fee is often 0.25% per quarter, and the bid may be outstanding for two quarters. Since there are usually numerous bids, all the banks make money on bid bonds with only a slight chance that the bid will be successful. Thus by and large the bid bond carries very little risk and pay the banks well.
- If successful, XYZ has to provide a performance bond of 5% of the value of the contract for the duration of the work plus one year. Performance bonds ensure that the state would recoup any losses stemming from incomplete projects, either due to unforeseen circumstances or contractor bankruptcy.
- XYZ, like most contractors, will ask for a down payment of 10% of the contract to be used to mobilize for the contract, i.e. buy machinery, import labor, build labor camps, etc. To obtain this 10%, the contractor will need to issue an advance payment guarantee (APG) for the amount of the payment. Each monthly payment under the contract will be paid

Table 6.5 Example of Banks' Annual Profitability From Documentary Credits

Assume Contract of $000		***$200,000***			
Documentary Credit Issued	**% Contract Required**	**Amount $000**	**Fee % p.a.**	**Outstanding for # Years**	**Bank's Income for First Year in $000**
Bid Bond	1%	$ 2,000	1%	0.5	$ 10
Performance Bond	5%	$ 10,000	1%	4	$ 100
Advanced Payment Guarantee	10%	$ 20,000	1%	1.5	$ 200
L/C facility	10%	$ 20,000	1%	1.5	$ 200
			Bank Profit on Cash Collateral		
Cash Collateral Held	10%	$ 20,000	1%	2	$ 200
Arrangement Fee on Facility	1%				$ 2,000
			Rate above Libor		
Average S-T Loans to Contractor	20%	$ 40,000	1.5%	1.5	$ 600
Total Bank Facility Required in 000s		***$ 92,000***			***$ 3,310***
Assumed Bank Asset/Net Worth	10				
Risk Imputed on Capital of Bank =100% of Loans +10% of DocsCred/Leverage of Bank in 000s		$ 4,520			
Net return on Capital Imputed p.a.					73.23%

(Continued)

Table 6.5 (Continued)

Lead Syndicator's Profitability			
Assume lead bank takes 20% of total risk			
Amount received for a year on Bank's Share of the facility			$ 222
Amount from Cash collateral held for syndicate			$ 200
Arrangement fee on share of facility		1%	$ 184
Praecipium of arrangement fee		0.25%	$ 184
Total yearly earnings by Lead Syndicator in 000s			**$ 790**
Risk Imputed on Capital of Bank for its 20% share of the risk =100% of Loans +10% of DocsCred/Leverage of Bank in 000s	$ 904		
Net return on Capital Imputed p.a.			87.39%

upon certification of work performed by the contractor and prepared by the independent consulting engineer chosen by the client. The monthly payment will be for the work performed minus the 10% paid in advance as part of the APG. Hence, the average amount of the APG will be for half of the contract since the sum it covers declines month on month.

- XYZ will need a letter of credit facility to import whatever material, parts, equipment etc. is needed, for about 10% of the contract. This will be outstanding for perhaps half the duration of the contract.
- XYZ will usually also need a short-term loan facility to tie it over until the payment by the client is received. The loan facility could often be for 20% of the value of the contract. On average, however, this loan would be outstanding for only half of the duration of the contract.

The bank fees will be negotiated by XYZ based on the credit worthiness of the company and all normal factors entering bank/client relations. A common fee structure is shown in Table 6.5 and is based on a 1% fee on whatever facility is needed. The bank will also often ask for a cash collateral account for security on which it will make whatever it makes on deposits- in this example, we have assumed a spread of 1% above cost of funds (usually LIBOR). The profit on the bank loan is also based on a spread of 1.5% above LIBOR.

From the banks' point of view, the risk involved is limited if they stick to reputable contractors. Furthermore, the experience of banks in the Gulf with documentary credits has historically been very good. Large contractors tend not to fail. If a large, reputable contractor got into trouble, the state client will in most cases intervene to resolve the issue. At times the client will push the banks to lend more money to the contractor or help the bank hire a partner for the troubled contractor to finish the project. In the end, banks do very well, even if at times it requires some heavy lifting on their part.

Profitability

When evaluating the profitability of the facilities, banks would compute their return on the capital they use to cover the risk. In the case of XYZ, assuming a large Saudi contract, the banks will only have to impute the loan against their capital. Hence on a return as shown in the table of US$1.1 million for the first year on a risk of US$4 million imputed, this corresponds to 73% return on capital.

However, if the bank decides to share the risk with other banks and lead a syndication, it will have to do all the foot work. The bank will strive to get a mandate from XYZ to arrange the facility. As lead manager, it will take a front-end arrangement fee, in this example 1%. The bank will keep only a portion of the risk, say 20% and syndicate the rest of the risk to other banks. It will often pass on ¾ of the front-end fee to the participants of the syndication, keeping ¼ of the overall fee, called the "praecipium" for basically having found and sold the deal to its colleagues. Since the bank is now only at risk for 1/5th of the total facility, its use of imputed capital is reduced accordingly and its fees relative to the risk increased substantially. In our example, the bank would earn over 87% on its imputed capital.

Of course, there are hundreds of permutations of the example shown, and it can be complicated *ad infinitum*. For example, the letters of credits fee could be higher or lower. There could be payment fees, foreign exchange profits on non-dollar transactions, the interest spreads could vary substantially, etc. Our example is merely a generic and simplified version of a complex, lucrative financial product that has become a mainstay of banks in the Gulf.

In all cases, however, large banks were greatly incentivized to seek mandates from contracting clients in the Gulf, as it would drastically maximize the bank's net returns on assets. The syndication system is mostly based on traditional banking relations between bankers and clients and between bankers themselves. Indeed, each syndicated transaction is presented in great details in various memoranda full of information on the contract, the client, the contractor and the bank itself. It is normally sent to numerous banks around the world, especially strategic banks with connections to the Gulf, and to the client and/or the contractor. The credit committees of the invited banks will analyze the syndication memos very carefully. They will decide whether their respective banks' can accept the risk and whether the expected profitability is sufficient to satisfy their required return on assets.

However, as in most credible transaction, the contractor will usually give the mandate to the bank he/she knows and trusts the most. For example, Rafiq Hariri, when he was the high flying head of Saudi Oger, would always give his mandates to The Arab Bank of Jordan where he was a board member and major shareholder. In turn, the bank will usually choose the members of the syndication from among the banks it has dealt with in the past, and whom it can rely on for relatively quick answers. The location of the lead bank is most important. Indeed, in spite of all the electronic progress, face to face contact between bankers who know and trust each other will achieve quick, efficient and very profitable results. Hence, the marketplace is vital to bigger deals. London, of course, has always been the center of the syndication business. Bahrain started to become an important regional syndication center, but as Bahraini politics interfered with how banks felt about the stability and credibility of the country, London regained its preeminence in Gulf deals.

Conclusion

Even with the recent trouble facing major Gulf contracting companies such as Saudi Oger and Saudi Binladin Group, from a bank's perspective the business of documentary credits has remained lucrative. Recent payment issues with these contracting companies affect their ability to meet payment obligations, and while this has been extremely detrimental to employees and could affect loan performance, it does not affect the business of documentary credits. Documentary credit fees are paid upfront, and the risk of payouts is minimized by the fact that most state clients rarely, if ever, call performance bonds. In fact, in the thousands of performance bonds in which Saudi Arabia has been the state client, only a handful have been called, even though there have been numerous performance issues. Instead, state clients often prefer to negotiate a settlement or alternative solution, such as extending financial assistance or locating an alternative contractor to complete the project. For the banks, this is always preferred, as it is significantly less costly than paying out a performance bond.

In the Kingdom of Saudi Arabia, as of late 2017, there were over US$280 billion worth of construction projects in the early stages of development.[1] In the state budget for 2018, there was an additional US$14.4 billion slated for new infrastructure projects.[2] All of these projects require the aforementioned documentary credits, ensuring that for time to come, banks can continue to rely on this lucrative practice.

Notes

1. Sean Cronin, "Saudi Budget: Builders to Reap Rewards of Record Spending," *Arab News*, December 21, 2017.
2. "Saudi Arabia Plans $14bn Infrastructure Spend," *Trade Arabia*, December 20, 2017.

7 Conclusion

The financial markets of Gulf have grown exponentially over the past forty years. They have gone from being a collection of quasi-medieval institutions to networks of highly sophisticated investment vehicles. They have been a buffer protecting the people from fluctuations in the countries' energy rents and allowed the Gulf states to take on an outsized role in global financial markets.

In hindsight, none of this was foretold. The overarching story painted earlier ebbed and flowed over decades, and within those movements were many minor setbacks and major crashes. Not all the markets were able to recover or grow to their full potential. Bahrain, once seen as the future for regional finance, has taken a back seat to deeper and larger financial markets next door. Saudi Arabia's financial markets, once dominated by money-changers and their outsized role in domestic banking, now has the most professional and powerful central bank in the broader Middle East and North Africa.

Alongside these variations have arisen a number of uniformities. All the financial markets in the Gulf allow for free financial flows within and across countries, in fact freer than in most other regions. There are no foreign exchange regulations, even at times of tight budgets. The currencies have remained tied to the US dollar in part because of the strong political links between the Gulf states and the United States but also because most of the former's income comes from oil and other energy-based products which are denominated in dollars. Similarly, most of their expenses are also denominated in dollars. This includes arms purchases, large civil works contracts and foreign investments. Any devaluation or revaluation would have only very minor impact on the local economies. Despite this, the Gulf states have been unable to set aside rivalries and fears of domination by each other to develop common fiscal and monetary policies. Nonetheless, through the common peg to the dollar, which was and has remained the common denominator, the US dollar has become the de facto regional common currency, making respective monetary policies across the Gulf states indirectly decided by the US Federal Reserve.

Also ubiquitous across all Gulf financial markets is the lack of taxes. Income tax on companies and individuals are nonexistent except for Zakat, a voluntary vaguely defined religious tax. It has been argued by the proponents of rentier state theory that a lack of taxes allows the states' leadership to control politics and that any creation of taxes would lead people to ask for representation. In reality, there are many states where people pay taxes and have no, little, or fake representation. In the Gulf the lack of taxes has come from tradition. In most Gulf states, if a ruler was seeking to establish taxes, the larger merchant families would move to another Gulf state and basically 'tax' shop. This process of tax or tariff shopping is what led to the growth of Dubai as a regional trading hub. While freedom of movement is no longer as easy as it was in the earlier centuries, the tradition of no taxes has remained, made possible by each state's income from oil and gas. This does not mean it cannot change. The latest efforts to start establishing a tax base, starting with a Value-Added Tax established in Saudi Arabia and the UAE on January 1, 2018, may be the first step to an evolution of mentalities. That said, the movement toward taxation is a paradigm shift, and accordingly will take time.

Amidst all this, it is clear that the hand of the state has been the guiding force in economic development. The ability to rapidly enact broad ranging economic policy has been integral to the region's growth. This has only been possible because of the tight control the state has had on key institutions in the market. In most Gulf countries the banks are de facto controlled by their regulators. In Saudi Arabia, the monetary agency had, and now PIF has, a large and controlling equity interest in the leading banks. This is key in times of budgetary stress, or global recession, when the domestic banking sector becomes integral to governmental economic policy. Whereas direct state-influence on banks may not be as extreme as in Saudi Arabia across the broader Gulf, the largest regional banks, including the National Bank of Qatar of the Emirates NBD, are closely related to the royal families.

Through this control of the banking sector, the state has essentially controlled the flow of funds across the private sector. In a similar way, the states have sought, and gained, influence across the regional capital markets. For a long-time, the stock markets in the region were not greatly encouraged because central banks could not easily control what de facto are platforms that allow the flow of funds directly between private individuals and companies. However, most firms that were initially in the position to float shares on the stock market were, and remain, dependent in some form on their relationship with the state which allocates contracts and transfers from oil/gas payments. Through this relationship, often times one that actually includes majority control (i.e. SABIC), the state has maintained a strong hand on the direction of capital markets. As these markets developed, the public and the state alike have required much more disclosure from the companies and therefore opened the possibilities of strong regulation on how the firms managed their capital issuance, dividends and ultimately management. This has provided the state more confidence in allowing the capital markets to grow unabated, a trend that many states—such as Saudi Arabia—view as a central part of future financial growth.

The telltale counterpoint to this control of banking and capital markets is Kuwait. It is there that the state has not had as free a hand in the direction of the financial markets. This has derived from a number of factors such as setbacks stemming from the Iraqi invasion, but most importantly because of the strength of the National Assembly. This legislative body distinguishes Kuwait from a political perspective, but also limits the ability of the monarchy to make economic decisions with wide implications freely. The classic example of this is the failed K-Dow petrochemicals project. But also, compared to its peers, Kuwait has no mega-planned cities or bustling free zones. In many cases this may be for the better, but equally, it has limited Kuwait's agility and competitiveness in the face of dynamic and rapidly changing financial markets, of course to the great benefit of its neighbors.

Despite the National Assembly and its impact on economic policy, Kuwait has an SWF that matches its regional peers in influence. These SWFs have grown into financial behemoths all their own. Common to all the region's SWFs has been deep opacity. Except for Mubadala the smaller, albeit powerful, SWF of Abu Dhabi, the Gulf's SWFs issue no financial statements, do not list in detail the assets they hold or how their investment decisions are made. Since, in principle, the SWFs hold funds in an effective trust for the people, it would make more sense if the SWFs were eager to show the citizens how they operate, how much money they make, and how they actually benefit the countries. However, the SWFs are operated without consultation with the people. The lack of public information and involvement in the management of the assets opens the door to speculation. Is it that the leadership wants to access the funds as it sees fit, regardless of the interest of the people? Is it afraid of the criticism that could be levied against them should the losses be too extensive? Or is it that they are merely trying to protect the funds from watchful, and often predatory, global financial actors? Whatever the reason for the opacity, the management of the Gulf's SWFs is far from the standards set by Norway's wealth fund, which is now the most transparent, successful and credible in the world. The Gulf SWFs' opacity also takes them far from the Santiago principles drafted by an assembly of SWFs in part led by ADIA. It would seem that large funds like ADIA or PIF would greatly benefit from following the Norwegian example. It would definitely improve their credibility and ability to influence and lead global markets.

Looking forward, perhaps one the most important developments for the region will be fluctuations in the reserve status of the US dollar. Principally, this change could happen with the rise of China as the prime buyer of Gulf oil and gas, and its efforts to change the payment terms to Renminbi. The Shanghai oil futures contract, known by the acronym INE, has only been active for a few months but is already becoming an important tool for Chinese oil companies, Gulf companies and most importantly Chinese speculators seeking to hedge the price of oil in Renminbi. If the countries of the Gulf find it convenient to price their oil in Renminbi rather than dollars, it will give rise to the Gulf states having large cash reserves in Renminbi, which in turn would benefit the Chinese firms selling goods in the region. The Shanghai market is unlikely to become as developed as the London International Petroleum Exchange and its contracts for Brent, or to the New York Stock Exchange for WTI, mainly because the Renminbi is not freely convertible. Other buyers and sellers will hesitate to have large balances in that currency until they know they can easily transfer it to their home currency. Nevertheless, as the Renminbi becomes more internationally exchanged, the Gulf states will have to move toward the Shanghai market, which will weaken the stranglehold of the dollar on international transactions. Since, as mentioned earlier, the Gulf states are de facto part of the dollar zone and see their monetary policies linked to the US ones, a successful contract for oil in Renminbi would have wide ramifications. The tight link to the US Federal Reserve monetary policy would diminish, large Renminbi reserves would naturally drive the region's SWFs to look increasingly eastward, and China itself would take on some of the influence the dollar holds in the Gulf today.

Whereas the aforementioned currency-focused developments are somewhat speculative, a trend that has already begun, and set to increase, is the diminishing importance of the state to the financial markets, especially in Saudi Arabia. It is true that the financial markets have served as the intermediaries between the states and the income from oil and gas to the population. However, as seen by the policies of SAMA in particular, the governments have used the markets to promote economic diversification and the great development of industrial projects. The growth in the non-oil economy has been staggering, even though today, the Saudi state still receives 85% of its revenues from oil income. However, with no tax (except for the small and voluntary Zakat), the State has not benefited from the major growth of the likes of SABIC and Ma'aden. With the expected privatization of Saudi Aramco, and the emphasis on developing the private sector industrial and service companies, the dependence of the people on the state could be replaced by the state depending on the people. All the efforts of Saudi Arabia to achieve Vision 2030 and be weaned from oil will happen through the financial markets: new share flotations, increases in loans, documentary credits, consumer finance, etc.

As major efforts, such as Vision 2030, are undertaken to diversify away from oil and gas, financial markets are becoming more reliant on the private sector and the role of young but ambitious entrepreneurs who are creating new industrial and service firms. In other words, the growth of a modern economy, one that is moving away from primary energy resources, is pushing the Gulf's financial markets closer to those of more advanced economies. These transitions are slow, and just as the last forty years of regional financial evolution have ebbed and flowed, the next forty will also ebb and flow. Regardless, the overall trajectory is toward more advanced, competitive and modern market structures. Political and financial analysts of Gulf affairs have often focused on large, blockbuster initiatives like Saudi Aramco's IPO, but this analysis risks missing the forest for the trees. Whether the IPO, or other large structurally important transactions, happen or not, what has already happened and is continuing to happen is that Gulf markets are taking on characteristics that, until recently, were reserved for Western economies.

Index

Page numbers in *italics* indicate figures and in **bold** indicate tables on the corresponding pages.

Taylor & Francis Group
an **informa** business

Taylor & Francis eBooks

www.taylorfrancis.com

A single destination for eBooks from Taylor & Francis with increased functionality and an improved user experience to meet the needs of our customers.

90,000+ eBooks of award-winning academic content in Humanities, Social Science, Science, Technology, Engineering, and Medical written by a global network of editors and authors.

TAYLOR & FRANCIS EBOOKS OFFERS:

- A streamlined experience for our library customers
- A single point of discovery for all of our eBook content
- Improved search and discovery of content at both book and chapter level

REQUEST A FREE TRIAL

support@taylorfrancis.com

Routledge
Taylor & Francis Group

CRC Press
Taylor & Francis Group